The Housekeeper's Tale

The Women Who Really Ran
the English Country House

By TESSA BOASE

Aurum
Press

Inspiring | Educating | Creating | Entertaining

Brimming with creative inspiration, how-to projects, and useful
information to enrich your everyday life. Quarto Knows is a favourite
destination for those pursuing their interests and passions. Visit our
site and dig deeper with our books into your area of interest:
Quarto Creates, Quarto Cooks, Quarto Homes, Quarto Lives,
Quarto Drives, Quarto Explores, Quarto Gifts, or Quarto Kids.

First published in 2014 by Aurum Press
an imprint of the Quarto Group
The Old Brewery
6 Blundell Street
London N7 9BH
www.QuartoKnows.com

This paperback edition first published 2015

© Quarto Publishing plc 2014, 2015
Text © Tessa Boase 2014

Tessa Boase has asserted her moral right to be identified as the Author of this
Work in accordance with the Copyright Designs and Patents Act 1988.

Every effort has been made to trace the copyright holders of material quoted
in this book. If application is made in writing to the publisher, any
omissions will be included in future editions.

A catalogue record for this book is available from the British Library.

ISBN 978-1-78131-410-4

Typeset in ITC Giovanni by SX Composing DTP, Rayleigh, Essex
Printed and bound by CPI Group (UK) Ltd, Croydon, CR0 4YY

MIX
Paper from
responsible sources
FSC® C013604

For my parents

Contents

Prologue

Hatfield House, Hertfordshire 1890

Good housekeepers are not easily got at.
JOHN STRIKE, FORMER HOUSE STEWARD TO LORD SALISBURY,
PRIME MINISTER

Housekeeper Wanted

On Thursday, 16 October 1890, an advertisement appeared in *The Times* and *The Morning Post*, London:

HOUSEKEEPER WANTED, for a large, country house. A person is required, of a good address, who has filled a similar position. Write, stating qualifications, to S.N., May's Advertising offices, 162 Piccadilly, W.

Fifty-nine women read the advertisement, considered their options and replied in slanting copperplate handwriting, stating their particulars.

'I am a Protestant', wrote Mrs Phillips, 40, from Lambeth, in quavering black ink, 'an abstainer, early riser, very methodical, punctual in all duties and judicious in supervision of servants.' She was experienced in looking after linen, valuable china and stores, she 'fully understood' cooking with economy and she required wages 'from £35' a year. That is around £2,100 in today's money. Mrs Catherine Coleman, housekeeper to the Lord Mayor of London at Mansion House, also applied for the job. She prided herself on being 'a careful and industrious manageress, possessing a large amount of discretion, tact and judicious firmness necessary to control servants'. She was educated, tall, 'of good appearance and address'. She was leaving the post because the Lord Mayor elect would be bringing his own housekeeper. From temporary lodgings at Kemp Street, Brighton Mrs Ridout wrote too. Well educated for her 'station in life', she thoroughly understood the making of 'all

Preserves, Marmalades, Cakes, etc'. She had been 'disengaged' at the precarious age of 50, and was hoping something would turn up.

There were replies that appealed to a prospective mistress's vanity, promising to pander to her every need. 'I shall not consider anything a trouble which will add to the comfort of the household', wrote Mrs Davidson of Mayfair. Kate Corrigan, manageress of the Mosley Hotel in Manchester, understood 'all the nice little refinements of a well-ordered establishment'. Her hotel was about to be pulled down and rebuilt; in any case, she would much prefer a position in a '<u>house</u>'.

There were replies from career servants seeking to better their position, such as Miss Bessie Kelly, writing from a 'gentleman's establishment' near Warrington, Cheshire. 'I want to change now to gain more experience.' My age is 38. I think I may say I have a very good address & appearance.' Mrs Jennings from West Dean Park, Chichester, was disgruntled with her current job as cook-housekeeper, wishing to drop the 'cook' part. 'I do not like the management of the cooking and it's more then I thought it would be, but I took the situation through the wishes of Friends.' She had been there less than a year.

The words 'large, country house' acted as a clarion call. This was the top job for a working woman in the nineteenth century. You could do no better, nor live more comfortably or with greater security, and all under your own steam. Uniquely, it was a life that had no need of a man – and was far more exhilarating, perhaps, than housekeeping for a husband. The Victorian years were the housekeeper's apogee, a time of supreme confidence and expansion for the English country house. She started the century a more subordinate, explicitly feminine figure – pickler, preserver, sweet maker, distiller; in charge of all store cupboards and material things, a large bunch of keys clinking at her waist as she checked her housemaids' work. She ended the century in a black silk dress, a senior management figure of absolute authority, whose wages might outstrip both cook and butler (at Holkham Hall, Norfolk in 1894 the housekeeper earned £65 a year to the cook and butler's £40).[1] She answered only to the mistress of the house, hiring and firing dozens of maids and controlling the entire household budget. She remains one of the most caricatured figures of the age.

The housekeeper is invariably one of two types. She is a stern-faced, elderly spinster dressed in black – meticulous, repressed, asexual, perhaps nursing some secret bitterness. Or else she is a bluff, apple-cheeked Yorkshirewoman, spaniel-like in her devotion. Dickens, himself the grandson of a country-house housekeeper, delighted in the caricature – in *Hard Times* (1854) there is the ludicrous Mrs Sparsit, a widowed gentlewoman fallen on hard times with a 'Coriolanian style of nose' and 'dense black eyebrows', her preposterous sights set on marrying her master, Mr Bounderby. In *Bleak House* (1853) there's her counterpoint: the inoffensive treasure Mrs Rouncewell, 'a fine old lady, handsome, stately, wonderfully neat', an indispensable part of the grand Dedlock Estate for fifty years. Scotswoman Mrs Hughes of the television drama *Downton Abbey* (loyal, astute, a spinster by choice) belongs firmly in this second camp.

She was a stereotype to her employers: in 1822 Lady Elizabeth Coke urged her new husband not to engage a gorgon; rather, she wanted 'a goody sort of person, who will occasionally make up a mess of broth or sago for the poor people'.[2] The stereotype extended to her staff. Typically, 'the under-maids were more afraid of her than they were of her Ladyship',[3] wrote ex-butler Eric Horne in 1923. The Victorian caricature persisted well into the twentieth century, when mistresses actively *looked* for a cliché to employ, as if ballast against the bumptious new generation of servants. The young, insecure Duchess of Westminster hired 'somebody completely out of Dickens' to run Eaton Hall in 1930; a 'stoutish character' dressed in floor-length black bombazine.[4] Then there is the most sinister and manipulative of them all: Mrs Danvers, housekeeper of Manderley in Daphne du Maurier's *Rebecca* (1938). Tall and gaunt, dressed in black, her prominent cheekbones and 'great, hollow eyes' give her 'a skull's face, parchment-white, set on a skeleton's frame'.

*

The replies to the *Times* advertisement of 1890 paint a rather different picture. It was the top job, but it seems to have been a tough job in every sense – from 'judicious control' of unruly servants, to getting down on your knees with a scrubbing brush yourself. 'She is not afraid to soil her hands,' reads the character reference for a Mrs Adams from Chorlton, Manchester. For all its status, it was a surprisingly insecure job (1890 was a year of sharp financial recession), many women blaming 'restructuring of establishment' for their being let go. It was also a job for the desperate: widowed and orphaned gentlewomen, young and old, down on their luck. Their letters make poignant reading.

On black-edged notepaper from Bridgnorth in the old county of Salop, a 24-year-old widow applied for the post. 'Owing to my husband's recent death I have been obliged to depend upon myself,' wrote Frances Christy in intelligent, legible handwriting. 'I have never been out before, but am a lady and used to house keeping of my own, and am fully qualified for the post, being used to a large house in China, and having the command of a staff of servants. If you think it likely I should do', she added, 'kindly let me know as soon as possible, as I am anxious to get something to do.'

'I am a widow and I have one child who is at school', wrote Mrs Cleary from Southampton, a 36-year-old with 'the highest references' from a canon of Westminster Abbey. She admitted that she had not worked since she was married, 'but I am a competent housekeeper and would soon get into the routine of a Gentleman's house. Wages, £50.'

Death, in this sheaf of replies, is everywhere. 'I am the orphan daughter of a Gentleman, of very good family and connections, many of whom have held important posts in the Army, Navy, Church, Legal and Medical professions', wrote the 'very energetic and cheerful' Miss E. Illingworth, aged 31, in a rather defensive four-page letter posted in London. Harriet Robinson from Micheldever, Hampshire is another: 'My father now dead was for many years in the Bank of Scotland, Edinburgh & a Notary Public.' She did not state her age but sent a piteous photograph, 'taken about 4 years ago': very young, very slim, with a frizzled Princess Alexandra-style fringe and a yearning face. She holds a portrait of her dead father. 'Salary £35 to £40.'

Just one woman, 54-year-old Fanny Tagg from Birmingham, asked for more information. 'Would you let me know what your arrangements are for Country House and what county it is in.' Where *was* this 'large, country house'? It was a fair question. And yet it was, apparently, irrelevant to most. Their employment histories show them to be continually on the move, travelling by the great Victorian rail network hundreds of miles to each new posting, one big black trunk in tow: two years here, four years there, from Salop to Sunderland, Dorset to Derbyshire. Location was of far less concern than wages, for once you were installed in the closed world of the big house and its estate, you rarely left it.

What none of these women knew, as they dipped steel-nibbed pens in ink and laboriously wrote out their particulars, was that their letter would be read by the Marchioness of Salisbury, wife to the Conservative Prime Minister. A housekeeper was needed for the Cecil family seat in Hertfordshire: that vast and historic Jacobean mansion, Hatfield House. Had these poor women known, they might have been too daunted to apply.

Fourteen women – none of the above – were shortlisted for the job. A small, stiff envelope arrived in the post from Hatfield House inviting each to a personal interview with the Marchioness of Salisbury in the last week of October 1890, all expenses paid. For four consecutive days Her Ladyship sat in her morning room while personal secretary Mr Gunton ushered women in and out in fifteen-minute slots. 'No good', she scrawled irritably on their application letters. 'Not much.' 'Won't do.' 'Very nice but wants experience.' She struck off the typed names on her list, one after another, as the women entered and departed. 'Good, but perhaps too small a woman', she wrote of Louisa Aylott, ex-stillroom maid of Hatfield House, who was terrified to find herself in front of her old mistress. The field shrank. A small, tentative cross was finally brought to rest next to the names of Mrs Neill and Mrs Prince.

Mrs Neill was a Scotswoman, a member of the Church of England; age 37 years, height 5ft 5½in. In her last job as housekeeper to Mrs Carlile of Gayhurst House, an Elizabethan mansion in Buckinghamshire, she was said in her reference to have assiduously 'studied the interests of the family whom she serves.' The story of Mrs Neill is a sad one, for clearly she was a woman qualified to do the job. Her superior earnings of £55 hint at her status: here was a top-flight housekeeper. The Marchioness interviewed her, liked her, but deliberated for several days. Mrs Neill waited anxiously, then finally left London and returned to her friend in Oswestry, Salop. Hearing nothing, she continued to apply for jobs.

On 7 November another small, stiff white envelope, grubby with several carriage and train journeys, was delivered to Oswestry by the Royal Mail. It contained a letter written a week earlier to Mrs Neill's temporary London address. 'Dear Madam, I am directed by the Marchioness of Salisbury to ask you to please to come to see her again tomorrow, Monday, between 11 & 12. Yours faithfully, R.T. Gunton.' It was too late. Mrs Neill was distraught. 'Sir, your letter was forwarded to me this morning, I beg to say that I waited in London till last Saturday expecting to hear from her Ladyship, she promised me her decision as last Wednesday week.' Since then she had accepted a situation in Scotland 'on speculation', and was to start in six days. 'I should have "preferred" her Ladyship's', she wrote.

Two days into her new job – housekeeper for an elderly widow at Stichill House, a turreted Victorian mansion in the Scottish borders – she wrote again to Mr Gunton. 'Sir if her Ladyship is still in want of a Housekeeper I should be glad to accept the situation as I find it would be impossible for me to remain here longer than my month as I should lose my good character' – her all-important reference. 'It is a very "<u>rough</u> place".' I beg sir to remain yours respectfully, A.S. Neill.' But that is the last Mrs Neill heard from Mr Gunton or from the Marchioness of Salisbury. A letter delivered late had changed the course of her life for ever.

The other woman to interest Her Ladyship was Mrs Prince. Her application letter is in large copperplate, bold, unhurried and confidently to the point. 'My Lady,' she wrote from Alcester in Warwickshire, 'I have just returned here after being in London and concluded that you had engaged as it was some time since your advertisement appeared. I have been living 5 years with someone your Ladyship knows well.' This was intriguing to the Marchioness, who wrote on the top left corner, 'Ask what family she means.' Mrs Prince was well connected: she had read the advertisement *and* she knew who had placed it. There was a network of gossip running between the housekeepers of Britain's great houses as taut and as time-sensitive, in its day, as Twitter. In London there were up to twelve mail deliveries a day, allowing for many on-going conversations.

She continued laconically: 'I wish to have £60 a year' – this is about £3,600 in today's money. (Lord Salisbury's annual income was £60,000: about £3.6 million today.) 'Have been used to a large country house and understand household bread also a dairy.' This, in Victorian country-house code, hints at a very large establishment. Mrs Prince was confident, and she was tough. Mr Gunton duly summoned this 48-year-old woman to Hatfield House for interview on Saturday, 25 October at 11 a.m., reimbursing her a hefty £2 for her expenses, about £120 in today's money. But once Mrs Prince had travelled all the way back to the Midlands, she received a regretful letter of rejection from Mr Gunton. The Marchioness had apparently decided against her.

The job was first offered to Maria Woods, 51, long-term house-keeper of Middleton Park in Oxfordshire for the influential Earl and Countess of Jersey, political allies of Lord Salisbury. It seems likely that Mrs Woods was coerced into meeting Lady Salisbury out of respectful deference – her own, and probably that of her mistress, who was 31 years old to Lady Salisbury's 53. It was not easy to deny the Prime Minister's wife.

But Maria Woods turned the offer down. The housekeeper wrote bravely to Mr Gunton, once safely back in the basement of her Georgian mansion, saying that 'after due consideration' she didn't think she would be 'quite strong enough' to manage such a large house as Hatfield, and that she was sorry to be obliged to decline the honour. 'Lady Jersey says she do not think I should be strong enough either.'

Who, then, was given the position?

In a box in an upper servants' hall at Hatfield House is a large brown envelope, dirty and frayed, whose contents chart the Marchioness of Salisbury's meticulous hunt for a housekeeper in that autumn of 1890. This basement room is now the archive office, and I sat at a long, polished dining table where once the housekeeper had sat with butler, lady's maids, valets and cook, and read through those fifty-nine letters. To Her Ladyship, Georgina, who saw the whole process as something of a chore, they were just letters. Divided into bundles, each is marked with her impatient writing: 'London ones', 'Country ones' and 'These are hopeless, to be burnt'. To secretary Mr Gunton, who kept them all, they were estate correspondence to be scrupulously filed. But to me, they were the first evidence I had found of housekeepers as *real women* – and as such, they were thrilling.

Behind each page of diagonal scrawl, near impossible to read, was a story. I could almost hear their voices: 'I am a careful and industrious manageress' . . . 'I presume you do not object to a Catholic' . . . 'I will do all in my power to merit your esteem' . . . 'I am a widow (40) and have no family' . . . 'I left through the breaking up of the establishment'. Behind each cramped or flowery signature – Mrs Boosey, Mrs Bouncey, Mrs Bocquet – was a personality, a woman with weaknesses, eccentricities, secret hopes and appetites. There was something very exposed and vulnerable about this collection of letters.

Hatfield House is still lived in by the Cecil family, and is today a heavyweight player in Britain's heritage industry. It has clanking suits of armour from the sixteenth century; the silk stockings of a youthful Queen Elizabeth I; a wooden staircase topped with snarling lions carved in 1611. The week I visited, a Hollywood crew was filming with Johnny Depp and Gwyneth Paltrow – location hire now all part of the reinvention of the English country house. But the woman who ran this vast and prominent house for the 3rd Marquess of Salisbury – three times Prime Minister to Queen Victoria – is entirely missing from the archives. There is a small, unexplained hole in the estate records between 1840 and 1928, a hole perhaps forgivable in an archive that goes back to 1610. The bundle of applications is unique in surviving at all, and the archivists haven't yet got round to reading it.

I put the letters back in their battered envelope and turned to my laptop, and to the Internet, to solve the mystery of who was appointed housekeeper in 1890. The website ancestry.com took me to the 1891 census, then to Hatfield House, Hertfordshire and its list of servants. The housekeeper ('in charge' written above her job title) was Ann E. Prince, a widow of 49 – the very same who had initially received a letter of rejection. There she was, with eight maids in their twenties, on that Sunday in April some six months after her appointment. The rest of the household staff were with Lord and Lady Salisbury at their London residence in Arlington Street. Mrs Prince, who had so boldly requested £60 a year, was born in Islington. She ended up working just twenty miles from her birthplace. Ten years later, at the 1901 census, she was there still – though her mistress had died in 1899. By 1911, eight years after Lord Salisbury's death, she had gone.

There is no evidence of what kind of person Mrs Prince was, or even what she looked like – whether tall and fearsome, or small and benevolent. This was the woman behind all those famous political house parties with their influential guests, the woman responsible for the care and conservation of so many extraordinary treasures. Yet it is as if she never existed. Whatever her story, however successful her tenure, there is huge poignancy in this fact.

In researching this book, I was less interested in the minutiae and logistics of running a country house than in the human stories: the women entrusted with that weighty job. It was, in many ways, an isolating role. She was too senior to fraternise with her maids; too dignified to let her hair down. 'A faithful and excellent housekeeper', such as that belonging to the 11th Earl of Pembroke at Wilton House, Wiltshire in 1800, was 'consequently well hated by a proportion of servants under her direction'.[5] She was mocked both upstairs and downstairs for putting on the refined airs and graces of her employers. She was trusted with the family's most intimate secrets; she handled huge sums of money – yet the housekeeper's position was ambivalent, even supplicatory. She was entirely at the mercy of her mistress's good humour.

I set out to try to bring to life a handful of these women from the past one hundred and fifty years, from her most modest Georgian origins, to her infinitely more powerful Victorian counterpart, to her undignified, diminished end, hastened by two world wars. What were the fault lines of this very particular role, and how did it change as time passed? What were the physical hardships and the emotional rewards?

Exhuming their stories was not easy. Most housekeepers were, naturally, the soul of discretion, unquestioningly loyal to the mistress of the house. If she wrote a diary it was usually trivial, preserved only if it threw light on other, more interesting people. (Sarah Wells, habitual diarist and housekeeper of Uppark, was mother to the Edwardian writer H. G. Wells; the forty-four diaries of Grace Higgens, housekeeper to the Bloomsbury set, are valued today for their sprinkling of famous names.) I trawled through the neglected archives of these great houses – the yellowing bundles of estate letters; the housekeeping ledgers, shopping bills and laundry lists; the photo albums crawling with dust mites – and I managed to find documentary evidence of that guard being dropped; odd letters or diary entries that made me witness to their innermost thoughts.

At times I felt like a detective pursuing the smallest shred of evidence, for servants pass like ghosts through most country-house archives. Where there were gaping holes I assembled the outside facts and used my imagination. To put flesh on their bones I visited the houses, breathed in the dank basement air of the housekeeper's sitting room, pictured what it might be like to push through that green baize door from a dark, flagstoned passageway smelling faintly of cabbage and into the elegant opulence of a stateroom hung with Gainsboroughs. I layered all these impressions one upon the other and tried to immerse myself in their world.

My housekeepers link arms in a chain through history, from the Great Reform Act of 1832 to decimalisation and the TV drama *Upstairs, Downstairs* in 1971. There is Dorothy Doar, Regency housekeeper for the obscenely wealthy Duke and Duchess of Sutherland at Trentham Hall, Staffordshire. There is Sarah Wells, a deaf and elderly Victorian in charge of Uppark, West Sussex. Ellen Penketh is Edwardian cook-housekeeper at the sociable but impecunious Erddig Hall in the Welsh borders. The First World War turned these country houses upside down – literally, in the case of Wrest Park in Bedfordshire, whose new role as war hospital was enabled by Scotswoman Hannah Mackenzie. The story of Grace Higgens, cook-housekeeper at Charleston farmhouse in East Sussex for half a century, has a different flavour – but is no less moving for its tale of stoicism and endurance.

The surprise is in the great hardship of their lives. History, fiction, film and television have led us to believe that these were secure and rather grand ladies, yet, as suggested by Lady Salisbury's bundle of replies, these women lived precariously. They were given immense responsibility for very little financial reward in a world with few choices. They suffered private hardships and crises while serving their families, yet often responded with heroic chutzpah. I discovered an unwanted pregnancy, an affair, two thefts and a court case. One housekeeper worked until she was 70; another crossed the Atlantic several times and died at 102, enjoying a daily bottle of whisky. The accounts of these women end for the most part badly and abruptly, but having examined the evidence and tried to understand their motives, I found myself cheering them on.

Part 1

Dorothy Doar

Trentham Hall, Staffordshire 1832

It is quite impossible in such an establishment to permit of her breeding.

James Loch, Chief Agent to the Sutherlands

Timeline

1830s – Stagecoach from London to Edinburgh takes two days as turnpike roads improve. 'Railway Mania' begins.

1830 – William IV ascends throne, aged 64. First D.I.Y. knitting book, *Ladies' Work for Sailors*.

1832 – Great Reform Act: men with homes with an annual value of £10 get the vote.

1835 – First pre-packaged baking powder on sale.

1836 – Dickens's first novel *The Pickwick Papers* serialised.

1834 – Poor Law Amendment Act: the destitute refused parish relief and forced into the workhouse.

1837 – Victoria becomes Queen, aged 18.

1839 – First Indian tea for sale in London.

1840s – Railways expand to most towns and villages. Food in tin cans becomes more widely used.

1840 – First postage stamps: Penny Black and Twopence Blue.

1841 – London's Reform Club installs gas cookers, among first in the country.

1842 – Beecham's Pills first marketed. Coal Mines Act: Women and children under ten prohibited from working underground.

1849 – Safety pin invented.

Abominably Rich

They made a formidable cabal, the five housekeepers of the Duke of Sutherland. Like pawns on a chessboard they were ranged across the country: Mrs Spillman sat at Dunrobin Castle in the far north-east of Scotland; Mrs Cleaver at the southernmost extreme, West Hill in Wandsworth, Surrey. In the capital, the tireless Mrs Galleazie reigned over Stafford House, scene of much entertaining. Mrs Kirke presided over the new hunting lodge, Lilleshall Hall up in Shropshire; and Mrs Doar sat plumb in the middle: keeper of Trentham Hall, Staffordshire.

Letters flew between these five women daily: hastily scrawled notes with advance warning of the family's imminent arrival or departure; requests to send Staffordshire partridge, kid boots from London, whisky barrels from Scotland, more ripe pineapples for this week's reception at Stafford House. Sicknesses were communicated, staff vacancies filled and in-house gossip quenched. A nobleman could not hope to employ five more discreet or implacable custodians.

This is the story of one of these women: a housekeeper who, after fourteen years' loyal service, fell spectacularly foul of her employers. The year was 1832, a time of great political upheaval in Britain. Dorothy Doar was a small but vital cog in the enormous machine servicing the richest, most powerful and probably most disliked family of her day. Given the size of this machine – the Duke and Duchess of Sutherland moved between not two, but five houses – it is by sheer chance that the sorry tale of Mrs Doar has survived at all. But, like a gnat squashed between the pages of a book, I came across her in a random bundle of otherwise dry correspondence between two land agents; a bundle tied with white ribbon and filed away in the vast Sutherland Collection at the Staffordshire Record Office.

Written over the course of two months in 1832, this series of letters is highly unusual – unusual because the housekeeper leaps brightly off the page. Dorothy Doar *lives*; her character and foibles are laid bare. Her tale unfolds in a drama that no wage book, store-cupboard inventory or housekeeping accounts book can hope to compete with. The letters throw light on basement politics between upper servants in the Regency era: back-stabbing, rumour spreading, leapfrogging for advancement. There are hints of sexual liberties; of houses so rarely visited by their owners that they develop their own unconventional codes of conduct. The letters show us, too, how the uber-aristocracy of the day treated their upper servants.

For such an important family, a surprising amount of time and energy was put into the relationship between mistress and housekeeper. You could not run five houses without the likes of Mrs Doar. She was somebody to be kept sweet: to be soothed, praised and assisted. The relationship was based on loyalty, honesty and trust – with the servant always aware of the immense gap between the haves and have-nots. No servant, no matter how senior, could take anything for granted – as Dorothy Doar was to learn to her cost.

Mrs Doar's job was to facilitate the most luxurious lifestyle pursued in Britain at that time. Her employer was George Granville Leveson-Gower (pronounced 'Looshun Gore'), known to his housekeeper in 1832 as the Marquis of Stafford, just one year off being made the Duke of Sutherland, the title by which this lineage is remembered. He had, by virtue of an astute marriage, created a dynasty second only in wealth to the royal family. Quite simply, the Staffords owned much of Britain, and as a consequence were hated and revered in equal measure.

They were not, like some aristocrats, cheese-paring. The Marquis's annual income was around £200,000 (£10 million in today's money), and his wife, the Marchioness, lived to enjoy it. At Stafford House, the largest and most sumptuous of London's private palaces, Elizabeth Leveson-Gower would host famously lavish dinners and late evening parties where the 'long succession of rooms, their spaciousness and loftiness has such an effect that people look like Lilliputians'.[1] The size and grandeur of the staircase alone made 'the whole company look both pigmy and dingy',[2] remarked a guest. The style of living of the Marquis of Stafford exceeded, thought one Lady Beaumont, 'everything in this country. No one could vie with it.'

Lilleshall, the smaller of their country residences, was so luxurious that Lord Stafford's sister-in-law Henrietta, Viscountess Granville, found herself beginning 'to wish for something to dislike, as I think my eternal raptures must sicken all my friends and acquaintances', she wrote. 'Lord Stafford is abominably rich.'

For a woman in Mrs Doar's profession, you could not hope to do better. The opportunities for job advancement, with so many houses, were endless (not just the family's own, but those of their in-laws – Castle Howard, Eaton Hall, Chatsworth House, to name but a handful). An army of staff was in constant employment and redeployment around the country. Loyalty was rewarded, glamour – at a distance – an exciting distraction from the daily routine. To come to the attention of My Lady Stafford, to worm one's way into her good books, was to be assured – one would have hoped – of protection in life.

At the hub of this great family's wheel of influence and patronage was Mrs Doar's fiefdom, Trentham Hall. Every dynasty must have its seat, and this chaste and elegant Georgian mansion, connected by scrupulously formal gardens to a mile-long, baguette-shaped lake, was where the important scenes of life were played out for Lord and Lady Stafford and the four surviving Leveson-Gower *enfants*, George, Charlotte, Elizabeth and Francis.

In just her second year with the family back in 1819, Mrs Doar helped prepare for the young Elizabeth's wedding at Trentham – a phenomenal strain for the servants, hundreds of mouths to feed and all eyes fixed on the 22-year-old bride, rumoured to have been presented by her new father-in-law, the Earl of Grosvenor, with jewellery worth £3,622 8s 6d (£180,000).[3] In 1828 Mrs Doar had helped contrive, with much sweat and labour, the euphoric celebrations at Trentham Hall for the birth of Lord Stafford's first grandson. Cannons were fired, feasts and games for the tenants laid on with no stinting, and 'spontaneous rejoicings' were reported on every Sutherland estate up and down the country.

It was an orderly world, tightly run by land agent William Lewis and his second in command, housekeeper Dorothy Doar: representatives of master and mistress in their absence. But for much of the year there would be a sense of suspended animation within the house. When would the family return? The Staffords loved Trentham Hall – a two-day gallop from London in the well-sprung family post-chaise – but they used it sporadically. Politics, St James's Palace, the London season (February to July), Scottish acres and grandchildren at Lilleshall all vied for their attention. They liked to spend September here after summer in the Highlands, but they were a highly mobile family and so there were no other certainties.

Country-house tourists who turned up at Trentham hoping for a glimpse of the legendary Staffords were shown round by the housekeeper. This was the Georgian way: a guided tour given in exchange for a tip. *Jones's Views of the Seats of Noblemen and Gentlemen* (1829) was the hefty guidebook of the day and it lists each of Trentham's 295 works of art. Visitors knew precisely which 'fine specimens of the best masters' they would find here – the Poussins and Watteaus, Tiepolos and Titians, Holbeins and Hogarths. Mrs Doar led a well-worn circuit around two dozen staterooms often shrouded in dust sheets. She learnt to pause on the curve of the great staircase to show to best advantage the Holy Family by Rubens; she allowed extra time in the Old Library for viewing of Holbein's King Henry VIII (a masterly copy). And she knew that the ladies in particular wanted to peruse her mistress's chambers, hung with family portraits and Her Ladyship's own watercolours.

Visitors made a refreshing change, but they were not Family. Mrs Doar expended a great deal of nervous energy in waiting; scrutinising the family rooms through her mistress's eyes, checking and rechecking the linen cupboard, sorting the translucent Staffordshire bone china and adding to the growing stock of rosehip, gooseberry and ginger wines which lined her still-room shelves.

Under her control were a kitchen maid, a laundry maid, three housemaids, a still-room maid and two dairymaids: eight young girls to be kept busy on 'board wages' in a house that was, essentially, killing time. Kept busy, and kept away from the butler's charges – four footmen, under-butler, steward's room boy, hall boy, boot boy and knife boy. Country-house staff the length of Britain routinely spent months on end similarly holding their breath.

It was imperative to be ready. When the family arrived, tired from bouncing along the turnpike roads, Trentham Hall must look as if it was always thus: no dust sheets on the furniture, fresh flowers in all the vases, writing paper and ink in the bedrooms, beds aired, linen crisply ironed and every fireplace scoured until gleaming with brushes, blacklead, emery paper and cloth. Nothing should jar or jolt the family's cosseted, infantilised sensibilities. No one must wonder at the frantic preparations behind the scenes.

No sooner had the family arrived than its departure must be prepared for, without knowing exactly when it would come. Mrs Doar was a swan, her feet paddling furiously. She was a magician, conjuring scenes of order and tranquillity. I imagine her heart frequently pounded beneath her whalebone stays while her face remained impassive. She lived and worked in an atmosphere of restrained upheaval.

The Staffords adored coming home. Favourite daughter-in-law Harriet wrote to her sister, on arriving at Trentham in 1828:

I rushed to the potager – you know my weakness – and walked up and down between spinach and dahlias in ecstasy . . . There is a repose, a *laissez aller*, a freedom, and a security in a *vie de chateau* that no other destiny offers one. I feel when I set out to walk as if alone in the world – nothing but trees and birds; but then comes the enormous satisfaction of always finding a man dressing a hedge, or a woman in a gingham and a black bonnet on her knees picking up weeds, the natural gendarmerie of the country, and the most comfortable well-organized country.⁴

Lady Stafford wrote of arriving at Trentham after an exhausting tour of the Scottish Sutherland acres in the autumn of 1831. She stayed at Dunrobin, where all was 'in perfect order, Mrs Spillman exceedingly active & happy but finding great difficulty in breaking in Cookmaids'. But she was greatly relieved to return, albeit briefly, to the Staffordshire seat. 'Here I am arrived', she wrote to her husband in London, 'and though it very provokingly is a rainy day, I must own I have not seen any thing comparable to it, in its own style since I left it, & hope we shall come here to stay in the summer.' She continues: 'I found Doar with everything ready for me & am to have a Partridge for dinner with a boiled Fowl in addition, some fish & an apple tart. Such good bread & butter!'

The menu, drawn up by Mrs Doar after long deliberation with the cook, was pure comfort food. The Marchioness was by this time a stout 66-year-old, known by gossips as 'old Mother Stafford'; yet there is a sense of her surrendering with pleasure to 'Doar' and her clucking ministrations.

II

Like A Dragon

We know a great deal more about Elizabeth Leveson-Gower, Marchioness of Stafford, than we do about her housekeeper. Dorothy Doar held one of the most senior posts of the period for a working woman. But in the annals of the Sutherlands she barely figures. If you want to track down her ghost today, to see where she worked, you will find that the house is gone. The far grander Victorian house that replaced Mrs Doar's Georgian Trentham Hall is gone too; just some pock-marked walls and a grassed-over bumpy footprint remain, overlooking the now restored formal gardens and lake. Yet there is a palpable sense, in the audacious scale of that lake – fed by the diverted River Trent, overlooked by a grim-faced 1st Duke of Sutherland on a Nelson-like column – of this family's tremendous self-regard. The house is gone, but an atmosphere remains.

Elizabeth, Marchioness of Stafford, was orphaned when her parents died of 'putrid fever', or typhus, while taking the waters in Bath in 1766. She was one year old. Her grandmother brought her up in Edinburgh, an only child, to inherit a wild, northern estate of one million acres and a castle, Dunrobin. Aged 20, Elizabeth married George Granville, then Earl Gower, a dull, nervous man with a large beaky nose and prim mouth, an obsession with collecting paintings and an aversion to the bagpipes (he swiftly converted Dunrobin's piper into a porter). With the blending of her Scottish acres and his Staffordshire and Yorkshire acres, they created the largest estate of any landed gentry in the country.

They passed two brilliant years in Paris where George was Ambassador, their four-year-old son romping with the Dauphin and Elizabeth confiding in Queen Marie Antoinette. Just before the Terror they beat a hasty retreat, but retained a love of French food, society and bons mots. Mrs Doar would have studied the French appendix of her manual *The Complete Servant* for help with the phrases that peppered her mistress's speech:

Outré – 'oot-ray'. Preposterous.
Ennui – 'ang-wee'. Tiresomeness.
Dernier ressort – 'dern-yair-res-sor'. Last resort.[5]

Elizabeth was everything her husband was not: brilliant, socially voracious, fun-loving, fearless. In her time she possessed great beauty – and many lovers. In 1799 Lord Stafford, his eyesight failing, was advised by his physician to 'strictly abstain from all conjugal intercourse with his wife' – who then, 'unluckily', fell pregnant. Lord Francis was born on New Year's Day of the new century, 1800, his father rumoured to be Lord Carlisle, Stafford's brother-in-law.[6]

This was her life – but what was she like to work for? Aged 50, she displayed a steeliness over the Sutherland Highland Clearances, done in her name, encouraging the crofters from the impoverished interior to the coast despite the Sellar affair (an agent who was put on trial for his cruel and needlessly violent evictions) She wrote to Loch, asking him 'to encourage Sellar in trouncing these people who wish to destroy our system . . . I do hope the aggressors will be scourged'.[7]

Physically she was large and indomitable. The Whig diarist Thomas Creevey wrote in 1833 of the newly widowed Elizabeth that 'it was as good as a play to see old Sutherland moving her huge derrière by slow and dignified degrees about in her chair'. Two years later he remarked that the Duchess-Countess of Sutherland, now aged 70, had 'all the appearance of a wicked old woman'.[8]

Her constitution was ox-like. She was the sort who mannishly pooh-poohed physical danger – as when she travelled by paddle steamer up the North Sea coast to the Moray Firth in October 1831. 'A delightful voyage', her scratchy letter to the ailing Lord Stafford began, on a gold-edged sheet folded like a book; 'I triumphant riding in the storm . . . All sick except myself who was famished & ate roast beef like a Dragon. No calm as yet. It is very odd that though tiresome enough it has not frightened me at all.' Her maid Betty, meanwhile, was 'Half dead'.[9]

III

Every Shilling We Have

Dorothy Doar came to work for the family in 1818: one year before the first steamship crossed the Atlantic; two years before the death of mad King George III; a decade before the first passenger railway. She was 27 years old, a Northumberland girl from the mining and foundry town of Long Benton, Newcastle-upon-Tyne. We don't know where she worked previously; the first census was not until 1841.

It was not unusual for girls to go into service at the age of eight; some started work at the neighbouring Stoke-on-Trent potteries and pits aged five. But Mrs Doar had a more fortunate start in life. Recruited from the preferred, steady ranks of the lower middle classes or from among the better of the working classes, she 'had her letters': she could write in a strong, slanting hand, she could keep an account book and she could spell, after a fashion.

The manual of the day – *The Complete Servant*, written by retired butler and housekeeper Samuel and Sarah Adams in 1825 – advised that the housekeeper 'ought to be a steady middle-aged woman, of great experience in her profession, and a tolerable knowledge of the world. In her conduct, she should be moral, exemplary, and assiduous, as the harmony, comfort, and economy of the family will greatly depend on her example.'[10]

James Loch agreed that the ideal housekeeper should be an older woman. In 1819 he wrote to a colleague about finding one for a Scottish cousin. 'She must be able to undertake the management of the kitchen when he has company and be a good Cook, but know how to pickle, preserve etc, be able to instruct the servants in baking and brewing and to keep monthly accounts, to take charge of the House & Linen.' His cousin would be willing to pay from 30 to 35 guineas a year (£1,300 to £1,500 today), throwing in the perks of coal, vegetables and milk. As for her type, 'he would prefer a woman who has served the most of her time in the country and she must always have been in a good gentleman's family . . . her age not under 30 nor above 45'.[11] Life expectancy at this time was 46; in Stoke-on-Trent's pits and potteries, just 37.

Did Dorothy Doar fit the bill, in Loch's eyes? She was on the young side, so might have worked her way up the ladder, moving on from cook, nurse or lady's maid. But she was also unusual in her air of maturity. She had indeed a 'tolerable knowledge of the world' beyond that of most servants. For Mrs Doar was a rare thing among female domestics: she was married.

This was unusual. For butlers, it was perfectly acceptable to be married. Employers liked it; it stabilised a man, as long as wife and children lived off site and out of sight. But it was an accepted certainty in nineteenth-century domestic service that marriage marked a definitive end to a female servant's career. A woman might return to service on the death of her husband, but for the most part it was premarital employment, a chance to save some money and learn domestic skills.

The downstairs world of the country house was something of a marriage market, what with so many visiting servants, and although flirtations were routinely sniffed out and quenched (one of Mrs Doar's particular responsibilities), things happened. At greatest risk were the teenage maids, giggling with the strapping footmen who lurked around the servants' hall and still room, hair pasted down, calf muscles nicely visible through white stockings.

'Avoid as much as possible being alone with the other sex, as the greatest mischiefs happen from small circumstances,' wrote Samuel and Sarah Adams, forefingers wagging. 'A reserved modesty is the best safeguard of virtue.'

Did Mr and Mrs Doar meet in domestic service, flouting the common 'No Followers' rule? Did she succumb to a suitor while working as a ladies' maid in a large London house – and was she then forced to leave her position? Dorothy married Mark, a 28-year-old Londoner, in Marylebone on 5 May 1818. A swelling bump was by now visible beneath her Empire-line cotton dress. It was remarkable, in the circumstances, that the Marchioness of Stafford considered Doar a suitable candidate at all – but then Elizabeth Leveson-Gower was by birth and instinct a Georgian – and in this pre-Victorian era, the servants' rulebook was less rigidly codified and prescriptive. Identical uniforms for maids had not yet become the norm; upper servants might wear cast-offs from their master and mistress's wardrobes. Moral attitudes towards domestic staff were far less censorious in the eighteenth century than they were later to become.

Mrs Doar arrived at Trentham Hall newly married – and newly separated from husband and baby. Emma, not yet weaned, was sent north to Dorothy's 34-year-old unmarried sister Elizabeth Parker in Newcastle-upon-Tyne. Two hundred miles now lay between her and her tiny daughter. Mark Doar took rooms in the village of Handford on the Trentham estate. The new Mrs Doar was free to work: she had her husband and her daughter's keep to pay for. And Dorothy was fiercely and unusually ambitious for her child. Her 'unfortunate' husband (as she wrote to agent James Loch) was unable to work, so it was down to Dorothy to fund her daughter's future. The girl was sent to school, which took 'every shilling we have'.[12] Very few children attended school at the time, and certainly not the offspring of servants. The lives of most children in this industrious part of the Midlands were unremittingly bleak.

Hundreds were employed in the printing rooms of the nearby potteries, cutting out decorative designs and sticking them onto ceramics. 'The printing room is indeed a bad school for children,' reported Dr Samuel Scriven to the House of Commons in 1841.[13] 'Their language is indecent and profane.' He found, in his research, 'mouldrunners' running back and forth with ware 'labouring like little slaves', and was troubled by the sight of so many 'dull and cadaverous countenances' – children suffering from lead poisoning.

Dorothy Doar's daughter was lucky: her mother's position meant she would not be gobbled up by Britain's Industrial Revolution. But there was little precedent at this time for putting a servant's daughter through full-time education. Not until 1833 would the Factory Act insist on just two hours' schooling a day for the over-fives. If you wanted to educate your child in the 1820s, you were usually middle class, your child was probably male and you paid heftily for the privilege.

Mrs Doar did not earn much. The richest family in Britain did not pay their female servants highly – perhaps even less than was normal at that time. By 1840 the Sutherland housekeepers were earning between

£31.10 and £63 a year (£1,400 to £2,800 in today's money) depending on experience, according to old leather-bound wage ledgers kept in the Sutherland archive.[14] The London house steward, butler and upholsterer, all men, earned twice as much. The various lowly maids got between £12 and £16 a year (£500 and £700), while the still-room maid (the housekeeper's personal assistant; three arriving and leaving within one year at Stafford House, which cannot have pleased housekeeper Mrs Harriet Galleazie) earned £14.14 (£650).

Bed and board was free, of course, and upper servants' perks were bumped up by gifts from employers and tradespeople. But still, William Lewis (agent for Trentham and Lilleshall) wrote to James Loch in 1832 that he considered 'Mrs Doar's wages too small for the faithful discharge of such a trust'. If you did not pay her enough, it was thought that the housekeeper might fall prey to temptation. At this stage of our story, Mrs Doar was held to be loyal, conscientious and above suspicion – but her low wage might have been a thorn in her side; the result of staying put for so very long. Yet once you found your place in a noble family, once you rose to their notice and approval, Mrs Doar was probably of the opinion that you'd be a fool to walk away.

Her young daughter was in Long Benton and her needy husband was in Handford, a mile from Trentham's gates. She was an absent wife, an absent mother: a housekeeper for an absent mistress. Mrs Doar had her share of anxieties, but she was required to sink herself into the minutiae of her work.

IV

Eight Slop Pails

The country house consumed material goods on a massive scale. It was a kind of firm devoted to *things*: getting them in, keeping them in shape. Such seemingly innocuous *things* were at the heart of Mrs Doar's downfall, so it is worth exploring exactly what they meant to her and her household.

Trentham Hall sat at the hub of a network of canals that carried a ceaseless traffic of cargo, both industrial and domestic. The lucrative Bridgewater Canal was the Marquis of Stafford's own, while the Trent and Mersey Canal, laden with Josiah Wedgwood's fragile wares, passed barely a mile east of Trentham Hall's front door.

Not far off was another Midlands country house, Dunham Massey, whose housekeeper Anne Calder would have been known to Mrs Doar. Though thirty miles apart, they shared several suppliers, and in this way gossip would pass between the houses as grocer, butcher and brushmaker sat in easy chairs sipping sweet wine and expounding on local news. Like Mrs Doar, Mrs Calder kept a detailed ledger of her orders. By accident it is Mrs Calder's ledger that survives. And so we know that in 1822 one local carrier on the Bridgewater Canal, a bargewoman called Mary Allen, handled no fewer than 177 different consignments for Dunham Massey – three or four a week – usually of several parcels, boxes, hampers, casks, crates or bundles at a time. These included barrels of vinegar, boxes of cheeses, nine fire-grates, seven coal boxes, bundles of carpeting and matting, eighteen chimney pots, eight slop pails, large parcels of sheet music, a hamper of soda water and a bag of feathers.[15]

Half a century later, one of Mrs Doar's successors at Trentham, Mrs Ingram, kept a bundle of crumpled receipts for the year 1874.[16] Passing through her hands was a complicated variety of goods, paperwork and money. The bills arrived from all over the country: 'Baby Linen Warehouse', 'Country Tea Warehouse', Clynelish Distillery in Brora. Through these receipts we can envisage the second Duke or Duchess of Sutherland airily waving a hand – 'Put it on the bill' – as they travelled round the country.

Mrs Ingram handled, among other things, kid elasticated boots, umbrellas, one dozen each of collars and cuffs, whalebone, velvet ribbon and hessian. She paid for thirteen easy chairs; for a gold clock to be repaired and cleaned; for moist sugar, lump sugar, Demerara sugar and arrowroot. There were heartburn lozenges purchased in Edinburgh, coke from the Newcastle Gas Works and two Minton busts of the Dowager Duchess of Sutherland commissioned in Stoke-on-Trent.

She ordered calf's head, sweetbread, tongue and suet; she paid for one box of cigars from Pall Mall, a firkin of ale and remedies from the Staffordshire local homeopathic chemist. For a certain Mrs Wills, who signed her receipt with a shaky cross – 'her mark' – she handed over £2 10s (£114) for a 'counterpaine knit for Dunrobin Castle'.

These were not just *things* to Mrs Ingram or Mrs Doar. These shopping lists were, to the housekeeper's eyes, minutely codified symbols of status. Everything – from the quality of the sugar in your tea to the stuffing of your mattress; from the type of painting hanging on your bedroom wall to the thickness of your ceramic soap dish – came down to hierarchy. Hierarchy lay at the very heart of the country house. As the manager of consumption, the housekeeper knew more about the multiple meaning of *things* than any other servant.

The order and structure of 'little things' was to become very dear to the Victorian upper and middle classes. Managing such household articles established 'bonds of appropriateness', so it was thought; bonds on which the whole order of society was built. Housekeeperly organisation and maintenance encouraged habits, 'without which man would tend to the savage state'.[17]

Outside Trentham Hall's brick walls lay the industrial town of Stoke-on-Trent. The skyscape of blackened brick 'bottle oven' chimneys and slag heaps contrasted starkly with the soft woodland mirrored in Trentham's still lake. Nothing could be less suggestive of beauty than this district of the Potteries: muddy and miserable, squalid and unclean. Here, people got by on bread and tea alone. A third of all children born didn't live past the age of five, victims of measles, scarlet fever, diphtheria and bowel disease. Lead poisoning (plumbism) and 'Potter's Rot' (silicosis of the lungs) saw to the rest. Life was savage indeed.

Trentham's elaborate table services, Her Ladyship's morning tea set, the translucent plate on which her partridge was served – all this came from Stoke, along with every chamber pot, slop pail and coarse, servant-friendly earthenware plate. Mrs Doar dealt in such hierarchies, and she was grateful to be on the right side of Trentham's gates. How lucky she was. Yet even so, her world was filled with insidious and occasionally demeaning reminders of status. The devil, as they say, is in the detail.

She had her own bedroom and sitting room; her maids had to share rooms (and often beds). Mattresses were stuffed depending on your place in the hierarchy: straw or horsehair, flock or wool – feather, naturally, for the family. According to an inventory taken of Trentham Hall in 1826, we know that Mrs Doar was rewarded with a feather mattress, but of the inferior one-shilling-per-pound variety (the family's stuffing cost twice as much). She also had a mahogany four-poster bed, five mahogany chairs, various stuffed armchairs, an oak chest of drawers, a mahogany fire screen and a white-covered sofa (a status-laden luxury in this climate of coal dust). There was a fitted carpet, window curtains and blinds.[18] It was a big room, and it is strange to inhabit it in one's mind; to view its contents like this, without having a clear picture of the woman who lived here. Physically, this is as close to Dorothy as the trail gets.

House steward Thomas Dodsworth had much the same, but in addition his room boasted a hearthrug, a walnut wardrobe and a writing desk with black leather top and inkstand. He was a man, and he was her senior – just. The maids' and footmen's rooms, by contrast, each contained one beech four-poster bed, one chair, one small table and a looking glass. A mean square of carpet partially covered the draughty floor. Just how far Mrs Doar had advanced in her own career was a fact daily on show, as much for her own benefit as for others'. Her clutter of armchairs, polished mahogany and soft furnishings was a reminder of her power – and, implicitly, her vulnerability.

On her soap dish was a subtly graded bar of soap, of better quality than the coarser maids' variety, yet not the coveted Rose or Windsor. It had been picked with a sense of entitlement from the store-cupboard soap boxes where best yellow, best mottled, Rose, Windsor, glycerin, white toilet, honey and soft soap lay cut in aromatic squares and wrapped in tissue.[19] When the house was full the chambermaids were wont to slip used nuggets of guest soap into their apron pockets, thumbing their noses at 'place'. Mrs Doar would turn a blind eye depending on her mood. She had her own porcelain washstand and set of chamber ware, more than the standard servant's seven pieces but some way short of the bedroom sets upstairs, which might consist of eighteen pieces of chintz-patterned china matching bed-hangings, curtains and upholstery.

Some markers of status were subtle, others less so. Trentham Hall in 1832 was not a comfortable house for servants. The wind in winter would gust along the flat Staffordshire acres, whipping up the long lake and moaning through doors and windows. On the wrong side of the green baize door the basement rooms were poorly lit and damp, the attic bedrooms freezing cold. Servants' privies, out in the muddy yard, were long-drop soil pits with a bucket of ash to sprinkle over your doings. Strips of newspaper hung off a nail for the fastidious.

House steward Thomas Dodsworth's room was detached from the Hall, next to the cowsheds, laundry and bathhouse and opposite the poultry. It was essentially an outbuilding and the air around it smelt of the farmyard, but this was 'Pug's Parlour' – a kind of senior common room where he, Mrs Doar and the other upper servants (cook, butler, lady's maids, valets, head gardener, coachman) took their dessert and brandy halfway through the midday dinner at precisely a quarter to one, parading out of the servants' hall and across the yard in strict precedence, holding bowls and spoons before them. This ritual was repeated at large country houses the length of Britain.

Neurotic attention was given to visiting lady's maids and valets, who, below stairs, took on their boss's status (and names). Servants' manuals devoted whole appendices to this irksome subject. Mrs Doar made it her business to know that an earl's eldest son always went *before* a bishop; that a duchess went *after* wives of the King's nephews. 'Excuse me, Mr Kirkby,' I can see her murmuring in the butler's ear, 'but I think you'll find that on this occasion, it's Grosvenor before Bedford.'

But for all the airs and graces, these upper servants were not dukes or duchesses. A list of the value of meals per head per day in the Sutherland household at this time allocates 22s for family (£55 per head in today's money), 4s for the steward's room (£10) and 2s for the servants' hall (£5).[20]

Mrs Doar's personal lair is not identified on the architect's floor plan of old Trentham Hall, but it would have been the hub of operations below stairs. This was the engine room of the house, where books were balanced, hopeful girls interviewed or dismissed, tradesmen met over glasses of sweet wine or brandy. As she talked through her requirements she would finger, like a gaoler, the bunch of keys that hung at her waist: symbol of her absolute authority.

The housekeeper's store cupboard boasted a filing system so elaborate that only she understood the nuance and specificity of each item. There were, for starters, a panoply of brushes – from banister to 'cow mouth' brushes, round-table to stair-carpet brushes. It resembled a tightly packed ironmonger's shop. Every Friday she would open it up, releasing the sweet-sharp smells of horsehair, beeswax and linseed oil, and would parsimoniously deal out the staff requirements (*Another* tallow candle, Paterson?). Scullery maids and chambermaids, footmen, boot boy and knife boy jostled in line as they called out: 'Blacklead, ma'am!' 'China cloths!' 'Beeswax!'

She guarded the linen closet more jealously still. Once a year, usually in winter, Mrs Doar would unlock its heavy oak doors and count over every item, entering it into a book with detailed notes on age, missing items, repairs and replacements needed. Fabulously wealthy the Sutherlands might have been, but old sheets and tablecloths were cut down and reused for children's sheets, dresser cloths and powdering sheets (for protecting the shoulders when dressing hair). The linen inventory taken at Trentham in 1803 includes 461 napkins (of two qualities), 172 tablecloths (three qualities, one horseshoe-shaped), 109 sheets (three qualities), 441 towels (four qualities) and 78 pillow 'coats'. There were 189 domestic cloths: china cloths, 'rubbers', pocket cloths, glass cloths, lamp cloths, dusters, horn cloths for polishing beer cups in the servants' hall.[21] 'The right cloth for the right job' might well have been Mrs Doar's well-worn mantra, mimicked by the girls as they flicked playful dusters. There were, as yet, no cleaning fluids.

She knew the hierarchy of each piece of fabric in her linen cupboard by its heft in the hand, its particular weave and lustre: damask, diaper, huckaback, fine linen, coarse linen. Guests were given best-quality sheets and towels, then came family, nursery, upper servants and lower servants. Bed sheets for servants were made of a rough hempen 'hurden', coarse calico, or unbleached linen that until well washed had the texture of cardboard. Their sheets were made up of two lengths of fabric seamed down the middle, unpicked and remade by Mrs Doar and the maids when threadbare. Nobody wanted to break in a new sheet; much better to inherit a slippery-smooth one slept in by the girl who did your job before you.

Mrs Doar would have felt her position in the very weave of the flannel as she wiped the back of her neck; in the thread count of the pillowcase where she rested her weary face. No tuck or fold or crevice of life was left unassigned or unorganised. 'A place for everything, and everything in its place' was the nineteenth-century housekeeper's catechism.

Except with Mrs Doar, things were not quite in their proper place. In September 1831, just before the Duchess's partridge-and-apple-tart visit, Dorothy Doar discovered that she was, once again, pregnant.

V

The Fear Of Contagion

Servants were not supposed to have children. It was an almost exclusively celibate occupation. With the reign of Queen Victoria, public censure of maids falling pregnant became ever more strident. Mistresses were neurotic in their determination to control not just their servants' souls, but their bodies too. The Countess of Carlisle would make a head housemaid in the 1880s report back that the under-maids were regularly washing their monthly napkins at Castle Howard because it 'proved they were not having a baby'.[22] Jane Carlyle's cook defiled the sanctity of her mistress's home by giving birth *in the house* – 'While Mr C was still reading in the *Drawingroom !'*[23] No matter what the circumstances – betrothed, seduced, raped – getting pregnant was grounds for immediate dismissal without reference.

As her mistress's eyes and ears, it fell to the housekeeper to keep these girls on the straight and narrow. The layout of country houses became ever more obsessed with creating barriers to intimacy. At Kelmarsh in Northamptonshire, tunnels were built to stop the laundry maids passing through the stable yard. At Lanhydrock in Cornwall, the housekeeper's bedroom guarded the entrance to the maids' dormitory. She was the sentinel. But who was watching *her*?

Of all the babies accepted by London's Foundling Hospital, Bloomsbury between 1821 and 1830, two-thirds came from servants. Of these, a disproportionate third are in the higher ranks of service (housekeepers, cooks, governesses, nurses, lady's maids): older women with better social backgrounds and greater literacy skills than the servant population at large.[24]

How did they become pregnant? Not through promiscuity – there was little opportunity for the upper servant isolated through her position. More often it happened through misfortune: when a long-standing courtship failed to end in marriage as expected. These women did not want to abandon their newborns, but they had no choice. Small, poignant mementos – bracelets, buttons, necklaces – were left with their babies at the Foundling Hospital. These children would, at least, have some kind of a future. Another way out was infanticide.

In 1849 the nation was gripped by a case of unusual horror in which a London cook-housekeeper was accused of a double infanticide: twice over seven years she throttled her child (one newborn, one two years old), boxed up the body and sent it to relatives in the country. 'The Child Murder in Harley-Street', as reported, paints 36-year-old Sarah Drake as 'inhuman', 'barbarous' and 'unnatural'. Celebrated Scotland Yard detective Sergeant Whicher investigated, and the trial was 'thronged with eager lovers of the horrible and mysterious', including many 'well-dressed females'.[25]

To public outrage, Drake was acquitted on the grounds of insanity. She did not hang. Instead she was sent – a 'criminal lunatic' – to Bedlam. 'She did not shed any tears', reported the *Bucks Herald*. 'But notwithstanding that, she was evidently suffering most acutely.'

Housekeepers were not supposed to bear children – but nor were they supposed to have husbands. Dorothy Doar was an anomaly in every way. One baby girl had already been born and put out to nurse. She knew that this pregnancy spelt bad news, both for her job and for her family's precarious finances. She did not inform the Marchioness of Stafford until she was six months gone.

Perhaps, first, she waited to see if the pregnancy would hold (by now Mrs Doar was forty years old). Perhaps she vowed to do it in the new year, but then was reluctant to trouble her mistress just then when the family was doubly preoccupied by the prospect of a London cholera epidemic and the long-anticipated Reform Bill.

I can see her walking the two miles round Trentham's long, island-studded lake, hands fretting inside her shawl, as she turns her situation over and over. It is winter, though unusually mild. In nearby Severn Stoke there are reports of an apple tree that has produced a miraculous, unseasonal crop of fruit. But down by the lake the wind comes from the north, biting the back of her neck as she makes the mile-long descent through woodland and birdsong, then comes again like a blade at her face as she rounds the tip and heads towards the house.

Who is her confidante? Can a woman in this position unburden herself without losing her authority?

That winter everyone was distracted. The whole house was on edge. This was a revolutionary time for England. Early in February, rioting was narrowly averted thirty miles to the north in Manchester by the police with 'a liberal use of their sticks', breaking up a mass meeting of the Political Union of the Working Classes.[26] The people had taken to the streets, agitating for parliamentary reform. It was thirteen years since Peterloo, but the memory of how viciously that demonstration was dealt with by the cavalry, sabres drawn, was still raw. The people of Manchester still wanted change. The previous October, Bristol had burned for two days, put under siege by enraged rioters looting, ripping up gas pipes and smashing windows. The enfranchisement of the working man was their goal. They wanted the vote. 'This is our time! Go it, go it, my lads!' was the cry of the mob.[27]

Then in mid-February came terrifying news from London. Mrs Galleazie, housekeeper at Stafford House, reported that the first case of cholera morbus has reached the East End. This was a new and sinister disease, known variously as 'Asiatic', 'spasmodic', 'malignant', 'contagious' and 'blue' (for the sufferer's corpse-like face and tongue). It had spread from India to Russia, from Russia to Hamburg and now by ships to London and the northern ports of Newcastle, Edinburgh and Glasgow. It was 'a disease which baffles human skill', lamented one MP at the passing of the Cholera Prevention Bill on 18 February, 'and therefore it must be considered an infliction of Providence.'

At Stafford House the Marquis reacted with patrician authority (and not a little horror at this working-class pestilence carried in the air, as the 'miasmatists' insisted, from the unthinkable slums of the East End). 'The Marquis of Stafford has adopted the greatest precaution to prevent the cholera morbus amongst his establishment', reported *The Times* on 3 March 1832.

All the servants have received the strictest orders that on no pretence whatever they go further eastward than Charing-cross, on pain of immediate dismissal, and that they are not to mix with any of the trades people. The post man now throws the letters into the house, and the newsmen, when they deliver the newspapers in the morning and evening, have to throw them over a wall, so great is the fear of contagion on the family of the noble Marquis.

Mrs Doar has heard of her boss's draconian measures via Mrs Galleazie, so when a newspaper finds its way to her sitting room she reads of 'The Cholera Panic' with knowing shakes of her head, although she has never been to London. Is Charing Cross far enough to be safe, she wonders?

A short stroll to the east took the then 21-year-old reporter Charles Dickens to the squalid streets and slums surrounding Drury Lane: theatreland. 'The filthy and miserable appearance of this part of London can hardly be imagined by those (and there are many such) who have not witnessed it', he wrote in *Sketches by Boz*. 'Filth', he noted:

filth everywhere – a gutter before the houses and a drain behind – clothes drying and slops emptying, from the windows; girls of fourteen or fifteen, with matted hair, walking about barefoot, and in white great-coats, almost their only covering; boys of all ages, in coats of all sizes and no coats at all; men and women, in every variety of scanty and dirty apparel, lounging, scolding, drinking, smoking, squabbling, fighting, and swearing.[28]

By the end of March the cholera was in Paris; 7,000 died in the first two weeks. Its savage spread made London look positively safe. The

British papers kept pace, publishing lists of high-born Parisian victims; lists anxiously scanned by the Marchioness. There were ghastly echoes of the Terror as she saw her old social milieu picked off one by one. All this is noted in Trentham's servants' hall, *The Staffordshire Advertiser* spread out on the scrubbed table after dinner. Mrs Doar recognises some of the foreign names; names often glimpsed on her mistress's prolific correspondence. Can contamination travel by post?

The Midlands sits between London and the northern ports. How long could it be, she asks herself, before the epidemic arrives? By now the nation is decidedly twitchy, any mild bowel problem suspected to be cholera. Mrs Doar is the first at Trentham to become ill. Usually so vigorous, the housekeeper's limbs feel weak, she sweats all day and has a nausea wholly unconnected to her secret condition. For the first time in many months she is forced to retreat to her bedroom. Then news comes from Lilleshall that housekeeper Mrs Kirke is ill – 'dangerously ill'.

In such a febrile atmosphere, Dorothy Doar does not willingly let go of the reins. She knows she should be overseeing her girls, but once she takes the weight off her feet she feels as if a great hand is pressing down on her, preventing her from moving. The Trentham maids have surely noticed her rounded figure. The land agent William Lewis, her close colleague, remains unaccountably unaware of her new shape, hidden as it is by stiff silk skirts, billowing sleeves and biting stays. As she lies sick and sweating in bed, she knows she must write to Her Ladyship. There is no more concealing it.

VII

My Heart Is Almost Broke

O n 2 April 1832 the Marchioness of Stafford attended a soirée at Downing Street given by the Whig Prime Minister's wife Countess

Grey (her old admirer Prince Talleyrand, the French Ambassador, proffering his arm in the absence of her doddery husband). The same day James Loch wrote a letter to William Lewis from his offices in Bloomsbury Square.

Her Ladyship desires me to say that Mrs Doar has announced her pregnancy – and that after deliberating very maturely on the subject she has written to her to say she cannot stay. I am quite certain that her determination is correct and I really gave it every consideration. It would be a bad example to others, and a Housekeeper who has Maids to look after should not be bearing children even to their husbands.

Lady Stafford wishes you to see her as soon after you get this as you can and to soothe her – she wishes the expense of her journey wherever she may wish to go to, to be defrayed.

Her Ladyship laments this circumstance exceedingly as I must say I do if this is of any importance, as she was a most excellent and zealous and faithful person and who did her duty fully, amply and conscientiously. Lady S wishes you to say so to her.

It had been a hard decision, even for a tough old Marchioness. The maternal cluckings of 'Doar' were now reversed: Lady Stafford wanted her 'soothed' as she knew exactly the damage this decision was about to wreak in her housekeeper's life. Even James Loch, who knew Lady Stafford of old, was impressed by her genuine regret. He added in a postscript, 'She does not wish her hurried away by any means.'[29]

Letters travelled fast in 1832. William Lewis received it the next morning and digested its contents with some surprise (how could he not have noticed?). He braced himself anxiously for a change of regime. What had Mrs Doar been playing at all this time? Foolish woman! Lewis put off knocking at her door until after midday dinner, as it was an interview he was rather dreading.

What were Mrs Doar's rights, as a pregnant servant? 'A Woman with Child may be discharged by a Justice', stated the legal appendix of *The Complete Servant*. 'Should a woman with child be hired for a term, and her master knew not of it, or should she prove with child during her servitude, he may discharge her, with the concurrence of a magistrate.' In modern terminology, it was a sackable offence with no compensation.

'But if, when he knows it, he does not discharge her before a magistrate, but keeps her on, he must provide for her till her delivery, and for one month after; when she is to be sent to her place of settlement.'

It was entirely up to the whim of the employer. Crucially, Mrs Doar had revealed her pregnancy. But beyond a few weeks' grace, she had only Lady Stafford's goodwill standing between a life of relative comfort and one of great difficulty. Lady Stafford was right: her housekeeper would require a great deal of soothing.

By next day's return post Loch received a letter from a distraught Dorothy Doar. It starts in a firm hand in flowing cursive script, but soon becomes incoherent and illegible, littered with spelling mistakes. It is the only letter in her hand to survive and it reads as a howl of despair, straight from the heart.

3 April

Sir

You will excuse my troubling you but having experienced great feeling and kindness of hart from you on former accations made me take the Liberty. I sincerely hope you will intersede with Lady Stafford on my behalf – you have hard from her Ladyship of my Situation. I was in hopes her Ladyship would have let me keep my Situation as usual – after my Confinement which will take place early in June I would put the child out to nurse so that it could not in any way interefear with my Buiseness.

I hope and trust Sir you will be my friend and prevail on my Lady to allow me to stay if its only for a short time as God knows what will become of me – my poor husband for a long time has been so very unfortunate and the Education of my Little Girl [now 14] has taken every shilling we had so that I have not the means of going in any way of business that I could be getting a little to inable us to live. Doar has got a Situation however and I hope he will be able to make it answer – but the sallery is low so that I must dow what I can to inable us to live.

She did have another plan, hatched with her husband. She had thoughts of opening a small shop in Newcastle-upon-Tyne, though she didn't know how she would manage it without help. But Mrs Doar's heart was not in this new career. She held out hope that Her Ladyship might reconsider, with Loch as her powerful go-between. The letter returns to the open sore of her dismissal:

I assure you at this time my heart is almost broke I have been upwards of 14 years in the Marquis of Stafford's family and it grieves me much very much indeed to leave it – indeed Sir to describe to you the distress I am in would be impossible – but I hope by leaving me case in your hand who I had always concidered my friend that you will be able to prevail on Lord and Lady Stafford to dow something for me.

I remain Sir your most humble and obedient servant

Dorothy Doar.[30]

James Loch was an exceptionally busy man. He had been with the Staffords for twenty years, and was at this time involved in a myriad other activities: pushing through the Scottish clearance systems, chasing rick-burners across rural Salop and Staffordshire, manoeuvring with the railway and canal men over Lord Stafford's awkwardly overlapping interests, keeping up with the auditing and administration of the various landed estates. All this kept him daily at his desk until late, much to his wife's chagrin. He was also an MP, for Scotland's northernmost constituency of Wick Burghs, and was immersed in the growing excitement of the Reform Bill question, a motion the Staffords supported unambiguously. At home his own family was getting larger: he and Anne now had nine children. In 1832 Loch was 52 years old and at the height of his powers, a managerial entrepreneur employed by a millionaire aristocrat. He was a man who held real power.

Mrs Doar's troubles might have seemed like a dot on the map to James Loch. But this was not how he treated them. Hearing again from Lewis that Mrs Doar seemed 'in very great distress' and had 'not saved a single shilling but is desirous of setting up a little shop in Newcastle to sell Groceries & confectionary goods', Loch – who is damned by history as the intransigent, inhuman architect of the Highland Clearances – turned his mind to extracting some good from this unfortunate case.

Our most intimate glimpse of Dorothy Doar comes from this series of letters between the two agents: the push and pull of power as senior and junior together decide her future. The letters sit in two musty bundles in the Sutherland archives, sandwiched between missives on animal husbandry, new roofs for the Lilleshall tenants, road-building projects and rick-burning culprits: the stuff of estate management. And at first it seemed as if this particular staffing problem could be dealt with in the same drily efficient way.

Lewis, anxious to help (and keen to avoid another emotional, recriminatory interview with the housekeeper), had got behind the shop idea: he'd already identified a vacant premises on Newcastle Road owned by Lord Stafford. 'I doubt not she would soon get a little business that would maintain her', he wrote to Loch. 'I should be most happy to throw my little influence in her favour for I do consider she has been a very good and faithful servant to Lord & Lady Stafford but of course I will not say a word to her on this subject until I hear from you.'

First, Loch had to contact the Staffords. On 6 April he replied, in his fast-flowing, rapid-thinking, almost illegible hand, to Lewis – three days before the Reform Bill's first night debate in Parliament. 'Your idea for Mrs Doar is upon the whole approved of', he wrote. Lord Stafford would help with start-up costs, providing the money didn't go straight into her husband's debts. It was a generous offer, and it was the final offer.

Both Lord and Lady S. are very sensible of Mrs Doar's being a very faithful servant – but it is quite impossible in such an establishment to permit of her breeding and bearing a family in the House and if she went away for a time who then would look after the girls – besides it would be an example for the other Upper Servants and it would be Castle Howard over again in its worst times.

(One wonders what sexual liberties the Georgian upper servants had been taking at Castle Howard, the Yorkshire seat of Lord Stafford's nephew George Howard, 6th Earl of Carlisle.)

'You may perhaps have an opportunity of explaining this to Mrs Doar', he continued, 'and tell her I have got her letter, that I shall be most happy to help her *in any other way but in the way she wishes*, and if she fixes upon going to NCastle we will do what we can for her.'

On 10 April Loch managed, in the midst of great political fervour, to talk to the Marchioness about her housekeeper's plan. 'You may take steps to put Mrs Doar into her shop and give her a little assistance', he wrote to Lewis; 'of course her own health and situation are to be first consulted – and let it be known that she has her Ladyship's support and that she goes on good terms.'

In the Midlands, Mrs Doar learns of Her Ladyship's financial and moral support and is a little mollified. She has a focus. She has a plan. A shop is not so very different to her various store cupboards; she will make a good shopkeeper. She'll be near her family. As she lies sick in bed, the baby kicking in her belly, I imagine her mind turning to the material world of stock and supplies. She begins, as is her way, to make lists. 'She seems now at rest in her mind,' Lewis writes to Loch, 'and is much satisfied with Lord & Lady Stafford's goodness toward her.'

So much oil poured onto troubled waters, so much soothing and praising of Mrs Doar's talents and loyalty. And yet she is to be let go, rather than be granted six weeks' leave. The Staffords are barely at Trentham for six weeks each *year*. Attitudes have changed since Dorothy bore her last baby: this time it is the principle of the thing that counts, not the logistics.

That evening, Lady Stafford left her husband at home once again to attend a ball at Westminster's Ashburnham House, hosted by Princess Lieven, formidable wife of the Russian Ambassador, famous for introducing the waltz to London society (and for the remark, 'It is not fashionable where I am not'). It was an evening 'numerously and elegantly attended' by a clutch of Marchionesses – Titchfield, Londonderry, Salisbury, Clanricarde . . . and of course that old intriguer and womaniser, Prince Talleyrand.[31]

A fortnight later, the Staffords took ten horses, four carriages and numerous servants to another of their splendid houses – West Hill, a mansion in leafy Wandsworth, just south of the capital. The servants' hall buzzed with talk of ill health. 'A Murrain appears to have got among our housekeepers', as James Loch puts it, rolling his Scottish Rs with enjoyment at the biblical term. A murrain: a *plague*. Poor Mrs Galleazie was virtually under house arrest in town, Mrs Kirke dangerously ill at Lilleshall, Mrs Spillman at Dunrobin was at increasing risk being so near the infected Scottish ports and Mrs Doar not just ill but *pregnant*. Who would replace her?

West Hill's housekeeper, Mrs Cleaver, was herself still learning the ropes. According to the servants' wage ledgers, we can see that she took over from Mrs Maben in January, a step up from her previous position at the Marquess of Landsdowne's house. Her old employer might be in Lord Grey's Cabinet, but the Staffords were incontestably Britain's most powerful family. No doubt she thought it most unorthodox that Trentham should have a married housekeeper: more still, one with a daughter and another baby on the way. But Mrs Cleaver prudently kept her council. She knew better than to gossip this soon into her tenure.

At West Hill the Staffords fall into a quieter regime, and Lady Stafford's attention alights on her new housekeeper, poached at new year from her acquaintance, Lady Louisa. Cleaver is, it must be admitted, an impressive figure: sensible, efficient, tolerably well educated. After not quite four months at West Hill she is running the house with far more zeal than old Maben who, for all her loyalty, had most definitely let things slip. Goodness knows, it was hard enough to find a replacement housekeeper, not once but *twice* in a year . . . and – if Lady Stafford is to act upon the plan taking shape in her mind – to have to start all over again at West Hill . . . *Quel ennui.*

Before she is called back to town for an intimate soirée at Kensington Palace (just the Duchess of Kent, the King and Queen and a dozen other titles) the Marchioness comes to a decision.

VIII

Eight Dozen Of Sweet Wine

Mrs Cleaver arrives at Trentham Hall with her bags after two days' travel by stagecoach. She has her instructions. She knows she is on trial, and that this could be an unprecedented chance for advancement. Gingerly, she knocks on Mrs Doar's door.

'Who is it?'

The housekeeper's voice sounds thin and strained to Mrs Cleaver's ears. She hopes Mr Lewis has paved the way for the transfer of power, as she doesn't want a fight on her hands.

On 9 May Lewis writes to Loch: 'Mrs Cleaver arrived on Monday.' He has also received a note from Lady Stafford, increasingly tetchy as the political tension mounts in London: 'Her Ladyship will never again have a married House Keeper it is attended with many bad consequences.'

Mrs Cleaver is put straight to work drawing up an inventory: every new housekeeper must know how things stand. It is a way of taking possession – to finger and itemise every sheet, every cloth, every teacup and saucer. No cupboard or room escapes her eye.

Lewis's letter, interrupted, continues in an irritable hand. 'I am this moment told Mrs Doar has packed up 8 dozen of sweet wine to be sent off. Is this allowed? Mrs Doar has not pleased me these last few days, for I think she does not estimate properly the great kindness shewn her by the family and thinking she ought to be continued.'

Dorothy Doar is still sick in her bed and won't be moved: it is her only way of hanging on. How *could* they bring in her replacement so quickly? After all these years! Her store cupboards, her systems, her girls, her rules. *Is* it her replacement? Mrs Doar finds Mrs Cleaver coldly efficient and reeking of ambition. She becomes resentful, contrary, territorial. But most of all she is frightened. It is time to stop procrastinating, as her uncertain future now stares her baldly in the face.

While Mrs Doar was packing up her ninety-six bottles of sweet wine, Britain was teetering on the brink of revolution. On 7 May Earl Grey, the Whig Prime Minister, requested an interview with the King and asked His Majesty to create sufficient Whig peers to push the Reform Bill through the House of Lords. It was a bill that aimed to enfranchise the growing middle classes (those living in homes worth at least £10 annually – £500 in today's money – which cut out most of the working classes) and give proper representation to the newly industrialised cities of the English Midlands and North – and thus far it had been systematically and cravenly blocked by the Tories.

William IV then had sudden doubts about meddling with Parliament. He misjudged the ugly mood of the nation and refused. On 9 May, with the Reform Bill vetoed yet again by the House of Lords, the Prime Minister and his Cabinet resigned in disgust.

On 10 May, town councillor Mr Lee wrote to James Loch from Birmingham, where the police were trying to prevent 'an explosion of public feelings'. 'Disastrous news from London. The country is I feel in an awful state of difficulty. People of England have lost their faith in royal pledges [and are] disgusted with privilege and aristocracy.'[32]

It was not a good time to be a lord. Nor was it a good time to be a king. William IV had mud slung at his carriage and was hissed at in public; Queen Adelaide was left with the 'fixed impression [that] an English revolution is rapidly approaching, and that her own fate is to be that of Marie Antoinette'.[33] Whig clergyman Sydney Smith described a 'hand-shaking, bowel-disturbing passion of fear' as London's streets crackled with anger.

On 10 May James Loch, sitting in his office in the well-to-do suburb of Bloomsbury Square, turned his rapid-fire mind to Dorothy Doar's health and the matter of the sweet wine. His suspicions were now aroused, and his tone had subtly changed. There was a clear wish to resolve this matter and move on. 'We are in a state of ferment on public matters,' he wrote to Lewis.

I have time only to say that Mrs Doar when she is *fully* able must go to her lodgings at Handford – she appears to repay badly her Ladyship's kindness – take care that directions are given that all her linen is kept separate from the rest of the household – and that Mrs Cleaver know that it is her Ladyship's orders that every thing in Mrs Doar's room be well scoured – let a temporary female wait on her and let the House Servants attend to their own duty.

He was slightly irritated by the detail of the wine. 'Surely the sweet wine must be her own making,' he wrote; 'she never could think of packing up his Lordships?'

The worry was that the housekeeper might have contracted the cholera morbus. But there was also a sense of wishing to erase Mrs Doar from Trentham Hall. She had become an embarrassment; she was surplus to requirements. As she went about her packing, sending box after box out of the back door with the help of the girls and the boot boy, gossip began to travel along the basement corridors.

Loch's letter crossed that of William Lewis, who was now obsessed with the sweet wine. If *he* didn't have access to such perks, why should

Mrs Doar?' Lewis tried to pull rank. 'Hope you will let me know if Lady Stafford allows her to claim the sweet wine. I should think not. But if so, such indulgences may and will lead to great abuse if House Keepers have such privileges.' The answer from the Marchioness – communicated to Loch before she readied herself for a splendid Friday-night 'tout' at Devonshire House – was not what Lewis wanted to hear. Do not interfere in this matter, came her instructions. It was, in all probability, some home-made wine of Mrs Doar's own. Let the housekeeper be.

By 12 May William Lewis's careful, audit-book mind felt under attack from conflicting sources of chaos. First the state of the nation, still without a government: 'The people are generally speaking very much disappointed and disgusted at the conduct of the Lords', he wrote to Loch, 'and it will be well if they in the manufacturing towns remain quiet under such a disappointment.' Stoke-on-Trent sat just outside the gates of Trentham Hall. What if the people were to storm this pleasure palace with cries of 'Go it! Go it! This is our time!'? Where would this leave the servants?

Within the house all was not well either. 'Mrs Cleaver has nearly gone over the inventory', he continued:

she seems a very correct & proper person. I am exceedingly annoyed at Mrs Doar's conduct. She has I understand behaved in a very unkind and improper manner to Mrs Cleaver. But Mrs Doar has told her to take upon herself the entire control and management of the house, which she has done. Mrs Doar has a person to wait upon her & the Girls are all kept to their own work. Everything will be well scoured that has been used or connected with Mrs Doar's rooms.

James Loch did not involve himself further with these acrimonious hints and allusions. He had his hands full. At Westminster the anti-Reform Duke of Wellington was trying in vain to form a new Tory Cabinet. Protesters with placards were urging a run on the banks: 'To stop the Duke, go for gold!' As frantic crowds cashed in their savings for solid gold, some £1.5 million was withdrawn from the Bank of England.

The Duke of Wellington, leaving St James's Palace in his carriage, was attacked by a mob which 'set up such an astounding hissing and yelling, as to frighten the horses; and in plunging about, one of them fell near the Queen's entrance'. Military precautions were taken 'to preserve the peace of the Metropolis'.[34]

On 15 May, Wellington resigned and Earl Grey was recalled to office. The news was greeted in the capital with peals of bells. Now that revolution was looking slightly less likely, William Lewis could contain himself no longer. Seventeenth of May: 'There has been some very unpleasant reports about Mrs Doar packing up and sending off some heavy packages from the Hall,' he wrote to Loch, enclosing a defamatory letter written by one Mr Kirkby, another upper servant, probably the butler. 'This is altogether a most distressing circumstance. If anything is wrong that the woman should have so far forgotten herself in the honest discharge of her duty – (I was not by any measure reconciled to the sending off the sweet wine . . .).' No longer able to arbitrate, Lewis appealed to his senior, Loch: what should he do next?

On the morning of 19 May Loch replied with customary sangfroid. He was reluctant to think the worst of the housekeeper. 'You will investigate carefully the stories regarding Mrs Doar & if after a calm and deliberate enquiry you think her conduct really liable to suspicion you may & should then give her the enclosed letter.' But he cautioned Lewis 'how easy a thing it is to whisper away a person's character – & how serious a matter it is to so do'. Recollect also, he advised, how some think they can gain favour by bad-mouthing others behind their backs; spreading rumours while seeming to 'fawn' before them.

Why suspect Mrs Doar, he asked, if her own mistress didn't? 'Don't forget that her place entitled her to certain perquisites, and that system being approved of by her Ladyship it cannot be thrown up against Mrs Doar.' As to Mr Kirkby's malicious letter: 'I must caution you also at being led away entirely by Kirkby – he is as honest a man as breathes, but he is a man of strong passions and liable to be prejudiced – & he never liked Mrs Doar for she resisted his authority.'

He concluded by placing full responsibility on Lewis's shoulders. You be the judge, he said. Give her my letter if you think she deserves it. But remember that this will reflect badly on your own character if she is found to be blameless.

By now the gossip lines between the Stafford residences were humming. Later that day, as the gas lamps were being lit in the square down below, Loch was forced to pick up his pen to Lewis again.

I regret to have to mention that various reports have reached me of Mrs Doar making up large packages some of which are already sent away from the House – including some wine. It is never my habit nor my inclination to listen to stories or suspect others upon loose grounds of improper conduct, but as these reports have reached me in a way that prevents my neglecting them, I must call your attention to them.

I confess that I am very slow & most unwilling to believe anything against Mrs Doar – I have always considered her a good & faithful servant, and being still of that opinion I am quite sure that she will not hesitate to show you what has been conveyed away & packed up and then put an end to all the stories that are propagated, and by doing so enable me to proceed in doing what I have been authorised to do for her.

And with this, after the near revolution of the past week, Loch the workaholic took three days' holiday.

IX

Every Article Necessary

The temperature was rising. Creamy May blossom had burst into flower on every copse and hedgerow. After so many weeks of suspense and anxiety, the people of Stoke-on-Trent and the surrounding villages turned their minds to new bonnets and spring fairs. Stafford's

May fair swung into life (no change in prices, noted *The Staffordshire Advertiser*, except for pigs which were 'very dear'). Outfitters Boulton and Robinson respectfully announced to the ladies of the Staffordshire Potteries that their 'extensive and elegant assortment of Fashionable Goods for the Spring Season' was now complete; 'comprising a splendid and novel collection of rich, plain, and figured Du Capes, and Gros de Naples, in all the fashionable colours'.

Now that the rioters had put down their cudgels, Stafford County Gaol was busy that week with its more usual suspects: Jon Atkins, charged with stealing a spade; Mary Hargreaves, charged with stealing two pair of stockings; George Woolley, a blind man, charged with assaulting nine-year-old Caroline Green.

James Loch returned refreshed to his desk in Bloomsbury Square to find an unpleasant saga developing at Trentham Hall – in the very way he had refused to believe possible.

On 23 May another letter from Lewis had arrived, as follows:

I duly received your very kind & feeling letter relative to Mrs Doar, and I really don't know that any circumstance ever gave me much more real uneasiness. She is certainly in great tribulation, still I find from her conversation *she does not wish the boxes opened* but only the hampers returned from Handford [her husband's village]. But in my opinion for a thorough justification of her conduct she should not hesitate to open every box & parcel.

He acknowledged that she was ill – but Lewis was now feeling quite out of sorts himself: 'the affair altogether so unlooked for proves very distressing to my feelings'.

The Marchioness of Stafford was to be spared the sordid details until the truth had been extracted. While Lewis had to organise the breaking open of Mrs Doar's trunks and boxes, his mistress put on her jewels and went to 'one of the most splendid Balls the annals of fashion could ever boast', thrown by the Duke of Devonshire at Devonshire House, a mere fortnight after his last rout. Starved of frothy celebrity tattle in this period of hard news, London's *Morning Post* gave it the full treatment: 'All the apartments in that far-famed mansion, glittering with gold and silver, were illuminated with wax tapers only, exceeding a thousand in number, placed not only in chandeliers, girandoles, and candelabras, but in massive candlesticks of the precious metals; even the architraves of the door-ways were refulgent with light', gushed the reporter.

'In unison with the scene were the *Ladies*' dresses, all gold and silver, or diamonds and pearls, with the ostrich plume of fourteen feathers . . . The Marchioness of Londonderry wore a cestus or girdle of brilliants which attracted every eye.' As for the food,

Every viand which art and nature could produce was to be seen there, arranged on gold, silver, and china; the dessert consisting of the finest fruits, pines, cherries, strawberries, peaches, nectarines, and grapes; and fifteen sorts of foreign wines, from the golden Burgundy to the Spanish Fontcarrel . . . Amid all these attractions the ball-room never for one moment lost its influence, for the 'mazy round' was kept up till long after five o'clock.

This was Regency entertaining at its most lavish.

Meanwhile, at Trentham Hall, I can see Mr Lewis and Mrs Cleaver sitting in the Pug's Parlour discussing tactics. Mrs Cleaver is all for bursting in on Mrs Doar and surprising her, for if she has warning, the housekeeper will surely conceal whatever it is she is up to. Mr Lewis demurs: Dorothy Doar is an old colleague and (so he had thought) a friend. He hasn't the stomach for it. He has also heard from the still-room maid that the door is now kept locked. Could not a search be contrived with civility? Mrs Cleaver thinks not. She stands, ties on her bonnet and stares a mute challenge at the Trentham agent.

The next day William Lewis sat down to compose the most unpleasant, if vindicated, letter of his career. Twenty-ninth of May:

After the examination of Mrs Doar's boxes yesterday which displayed a disgraceful scene of robbery, I was so much agitated & affected that

I was really unwell all day – the Hampers were examined first and contained some dozens of home made wine such as gooseberry, ginger. The boxes being after opened, contained nearly a general collection of every article necessary for Housekeeping many of which she claimed as her own property which, however doubtful, Mrs Cleaver & I did not feel disposed to dispute with her. Except as far as the linen went . . . she gave them up as Lady Stafford's property. There is still a very great deficiency in the linen.

We received from out of the boxes 10 Dinner Damask napkins, 7 Table Covers, 35 Chamber towels, 3 Pillow cases, 8 waiting napkins, 1 Damask table cloth, 9 table cloths for Stewards or Housekeepers rooms, 2 Glass cloths, 3 plain sheets. She also exhibited from the boxes quantities of Tea, Sugar, Coffee, foreign wine, soap, candles, mops and many new brushes for shoes & house cleaning, all which she acknowledges to be the property of D Stafford.

It is dreadful to contemplate such proceeds & to witness such depravity in one who has every confidence placed in her, and it was amazing how hardened she appeared. As for the linen she said it was old & she was entitled to it. But Mrs Cleaver told her that she had taken the best & left the old! Mrs Cleaver is to be again amongst the linen today & will be able to give some account of what is deficient. I can assure you I am much pleased at the conduct of Mrs Cleaver in this affair and it is most desirable for her comfort & the peace of the establishment that Mrs Doar should be removed from the house. She is quite able to be moved but of course I also wish your decisive answer.

The articles enumerated (except the linen) remain in Mrs Doar's bedroom. Please say how I am to act with them & her. I never was so deceived in a character in my life.

Were these things hers, or weren't they? The slippery subject of 'perquisites', or staff perks, was broached in one of the more abrasive little manuals of the era, *Domestic Servants As They Are & As They Ought To Be*, written anonymously by a 'practical mistress of a household'.

'The term "perquisite" is so comprehensive, so elastic, and accommodating', the author writes,

that it is made to embrace and signify almost everything in the various departments of the house; anything, in fact, convertible or transferable, from damask clothes and silver, to rags, old brass, and metal of every description . . . Thus, glass, china, &c., often gradually disappear till, the numbers becoming visibly few, an enquiry is instituted, and the missing articles are reported as 'broken'.[35]

There was an ambiguity to ownership below stairs. Much of a housekeeper's reward came not as cash but as comforts. Favoured suppliers would butter her up with gifts; the best cast-off furniture, clothing and linen from the family was usually passed her way; and at retirement (if she retired – many worked until death) housekeepers to the aristocracy could expect an estate cottage and a pension. Many amassed large savings, as they did not need to spend. Mary Webster of Erddig Hall, who stayed thirty years with the family until her death in 1875, left £1,300 in her will (£60,000 in today's money).

But Mrs Doar had no savings. She had a daughter's keep to pay for, a feckless husband, rent due on the family lodgings, a baby on the way in a matter of weeks and her long-term job and all future security snatched from her. Pregnancy hormones raged through her body. As she squatted heavily and packed her trunks, one thing must have led to another. She finally gave in to temptation. They were not her things, and yet in a sense they *were* her things: she had ordered them, cared for, catalogued and stored them; mended and marked them; ground and sifted them; bottled and corked them. Each item (candle, banister brush, pillow case, tea caddy) had its own complex emotional significance to Mrs Doar, powerfully felt through daily use.

This is what she might have persuaded herself as she hastily wrapped brushes in sheets and bottles in tablecloths, squashing things flat in wicker hampers and tying them with rope. A small voice in the back of her head told her that this was not right; this was no way to repay the kindness of the noble Staffords. Another, more insistent voice, said – but it is not *fair*! She had served this family for *fourteen years*, through the reign of three different kings; and now, abruptly, she was to be shown the door – all for wanting just six weeks of leave. And what was it to them anyway, a handful of mops and dusters? Her Lord and Lady ate breakfast off solid-silver plates under a Poussin and a Gainsborough. All this – stock for her little shop, or there would be nothing to sell and therefore nothing to eat – was mere chicken feed.

So Mrs Doar might have told herself. But how wrong she was.

X

The Connivance Of The Girls

The day the housekeeper's boxes were prised open, 28 May, was the King's sixty-seventh birthday. The Marchioness of Stafford joined the crowds of grandees at a one o'clock 'Drawing Room' in St James's Palace. So thronged was the grand staircase and Throne Room with obsequious aristocrats that the Queen was a full three hours receiving guests. *The Morning Post* went on to give a detailed sketch of each noblewoman's outfit. Dorothy Doar's mistress wore

A dress of rich white satin, elegantly embroidered in gold lama; the corsage and sleeves handsomely trimmed with beautiful blonde lace; ornamental vandyked stomacher, with gold, enriched with diamonds and emeralds, very superb; train of Acanthus green moiré, lined with white satin and embroidered with a rich gold lama bordering to correspond. Head-dress, gold, with plume of feathers and costly diamonds.

On her return, she learnt of Mrs Doar's crime.

On 29 May, James Loch replied to William Lewis. 'The accompanying letter contains your instructions regarding Mrs Doar – who has by her conduct forfeited all the favour of Lord & Lady S.' They would not now help her in any way. She had burnt her boats. 'You will tell Mrs Cleaver that her Ladyship approves much of her conduct as reported by you. Let me know whether you (privately) think Mrs Cleaver's wages are enough – to make people honest & above suspicion they should have enough.'

The thought that nagged at the back of Loch's brain was this: Dorothy Doar had been underpaid. As a father of nine children, he knew only too well how money simply disappeared. James Loch condemned, but he also understood her crime. Regrettably, the woman had fallen prey to temptation. On a fresh sheet he wrote another letter addressed to Lewis, to be read out to Mrs Doar. She had now passed the point of meriting direct correspondence.

I have received your letter about Mrs Doar with the most sincere concern and have read it to the Marquess & Marchioness of Stafford, who desire me to express their severe disappointment that a person in whom such confidence was placed for so many years, should have behaved so little worthy of it.

They desire me to say that they cannot agree to her remaining any longer at Trentham and that you intimate this to her. And they have further told me that they cannot now agree to that being done for her which they have previously ordered for her. In regard to the things that she has taken, it is their wish that what clearly belongs to the house should be retained . . . They commend your conduct in this most distressing affair, feeling that while you maintained their interests, you have done so without any unnecessary vigour or hardship.

Perhaps Lewis wonders whether he should have been more vigilant. How long has this pilfering been going on? Days? Years? He stations a grim-faced Mrs Cleaver and one of the more sharp-witted girls outside Mrs Doar's bedroom door while he deliberates on what to do next. Lewis is a decent man, a man with a natural delicacy of manner and all the proper inhibitions surrounding women and bedrooms. For Loch's sake, he must personally see this excruciating matter to its close. But inside that room is a crumple of unwashed bedding; a heavily pregnant woman with flushed cheeks and hair awry; the sweet smell of the sick room. He cannot bring himself to conduct a final search of Mrs Doar's boxes and bedroom on his own.

The lowest point of Mrs Doar's long life in service comes that afternoon, on the first day of June. There is a knock at the door, and a man's voice: 'Dorothy?' It is her husband. Behind him is William Lewis, unable to meet her eye, and behind Lewis crowd Mrs Cleaver and that maid, on tiptoe, craning to get a look.

By six o'clock that evening, she is out.

Lewis woke at dawn after an exceptionally bad night. He drew his chair up to the black leather-topped desk, dipped his pen and wrote one further, detailed letter to Loch. Pray God the last.

The second of June:

It was necessary for securing back what belonged to the family to have another examination of the boxes and a general look through every drawer in the room which took place yesterday. I thought proper to send for the husband – he came and went through the unpleasantness with me and behaved himself with much propriety – the articles which we claimed were taken from her & the boxes again packed.

I would not allow Mrs Cleaver & one of the Girls to leave her until all was packed and her out of the house. I went to the inn for a room for her it being a wet day. She goes off tomorrow to her friends in the north. I of course told the husband that Lord & Lady Stafford could not be expected to do anything for her after her infamous conduct.

Lewis blamed 'the connivance of the Girls' for letting Mrs Doar pack up and send away so many things. 'This deficiency annoyed me much,' he wrote, 'and when the Girls were told of it by Mrs Cleaver they all declared their innocence.' The Girls, for their part, had no doubt long known about their housekeeper's growing belly and had imagined, as girls do, petting and spoiling the baby when it arrived. Of course they closed ranks against Mrs Cleaver.

The woman that attended the wretch, for I can call her nothing else, was also examined & from her we found that she had been sent out of the room and on her return found the room in an untolerable stench such as if from burning hair brushes, mops and flannel. Glass had been found in the ashes and the nail of a new mop. Not a doubt remains in my view but that the vile wretch had committed many articles to the flames.

His Lordship may here say that I ought to have taken the boxes away out of her room. But the whole was so bundled up with her own apparel that I felt a delicacy in doing so.

Lewis was deeply shaken. He blamed himself, but couldn't see how he could have done anything differently. That he had trusted her, wanted to help her – then had to search, accuse and banish her! 'Who could have guessed of such depravity?' he wrote to Loch. 'Who could guard against such a Devil?'

On 4 June, the day the Reform Bill was finally passed in the House of Lords by 106 votes to 22, James Loch wrote the last letter on the matter:

The disposition that could have led to the destruction of the things you mention must have been of the worst description. I am only thankful that it has led to nothing worse or more criminal – I say so most sincerely. As to yourself, I only know I should have acted entirely as you have done. No one could have expected such depravity.

*

The housekeeper set off the next day in the rain, in a jolting public carriage. She was heading for her family, 200 miles to the north.

Within the year her employer, the newly titled Duke of Sutherland, was dead. His son George set about flexing his muscles. The family seat should, he felt, reflect more sumptuously the status of its owner. His wife Harriet (pregnant with her seventh child) agreed. Within two years Trentham Hall was reduced to a shell. Like its cast-off housekeeper, it seemed to belong to a different world. On its footprint, and around

45

its old walls, rose a swaggering chunky Italianate palace with a square tower at one end, designed by the man of the day, Charles Barry. Few staff at Trentham survived the change of regime, and not Mrs Cleaver. When the new house threw open its doors to guests in 1840, a young queen was on the throne and a wholly new team of professionals was at work in the back of the building.

I searched at length for Dorothy Doar, post-Trentham Hall. Civil registration did not start until 1837 and the first census took place in 1841, but neither of these produced the woman I was looking for. I tried parish registers, records of baptisms, marriages (in case she had remarried and changed her name) and deaths. I looked in local newspapers, lest she was involved in some tragedy or crime that might be reported. I combed through emigrations records and digitised workhouse records. Like her ghostly presence in the Sutherland archive, I felt sure she was languishing in an un-indexed parish register somewhere, her name so badly misspelt that it couldn't be found.

And so Mrs Doar slipped away without trace. Did she manage to make a new life for herself in the north? Could she fit back in with her old family, after 14 years with the Staffords? Did Mark Doar leave his new and hard-worn situation to come with her? Did Dorothy survive childbirth? Did the baby live? Her attempted crime denied her the chance to work again in a country house – and most certainly not as an upper servant, lacking as she did the all-important reference from her mistress.

Perhaps the Doars emigrated to Canada or America, crammed in squalid conditions on a passage lasting several weeks. Today there are more Doars living in the US than there are in the UK; the family might have been part of the Doar diaspora from the north of England across the Atlantic. More likely, though, it was worse.

When health failed, savings were exhausted and the last bit of respectable clothing was pawned, the workhouse was almost inevitable. In 1832, the year of Mrs Doar's disgrace, it was still possible to seek financial support directly from one's parish of birth. Under the Poor Law Amendment Act of 1834, the only relief possible was to be found within a workhouse. Did Mrs Doar exchange her black silk for a prison-style uniform and give up her husband and two young children to the rules of segregation? Did she finish her days eating gruel?

Just two months before her downfall she was held to be 'a most excellent and zealous and faithful person who did her duty fully, amply and conscientiously'. Then, almost overnight, she was converted in their minds to a 'hardened' wretch; a 'devil' to be ejected swiftly. Agent William Lewis seems to have thought Dorothy Doar got off lightly thanks to the aristocracy's aversion to scandal. She was a thief, and as everyone knew, *Embezzlement of a Master's property is Felony*. "If he shall purloin, or make away with his master's goods to the value of 40s it is felony, and he shall, himself, his aider, or abettor, on conviction, be transported for 14 years.'[36]

But thieving alone cannot explain how *molested* the Trentham agent felt. It was as if the whole house and the society it sustained, with all its elaborate hierarchies and rules, had been violated. One moment Mrs Doar was one thing, and then – suddenly – she was another. By dropping the mask of duty and subservience so readily she had somehow conned Lewis. This 'good and faithful servant' had roundly duped him, and he was furious.

Mrs Doar's duplicity threatened all that the nineteenth century would come to hold most dear: the sanctity of the home. The black bombazine dress and bunch of keys – symbols of sobriety, dependability, morality – were revealed to be just a cloak, a veneer. Inside, she was human.

Postscript 2015

The unfinished story of Dorothy Doar haunted me as I wrote the rest of this book. She seemed to hover over its pages like a ghost. Had I denied her a happy ending? My instinct was that this tale did not end well, but where was the evidence for this? I returned to the Sutherland archive to see if I might have missed something.

There was one letter that had puzzled me, sent on 9 May, three weeks before Mrs Doar's disgrace. It was a seeming non-sequitur from agent William Lewis to James Loch: 'Her Ladyship will never again have a married House Keeper it is attended with many bad consequences.' *Many* bad consequences? I searched again in fraying bundles for letters written around this date. And then I found it: a letter written by William Lewis to the Marchioness of Stafford herself. It is a letter that changes everything.

My Lady – It is my painful duty to inform your ladyship that Mrs Doar was taken in premature labour yesterday morning and was delivered last night of a stillborn female child - seven months gone. Mrs Cleaver is very much put about as nothing could be done yesterday, but she will commence this morning with the inventory.

My Lady, Your much obliged servant, William Lewis.

They wanted her out, with or without a baby. Her replacement was already at the Hall, preparing for take-over. How raw must have been her agony. Today we might call it post-natal depression, the strange and desperate behaviour of Dorothy Doar: stealing from her own store cupboards, burning the evidence in her grate. This woman was out of her mind – with sickness, with fear, with the trauma of delivering a stillborn tiny girl onto bloodied sheets. It is appalling that her ordeal should be judged an *inconvenience* to Mrs Cleaver. That Mrs Doar, housekeeper of Trentham Hall for 14 years, was *still* to be cast aside. As for the Marchioness of Stafford… Dorothy's mistress does not come out of this looking good.

The missing letter once discovered, other stray ends came together. I found Mrs Doar in a parish graveyard register for St Bartholomew's Church in Long Benton, Northumberland. She died in September 1832, three months after her expulsion from Trentham. Her first-born, Emma Doar, kept house for her ageing aunt and uncle for the rest of her life. She never married. Like Dorothy, she died at 40.

Mother and daughter, strangers to each other while living, now lie side by side in St Bartholomew's graveyard.

Part 2

Sarah Wells

Uppark, West Sussex 1880–1893

How dark in these underground rooms.

SARAH WELLS

Timeline

1851 – Great Exhibition in London's Hyde Park attracts six million people.

1856 – The cage crinoline, worn by all classes of women, reaches six foot in diameter.

1857 – The Matrimonial Causes Act: divorce made easier and woman can retain earnings.

1858 – Can opener invented. Preserving jar with screw lid patented.

1859 – Houses of Parliament adopt gas lighting. Domestic homes swiftly follow.

Most new middle class homes have a water closet.

1861 – Isabella Beeton's *Book of Household Management* published.

1866 – First chocolate bar: Fry's Chocolate Cream.

1870 – Married Woman's Property Act: Women can inherit property. The corset grows longer and more rigid: hips and bottom are squeezed backwards.

1872 – Hair crimper invented.

1876 – Bissell's carpet sweeper patented.

1879 – Europe's first telephone exchange opens in London.

1885 – Invention of the motor car, and first 'safety bicycle'. The Singer 'vibrating shuttle' sewing machine patented, the first practical sewing machine.

1893 – Chatsworth in Derbyshire installs electric lighting using water turbines, the first great house to do so.

1897 – Millicent Fawcett founds the National Union of Women's Suffrage Societies.

I

The Worst Housekeeper

The second half of the nineteenth century was a golden age for the housekeeper. This was *the* era of wealth creation for the Victorians: the railway age. The moneyed classes built new houses, refashioned old ones and filled them with the spoils of Empire. To run them they employed many more servants than before. According to the national census, between 1851 and 1871 the number of housekeepers tripled, from 46,648 to 140,836.[1] This ranged from women working in middle-class homes to those employed by the great estates. And as houses got bigger and more and more crammed with furniture and ornaments, so the housekeeper's responsibilities grew.

The male house steward at the head of the household receded into the past. An all-powerful domestic matriarch took his place. The housekeeper commanded more girls – many more girls, each with specialised skills and separate areas of responsibility. A brisk new air of professionalism imbued her team. Maids' uniforms become absolutely codified (print dresses for the dirty work of the morning; black dress with lace cap and apron for the afternoon); surnames rather than first names were used; salaries rose according to fine gradations laid out in a spate of domestic manuals.

But country houses also resisted change. For every Trentham Hall or Highclere Castle undergoing a fashionable Charles Barry rebuild, there was an Uppark. Change on a country estate usually came about with a new male heir, but Uppark had no new lord of the manor. During Queen Victoria's reign it languished in a time warp. The outside world was moving swiftly on – gaslighting, central heating, hot-water plumbing, elevators – but Uppark slumbered in its green acres, oblivious to the modern era. It might as well have been situated in the remote Scottish Highlands rather than West Sussex, fifty miles from London on the steam locomotive. While recruitment agencies began to promote a new breed of 'first class' professional servant, at Uppark the approach was more arbitrary – and the choice of housekeeper was, arguably, reckless.

According to her son's autobiography, Sarah Wells was 'perhaps the worst housekeeper that was ever thought of'.[2] This has become the accepted view of Mrs Wells's tenure at Uppark, which ran from 1880 to 1893. She was bad at accounts, she was bad at managing her girls, she was ill experienced in buying stores and economising – so said her son, the writer H. G. Wells. If you visit the house today, push past the brass-tack-studded red baize door, descend the eighteen steps to the basement and peer into her little sitting room, this is the line that the hovering National Trust guide will give you: here sat Mrs Wells, the very worst of Victorian housekeepers. But is this fair? It seems nobody has really looked at the evidence. We have unquestioningly swallowed the judgement of her son, the famously prolific Edwardian novelist.

Fortunately, there is another source for Mrs Wells's story: her own version of events. She was a habitual diary keeper, jotting down a few repetitive lines each night before climbing wearily into bed. Unlike so many housekeepers' personal records, these have survived because of the fame of her son. Today they lie in the university library of Illinois, handled with reverential white gloves by scholars hoping to find insights on H. G. Wells. The diaries have also been photocopied by the West Sussex Record Office, and it was here, in Chichester, not ten miles from Uppark, that I laboriously read through hundreds of pages of her quavering copperplate script.

Using the five unpublished diaries of Sarah Wells, the Uppark archives and her son's letters, I set out to resurrect her world and reassess her performance. Truthfully she should never have taken the job: she lacked the qualifications. But Mrs Wells was eager to make the best of it, elated at her apparent great change in fortunes. The reality of her daily round, in this twilight world below stairs, turned out to be relentlessly hard for a frail woman in her sixties – and nothing like the Victorian caricature of the housekeeper, haughty in her black bombazine dress and clinking keys, directing work from the comfort of a wing chair in her sitting room.

The story of Mrs Wells is one of unexpected physical labour and of humiliating old age. Women like this had to work to the bitter end; they had no financial cushion or job security. We find her organising the annual spring cleaning at nearly seventy years old, her rheumatic joints so tender she can hardly walk. She spends her working days, up to fifteen hours long, underground in the servants' quarters at Uppark – sewing, linen checking, sugar pounding, writing off for replacement maids, bookkeeping. She must also deal with an endlessly quarrelsome tribe of maidservants and a more than usually prickly mistress. Our housekeeper works, most remarkably, for a lady who was born a dairy farmer's daughter.

In trying to understand the particular nuance of Mrs Wells's story, we need to consider what preceded it – the extraordinary marriage made by the master of Uppark, Sir Harry Fetherstonhaugh, to the estate dairymaid Mary Ann Bullock half a century earlier. It was a marriage that jolted everything out of its place, with implications for the mistress–servant relationship ever after.

II

1825: The Dairymaid

For the price of one penny, No. 8, Vol. 13 of the *Princess' Complete Story' Novelettes* (1886) tells the story of Kitty, a demure country girl who goes into service as a maid, falls in love with her mistress's son and ends up as Countess of Masborough. 'Penny Dreadfuls' such as this were written for young maids in cold attic bedrooms; girls with no more chance of walking down the aisle with the lord of the manor than being given a morning lie-in. Things like this didn't happen in real life.

But at Uppark, back in 1825, they did. When Sir Harry Fetherstonhaugh, 2nd Baronet, tired of gambling and gallivanting (and when society tired of him – 'the greatest goose that ever existed', thought one), he turned his attentions to home, and to marriage. He was a red-nosed, haw-hawing old Etonian of 71. She was an illiterate, 20-year-old local girl, and she worked in the cool, tiled dairies of Uppark in West Sussex. Sir Harry took to sitting outside the dairy entrance in Sir Humphry Repton's inspired little shelter – a curved white roof over four slender white pillars – resting his gout-ridden hulk on a white slatted seat while indulging in a Devonshire cream tea from the home farm. Before him was the far ridge of the South Downs; behind, the dairy's showroom for visiting ladies, with decorative pitchers and earthenware bowls laid out on shelves. The working dairy was one door further in: worn paving slabs, the slap of butter pats, a sour smell in the air and the chatter of female voices.

One voice stood out for Sir Harry. Mary Ann Bullock was proposed to by His Lordship while standing at the door of the dairy, her skirts hitched up into her apron. 'Taken aback, like,' was her reaction, according to a workmate. 'Don't answer me now,' said Sir Harry, 'but if you will have me, cut a slice out of the leg of mutton that is coming up for my dinner today.' Miss Bullock was no fool. When the mutton arrived, the slice had been cut.

The upper-class rumour mill ground into life – and as with any good rumour, they got the gist but were hazy on detail. 'Sir Harry Fetherston, 76, has married his kitchen maid, aged 18,' wrote Mrs Arbuthnot in her racy journal (the political hostess went on to note several other 'quite curious' marriages between 'old men' and younger women that year).[3] The Sussex County set snubbed Sir Harry's new wife, while Uppark's servants sniggered behind her back. A footman was dismissed on the spot by Sir Harry for laughing at the new Lady Fetherstonhaugh as she alighted from her carriage. It was so hard to take her seriously.

Mary Ann was sent to Paris to have her manners gentrified. She learnt to read. She learnt to write a good hand. She was also taught to embroider very precisely in wool, and once back at Uppark busied herself decorating fire screens and footstools. 'I've made a fool of myself, Legge,' Sir Harry reportedly told his old gamekeeper – but the goose was cooked. He hit back at unkind snobbery with his own brand of snobbery, negotiating with the College of Arms for the registration of the 'Arms of Bullock' so that he could have them 'impaled' with his own (Gules on a Chevron between Three Ostrich feathers Argent a Black roundel, with an escutcheon of Ulster').

Casting around for companions for his isolated bride, Sir Harry brought into the house Mary Ann's younger sister, Fanny Bullock, a pert country girl in want of refinement, aged around eight. He also brought in his protégée (and illegitimate daughter, reportedly), 20-year-old Ann Sutherland, to educate young Fanny. The unlikely new family was complete – and stayed this way for the next twenty-one years. No heir was born to Sir Harry. He died aged 92 in 1846, an enormous man of reduced fortunes, confined to a large Bath chair, surrounded by women and beautiful objects.

III

1874: Hedward and 'Enry

Uppark is a pleasing dolls' house of a country house, as neat as an iced cake, set high on the West Sussex Downs with views, on a clear day, over the Solent to the Isle of Wight beyond. On a grey day the wind buffets the symmetrical, pink-brick Georgian facade and the immense, open prospect south seems bleak and forbidding. Behind are softer, gently enclosing beech woods, bluebells in May and herds of fallow deer. It is a place apart: an enclosed world with no other dwelling visible from its ninety-five windows.

Inside are all the spoils of several Georgian grand tours: two generations of voracious Fetherstonhaugh collecting. There are Canalettos, Batonis and Giordanos; there are chinoiserie lacquered cabinets, Dutch still lives, ormolu horses, Flemish tapestries, rococo giltwood mirrors, blue Sèvres vases and an immense quantity of Waterford chandeliers. There is a Saloon the size of half a tennis court, a Red Drawing Room, a Little Drawing Room and Little Parlour – 'little' being a relative term.

Tea, in the Victorian era, was served by the butler from an urn on a finely worked silver salver. There were grape scissors and asparagus tongs on the dining-room table and Dresden washbasins painted with Meissen jonquils and roses in the bedrooms.

Presiding over all this in the year 1874 was Mary Ann's younger sister – the living embodiment of High Victorian paranoia about class and transgression. The 1871 census has her down as Fanny Bullock, a name redolent of the farmyard, but three years later she is *Frances Fetherstonhaugh*. When Mary Ann died that year, aged 69, her will was very precise. Her sister Frances was to inherit her name, her coat of arms and the big house. And so this 55-year-old spinster vaulted all the rungs of the social ladder in one single, audacious leap.

But running a big house on a fairly frugal inheritance was a trial. Frances and her faithful older companion Ann Sutherland (rightful inheritor of the house, some thought, but anyway, permanently installed at Uppark and now aged 69) were not naturally authoritative with the servants. These first few years were thought to be something of a golden age in which to work below stairs at Uppark, because, so they said, you could get away with anything. The ladies muddled through. It was rumoured that they called the two footmen, who wore long-stemmed hothouse flowers in their lapels, 'Hedward' and ''Enry' (no matter what their real names were) to save confusion. Servant turnover was high. The new Miss Fetherstonhaugh took to using Sir Harry's

Queen Anne silver christening bowl as a washbasin in her bedroom; tongues started wagging in the basement and beyond. As with her sister, Frances was still snubbed by much of society.

She had lived an uncommonly insular life for a country-house inheritor. There had been few suitors for her or for Ann Sutherland. No breath of change had penetrated Uppark, which remained apparently frozen in the eighteenth century. There was no gaslighting, no flushing sanitary closets or hot-water pipes. Visitors noted the quaint lack of contemporary taste: there were no aspidistras, no antimacassars, none of the obligatory three cushions per chair thought so essential to the High Victorian aesthetic (by this time all padding and plumpness, drapery and ornament). Unkind gossips laughed at these unworldly ladies conspiring to keep the house as it had always been – to "ave everything as Sir 'Arry 'ad it' (The two did not, as it happened, talk like this, but it was *such* fun for County wags to imagine that they did.)

Intimidating masculine decor loomed down at the ladies from every wall – antlered skulls, portraits of horses, still lives full of dead deer, lobsters, slaughtered boar and limp partridges. Above the Red Drawing Room fireplace hung a large oil painting of Sir Harry in his vigorous, curious youth, a dog at his side. A portrait of George III dominated the grand Saloon. Frances and Ann holed up in the Little Parlour, a calm, sunny, double-aspect room with a rare quality of cosiness. They were literally cornered – in a house too big, too grand and a touch anonymous. The ladies sat in gilt armchairs with their backs against the wall, on an uneasy footing with all around them.

In another life, Fanny Bullock might have become housekeeper of Uppark, had she gone into service like her sister. Now, six years into her tenure, she decided she needed one herself, as a marker of the social pretensions of the household. Miss Fetherstonhaugh, as she was now called, wanted to be treated with due respect as lady of the manor both by outsiders and insiders. She needed a go-between, a confidante; a cushion between her and the world. She longed, too, to be free of the bother of dealing with servants.

In her choice of housekeeper, Frances Fetherstonhaugh gave away both her ignorance and her insecurities. Rather than appoint an efficient professional with excellent references from another big house – a woman who might make her feel socially uneasy, threatened or displaced – she decided instead to give the job to someone from her past. Someone who would protect her. The new housekeeper's name was Sarah Wells, and she was born an innkeeper's daughter in Midhurst, seven miles away.

IV

1853: Others Have Servants

Some thirty years earlier, this same Sarah Wells had arrived at Uppark to take up the post of lady's maid to Fanny Bullock. They were close in age (27 and 30), and natural companions in a household that Sarah recorded in her diary as 'very quaint and feeble,' though she 'got gradually used to them.' Fellow servants included lady's maid Anne Austin, 64; laundress Sarah Blackman, 72; housemaid Sarah Horwood, 45; and nurse Sarah Chitty, 53.[4]

Sarah Neal, as she was then called, came via Miss Riley's finishing school for middle-class girls, followed by a four-year apprenticeship as a dressmaker and a spell with one Lady Forde in Ireland. She nursed ambitions to learn French and to travel. What she got was Uppark's under-gardener Joseph Wells. And with their engagement announced, she had no choice but to leave. It was not done to continue in service as a married woman. Having become 'greatly attached' to her mistress (as she recorded in her diary), the two parted with 'deep regret . . . most reluctantly.' Miss Bullock, now aged 34 and unlikely to marry, watched her friend go off to the satisfactions of homemaking and babies, a life peculiarly out of her reach. Fanny Bullock might have thought her own good fortune a kind of curse, but she would have been wrong. The life Mrs Sarah Wells went on to lead was wretched by comparison.

The year she left Uppark, both Sarah's parents died within three months of each other. Joe was unable to find long-term work, employed for a time at the gardens of Trentham Hall in Staffordshire while his new wife lodged with relatives, 'spirits sadly depressed'.

Her husband's fecklessness began to dawn on her. 'Not quite pleased with what I heard', Sarah wrote in her diary; 'JW [Joseph Wells] had an appointment with Miss Burdett-Coutts' – the Victorian banking heiress and philanthropist. 'Too late the situation had gone. Oh, how disappointed we were, flat very low and dull.'

Things did not get much better. A habitual diary keeper, she packed fifteen years of married life into one battered volume, a line or two for each day. Days before giving birth to her first child in January 1855, Sarah Wells was on her knees scrubbing the floor. 'Felt it so hard to have so much to do, but I know Dear Joe cannot afford a servant.'

On giving birth, the first thing she heard was a voice saying, 'It is dead.' But then the midwife hit the baby, plunged it in a warm bath and brought it back to life. She called the child Fanny, after her old mistress, and she turned into a delicate little girl, prone to whooping cough and chest complaints. Two more children followed; Frank in 1857 and Freddy in 1862, and life settled into a grimly circumscribed routine.

Did not take children out today.
Did not get out. Cold snowing.
Boisterous winds did not go out.
Took children out after dinner. JW Cricket.
Ironed. Did not go out today.

Joseph Wells worked as a haphazard market gardener then as a shopkeeper and china salesman, but above all he was a cricketer. He was an extraordinarily fast round-arm bowler, and he played for the West Kent Club and the County of Kent, travelling the country each summer and earning what he could, bowling on village greens under scudding clouds and blue skies. The indoor life of his wife stood in stark contrast to his own. 'Busy preparing the children's winter clothes,' she would write in her own. 'I feel I cannot work fast enough.' Or, 'Char woman ill, had all my work to do myself – very tired – oh how hard I work, others have <u>servants</u>.'

On 26 June 1862 Joseph Wells made history when he bowled out four Sussex batsmen in successive balls. It turned him into something of a local celebrity. People visited his china shop in Bromley just to see this bowling legend in the flesh. Working in the background was Sarah Wells, long resigned never to learn French, own a silk dress or be waited on by a maid while genteelly entertaining relations in the front room. There was no front room: it was given over to the shop.

In 1864 nine-year-old Fanny Wells came home from a birthday party with a stomach ache. Three days later she died of 'inflammation of the bowels' (as appendicitis was called). Sarah Wells recorded her daughter's death as it happened, on a blank sheet of paper, as she sat in the sick room. This sheet, marked with tear stains, she then copied conscientiously into her diary word for word, as if this was a way of making things *count*.

My firstborn child expired in my arms. God's will be done.
My darling dearest pet pet, in her coffin, my darling only child.

Fanny was not her only child, but her favourite: her close companion. Sarah Wells needed to hold herself together for the sake of her boys and her husband, but she unburdened her grief in a series of agonised diary entries.

Oh never did I feel such sorrow – my own beloved mother dearest was severe. But this. Oh this. Is worse. Oh God . . .
It's like a dream, her toys & little clothes lying about . . . her precious drawings . . .

In a diary that confines itself largely to the mundane, her raw emotion is shocking. High child mortality is one of those Victorian statistics trotted out by historians – but here we get a glimpse of how it *felt* to be the mother of that child. It was common, but it was still appalling to go through.

Two years later another child was born to Sarah and Joseph – Herbert George or 'Bertie'. This son grew up to be H. G. Wells, phenomenally successful Edwardian author of novels such as *The Time Machine*, *The Invisible Man*, *Kipps* and *The War of the Worlds*. He was an observant child from the start.

The family home was Atlas House on Bromley High Street in Kent, a 'gaunt and dismal' place, according to Bertie, with a china shop at the front, a business bought from a cousin that proved impossible to invigorate. 'My mother in my earliest memories of her was as a distressed overworked little woman, already in her late forties', wrote H. G. Wells in his *Experiment in Autobiography* in 1934. 'All the hope and confidence of her youth she had left behind her.'

In 1866, the year of Bertie's birth, she recorded buying two pairs of sheets and three pillows – 'the first since I married, poor dear mother's nearly all worn out, how poor we are, not able to buy common necessaries'. She also went to London 'about my teeth', which were falling out. 'Had nothing done, expenditure great.' A note of desperation and injustice had by now crept into his mother's diaries. 'Very boisterous dark day . . . what a miserable house this is to live in and how hard I work. What shall I have to do soon!! God help me.'

By the summer of 1880 Mrs Wells was a thwarted, worn-out woman of 57. Her two eldest sons, adults now, were in and out of employment. Bertie was 13 and unhappily apprenticed to the Southsea Drapery Emporium, where he worked a thirteen-hour day and slept in a dormitory with other boys. Her husband was unable to play cricket, having broken his thigh bone falling off a ladder in 1877. The family's supplementary income gone, they were barely scraping by.

'And then suddenly the heavens opened', wrote H. G. Wells, 'and a great light shone on Mrs Sarah Wells.' A letter arrived in the post, stamped with a coat of arms, written in ink on heavy cream paper. It was a letter from 'Miss Frances Fetherstonhaugh', and it contained the suggestion of a plum job at Uppark. Mrs Wells had no experience of housekeeping for a country house, but she was in no position to turn it down. She snatched at the offer like a drowning woman.

V

1880: The Return

Mrs Wells must now journey from Bromley in Kent to Petersfield in West Sussex, to take up her new position. Much has changed since the young lady's maid left Uppark by pony and trap twenty-seven years ago; there is now a train station at Petersfield (and two at Bromley, for that matter), so she will travel into London and out again.

The London newspapers of the day record Wednesday, 4 August as a cool day of thundery showers. Mrs Wells anxiously bids her husband and sons goodbye, unsure when next she will see them, as this job comes with a harsh, if common proviso: *no attachments*. I have tried to imagine her journey back to the big house – an important one in every sense. She boards a steam train at Bromley North for distant Charing Cross, then jolts in a horse-drawn hackney cab over the River Thames to Waterloo Bridge station. There are omnibuses making the same journey, but Mrs Wells has a large black trunk with her and so must pay for a cab. One of her older sons is there to help her, for this is an immense journey for a woman who has scarcely left her basement kitchen for almost thirty years.

Mrs Wells dreads missing her train. The Central station is cavernous, echoing with shrieks and hisses, shouting porters and the urgent, clicking heels of men in bowler hats. She has on her best and only black dress and bonnet, which makes a pretty poor show next to the fashionable ladies in elaborate hats and bustles (the 'mermaid's tail' being the latest trend, with thirty-six yards of fabric cascading from the rump).

She runs anxiously after the porter as he trundles her poor old trunk down the platform and onto the train. Is it the right train? The whistle screams. Frank, or Freddy, waves her off with his handkerchief. She pokes her bonnet out of the wood-framed sash window. 'I'll be sending money! Look after your father! Remember to go to church . . .' Her eyes fill with tears. But still – what an adventure! For two hours she clickety-clacks south into the new commuter belt of lush and prosperous Surrey: Surbiton, Woking, Guildford, Godalming . . .

I can see Mrs Wells shaking out her copy of *The Standard*, bought at Waterloo and all her own to savour. Cowes Regatta began yesterday, she reads, while over in New York Dr Tanner's 'Fasting Experiment' is now in its fifth week (he is said to resemble a desiccated side of bacon). Poor Mr Gladstone, 70 years old and just two months into his second tenure as Liberal Prime Minister, is seriously ill in bed . . . Meanwhile various bills are being rushed through Parliament: the Irish Disturbance Bill, the Employers' Liability Bill, the Hares and Rabbits Bill, the Burials Bill. As to the interminable Afghan war, General Burrows has been defeated at Cabul and Candahar: driven back by savage enemy forces of 12,000.

With a jolt Mrs Wells sees she is drawing into Petersfield station in West Sussex. Here she is met by Miss Fetherstonhaugh's own carriage, not any old pony and trap. Coachman William Gray gives her the once-over: patched and dusty travelling coat, boots in need of resoling, trunk positively ancient. So, this is the new housekeeper.

It is a six-mile ride to the village of South Harting, at the base of Uppark's beech woods, and as the horses strain up Harting Hill Mrs Wells begins to remember with fond nostalgia her old mistress and the great house. The gardens are entered through a pair of golden gates – gilded ironwork in delicate scrolling curls – and it seems to Mrs Wells that, at last, some kind of fairy tale might be about to begin. Her life is about to turn good again.

She is shown by a maid into the sunny Little Parlour on the ground floor, where her mistress is waiting. How is their reunion, after all this time? I imagine the two women looking at each other with keen curiosity. Miss Fetherstonhaugh surveys a small woman whose face is lean and worn, with brows knit deep and blue eyes narrowed against misfortune. She has cheeks slightly sunken due to lack of teeth, and has learnt to press her lips together to hide the gaps. Mrs Wells stretches out both hands to clasp her mistress's in delight: hands enlarged and distorted by years of scrubbing and damp. Should she curtsy? A moment of hesitation. It's been decades since last she curtsied, and her knees are rather stiff.

'Dear Miss Bullock!' she begins.

'Miss *Fetherstonhaugh*,' murmurs old Ann Sutherland from behind, just a touch reprovingly.

Fanny Bullock was never a beauty – her eyes are somewhat dull and impassive, her nose beaky and cheeks rather heavy, much like her elder sister's. But life has not been exacting for this 61-year-old spinster, and she has aged well. Photographs show that her skin is pale and doughy, her forehead smooth, if framed by grey. Her hands, to the touch of Mrs Wells, are exceptionally soft. Both she and Miss Sutherland are dressed in black velvet (this does not vary), and the effect is somewhat stern.

So much has passed in two decades, Mrs Wells does not know where to start! Marriage, motherhood, bereavement and two grown sons out in the world. But something in Miss Fetherstonhaugh's impassive gaze discomfits her a little, and she finds herself looking around the room instead and exclaiming how nothing has changed; it is all exactly as it was. The gilded head of Bacchus and his succulent golden grapes carved into the chimneypiece; the little mahogany corner cupboard with its trinkets.

Should they talk of the past, or the present? What are her duties, as housekeeper? Mrs Wells has a rather hazy idea of what might be required – and Miss Fetherstonhaugh is, as it turns out, equally vague about her daily routine. But she is clear about one thing: the appointment of Mrs Wells as housekeeper, at £35 a year, is to mark a new era of prudence and sobriety at Uppark.[5] There are to be no more rampant expenses, no more wads of cash handed out willy-nilly. Accounts are to be meticulous and servants brought under control. A new cook, Mrs Stewart, was installed just yesterday, and the butler, Mr Lambert, took up his post a fortnight past, replacing doddery old Mr Friend. Mrs Wells's bonnet nods in assent and a note of panic rises in her chest.

I imagine a pause, the moment at which teacups might be refreshed. Instead, with a nod to the footman, the ceremony is over. 'Old Anne', the head housemaid, is called for and Mrs Wells – the new broom – is shown downstairs to the housekeeper's room.

Tucked away to the left of the entrance hall at Uppark are eighteen wooden stairs leading down to the subterranean basement. Here, three corridors of service rooms are set like a horseshoe around an inner, whitewashed courtyard, sunk below ground level, and the visitor today can do the rounds much as Mrs Wells would have done on this cool Wednesday in August 1880. First on the left is the still room. It was gloomy back in the 1850s, and it is gloomy today, notes Mrs Wells, observing paint bubbling up on dun and cream walls. Water has darkened the flagstones in the adjacent scullery where a length of duckboard is set down on the floor by the sink. Rank coconut matting covers the floor around one large central table.

As a lady's maid she had little to do with this room, where breakfast, tea and coffee trays are laid and rushed upstairs, cakes and sweetmeats produced, wines bottled and fruit preserved. Now it is to be her domain. She takes in the three high windows overshadowed by bay trees and the black kitchen range, decades old. A great wooden dresser takes up one wall, set with copper pans. It is dark in this room, and it is to get darker still as night draws in and oil lamps are lit. The clock ticks. Mrs Wells smiles with what she hopes is authority at the two girls uncertainly pounding lump sugar, and determines to keep cheerful. Why, you could fit her old Atlas House kitchen four times over into this great room.

Past the butler's pantry (dun and brown walls, Windsor chairs and a green baize table for shining up the plate), past the lamp room and silver safe. And here, at the southern corner, is the 'housekeeper's closet' (more walls blistered with damp; industrial-sized jars and tins lined up on shelves; a strong smell of spice) and the housekeeper's room. Here, I imagine relief flooding through her.

This is a pretty, double-aspect room, directly beneath the ladies' Little Parlour (though with none of the sweeping views). The late-afternoon sun makes its way through the high, cross-barred windows – in need of a little brightening, thinks Mrs Wells, her mind running through possibilities with leftover chintz. She would also like to paint the walls white; get rid of this dreary goose-muck green that makes the spirits sink. On the dresser are blue-and-white patterned Dresden cups and saucers; the fire is lit and a tea tray has been set next to two easy chairs. Mrs Wells, weary from her day of travel and extremely anxious about her role, wants to lower her poor old body into one of those chairs, rest her feet on the fender and wait for the kettle to sing.

But the tour is not yet over. Old Anne (65 years old or thereabouts, an illiterate Sussex girl who's spent a lifetime in service) takes her past the bell passage – fourteen bells for upstairs, much the same as two decades before – and past the large, vaulted distillery; set with great wooden barrels and brick bins for storing wine, to the upper servants' hall. Mrs Wells remembers this comfortable, well-proportioned room with a shock. The lean years at Atlas House have erased the memory of that large, round mahogany table set with a dozen dark chairs and one armchair (for the butler); that worn but thick Brussels carpet; the walls hung with murky oil paintings; the gilt mirror over the fireplace and the porcelain on the mantelpiece.

She fancies she sees the ghost of her younger self, a short, shy lady's maid in awe of this team of butler, under-butler, housekeeper, valet, head housemaid and Lady Fetherstonhaugh's sharp-tongued personal maid, the elderly Miss Anne Austin. As lady's maid to Miss Fanny Bullock, she had always been the most junior of the tribe. Now she would be joining the butler at the head of the table. Mrs Wells grips the back of a mahogany chair and blinks hard as this fact sinks in.

Finally she is led to the servants' hall for the lower tier of domestic staff, set well apart from their superiors in the north-west corner of the house, with the advantage of three tall windows at normal height. You can actually see out. Over the fireplace is a goulish stag's head, a kind of bas-relief trophy sliced through the cheeks with shrivelled ears and bits of flat wood in its eye sockets. Eight more pairs of buck's horns decorate the room, which is starkly furnished with one long table and two benches. At any rate, she won't be spending much time in here.

The sun is setting, and Mrs Wells yearns to walk up those eighteen stairs and breathe in the old South Downs view. She wonders how the gardens have changed since Joe worked on them. Back then the fruit won prizes, it was so perfect: grapes and pineapples so sweet you couldn't believe the taste of them, all grown in the glass-roofed hothouses. She remembers honey and figs, and deep-yellow milk from the Uppark Guernsey herd. She recalls pot-pourri jars in every room upstairs, filled with vivid carmine rose petals from the garden that never seemed to lose their fragrance. If only she could walk a little now and smell those summer roses once again!

But first the cook, Mrs Marion Stewart, is to be met. It is a little unfortunate that Mrs Stewart should have started her tenure one day before Mrs Wells, as this gives her an advantage she is likely to exploit (this, and the fact that her wage matches the housekeeper's, though she is technically inferior). Miss Fetherstonhaugh had implied she'd had a run of ill luck with cooks in the years since her sister's death, but Old Anne rolls her eyes and says not even a saint would last more than a year in Uppark's kitchens, her mistress has become so particular.

To reach the kitchen they must take to the service tunnels. These are, at first sight, rather quaint: underground vaulted passages punctuated by light wells, leading in one direction to stables and dairy, in the other to kitchen and laundry. They are not quite long enough to be claustrophobic, nor dark enough (at least in daylight) to be macabre.

They run directly beneath the gravelled entrance court to the big house, their light wells hidden around a central flowerbed planted with lavender. As servants make their swift and invisible way below, the well-shod feet of guests might crunch on gravel up above and the staccato strains of small talk float down the air vents.

The arched brick roofs and walls of the tunnels have been white-washed – some years ago, thinks Mrs Wells, judging by the dank and mossy walls. Water pools on the flagstone floor, and the air is damp and chill. Better take a lamp, says Old Anne – there are bats here at night. A shrew skitters out of sight as the two walk the fifty yards to the kitchen, their footsteps and voices echoing. They hitch their skirts up out of the puddles as they go. How intimately Mrs Wells is to get to know these underground passages – and how she will come to curse them.

VI

What A Party Of Women

There were ten women working under the housekeeper at Uppark; ten women plus a cook. Mrs Wells was to oversee one lady's maid, three housemaids, two laundry maids and one each of still-room, scullery, kitchen and dairymaid.

Back in the 1850s, as Mrs Wells remembered, the servants were drawn from Harting village with a handful from Petersfield and Chichester. By 1881 the census return tells us that they came from all over the country. There was the cook, Scottish, aged 26. There was her mistress's maid, Emily Dyson, 29, from Suffolk. The young dairymaid, Mary Drinkwater, came from Cheshire and talked broad, as did the other footmen Frederick Dunnett and Walter Larner, one from Norfolk, the other from Gloucester.[6] The girls were mostly very young – 17, 18, 19 – and they left after a few months, a year at most. No one really wanted to *settle*, it seemed to Mrs Wells; they were always imagining the grass was greener at some other big house, or wanted to try some of this new shop-girl or factory work. A thoroughly modern 'International Stores' had just opened in Chichester, where Shippam's meat-paste factory was also recruiting. As soon as you'd broken them in, they were off. By December of her first year, two of the young maids had gone and three more had been appointed. It was all very wearing.

With half an eye on the young housemaid who cleaned her bedroom up in the eaves, Mrs Wells managed to keep up her daily diary entry over the years that followed. She alluded warily to the hothouse of warring females she now found herself in.

Oh how I long for a quiet house.
The Cook disagreeable to Miss F.
No peace with servants here.
E & D most disagreeable. What a party.
Engaged kitchenmaid. Mrs Holmes gave warning.
To the Dairy. What passionate women, I never can think the end of it all.
The Poor Cook kept under by that horrid woman in the Dairy who can Pass it over!!!
What a party of <u>women</u> I am surrounded with.

'Women' is thrice underlined. Uppark was a house full of women. Mrs Wells's closest colleague, the one she might expect to share confidences with, was the butler, Mr Lambert. But Edward Lambert (on £40 a year) lived in a flat over the laundry with two young babies and Frances, his wife. Even when in his pantry, his mind was elsewhere; he was his own agent. Grooms, coachmen and gardeners likewise, all lived out. Sarah Wells was used to male company: she had three grown sons and a husband. To start with, she might have fancied herself on holiday from all their noise and need and mess. She wrote daily to her sons, yet was surprised to discover she didn't pine for her husband quite as much as she felt she should. But once she had fitted out her private quarters and arranged her books on the dresser just so – an old Peerage, Crockford's Clerical Directory, her yellow Bradshaw railway timetable, the Whitaker's Almanack, Old Moore's Almanack, an eighteenth-century dictionary and her well-thumbed Bible – the novelty soon wore off and she found that she missed them.

She had kept her own house for twenty-seven years. Now she must keep another's, without any of the satisfactions of ownership. Neither the preserving jars of strawberry jam laid down on the shelves, nor the fine towels hand-hemmed and monogrammed, were her own. All her activity was directed towards the comforts of another. And, proudly independent woman that she once was, a certain sense of resentment began to grow.

Did not move out, busy all day, supposed to do nothing.
Busy cutting out fine towels.
Busy with goods from the stores, did not go out. Busy making up wages book.
Busy put Red Currant Wine in Cask about 5 gal.
Strawberries sent in for preserving. Busy all day did not venture out.
Lovely day.

Not even the lovely day was hers to enjoy. However well she performed her duties, Mrs Wells could not break through the glass ceiling. There was no further promotion for a housekeeper, and none that would pluck her permanently from the basement.

Mrs Beeton's description of the ideal housekeeper in her *Book of Household Management* (1861) has a poignant resonance for women such as Mrs Wells who had kept their own house. 'The Housekeeper must consider herself as the immediate representative of her mistress, and bring to the management of the household all those qualities of honesty, industry, and vigilance in the same degree *as if she were the head of her own family*. Constantly on the watch to detect any wrong-doing on the part of any domestics, she will overlook all that goes on in the house.[7] For a woman who had been her own mistress, no matter how shabby her domain, this sudden lack of any real autonomy must have been both demeaning and frustrating.

The respectable, much-sought-after position of housekeeper might well have seemed the answer to a certain sort of woman down on her luck – but the reality could be unexpectedly crushing. *The Times* carried dozens of advertisements placed by needy middle-class women, often widowed, seeking the job of housekeeper. 1850: 'Wanted, by a highly respectable middle-aged country person, a situation as housekeeper in a tradesman's family, or in any capacity of trust and confidence. She would prove a great acquisition. The advertiser is a widow, truly, domesticated, and, having a small independence, salary is not so much an object as a comfortable situation.' Here is another from 1870: 'A widow lady, age 38, well educated, musical, with a good knowledge of French, domesticated, and fond of children, seeks an engagement as housekeeper to a gentleman.'

Innkeeper's daughter Sarah Wells, with her finishing-school education and her long-buried aspirations to learn French, was of perplexingly similar social standing to Miss Fetherstonhaugh, daughter of a dairy farmer. The housekeeper occupied Uppark like a troubling mirror image, or understudy, to her mistress – reminding her how far the one had travelled and how far the other had sunk. The relationship was never straightforward, and was frequently fractious.

VII

How Dull I Am!

Sarah Wells desperately needed this job: her family needed it, and she took from it what she could. She used Miss Fetherstonhaugh just as Miss Fetherstonhaugh was using her. Within days of arriving at Uppark, she parcelled up and sent off a great quantity of broken chinaware to be mended by one Joseph Wells of Bromley, 'Dealer in China, Glass, Earthenware, & Cricketing Goods'. A receipt duly came back from her husband, rather smudged and stained, dated 3 September 1880, for £1 14s 9d⁸ (around £85 in today's money). In a musty box of accounts for Uppark in the West Sussex Record Office – twenty-six bundles for the year 1880 – I found several more such receipts from Mrs Wells's husband. This opportunism continued until Joe's business was finally wound down in 1888, despite the one-shilling carriage fee from London – and the glaring fact that Petersfield had china dealers of its own.

Then there were her children to consider. 'We infested the house', remembered H. G. Wells. During school holidays and periods of unemployment, unless mistress and housekeeper had fallen out, Frank, Freddy and Bertie used Uppark like a free boarding house. At the start of her tenure they were 23, 18 and 13 years old. Like cockroaches or black beetles, the trio of male Wellses entered at basement level to undermine subtly the great house and its social pretensions.

This is the closest any of the boys had got to the gentry, and it came to them at one remove. 'There came and went on these floors over our respectful heads, the Company', wrote H. G. Wells. 'People I rarely saw, but whose tricks and manners were imitated and discussed by their maids and valets in the housekeeper's room and the steward's room.'⁹ Like a sponge, the teenage Bertie soaked it all up – and some twenty years later put his observations to comic effect in the novel *Tono-Bungay* (1909). Here, Uppark was reimagined as 'Bladesover', his mother as housekeeper Mrs Ponderevo and himself as George, her unruly only son. 'George' is as tickled by the servants' politics as he is by the goings-on upstairs: 'After Company, I remember, came anxious days, for the poor old women upstairs were left tired and cross and vindictive, and in a state of physical and emotional indigestion after their social efforts.' Each side of Uppark's red baize door seemed equally ludicrous to young Bertie. In the face of her young son's ridicule, Mrs Wells was required to take sides, and she sided with her mistress – if she didn't, after all, her life would be lived in vain. She absorbed the snobberies, became expert in 'the ranks and places of the Olympians' and deft in placing people's servants about her tea table, where the etiquette was strict. 'I can see and hear her saying now', wrote H. G. Wells of her fictional counterpart in *Tono-Bungay*: '"No, Miss Fison, peers of England go in before peers of the United Kingdom, and he is merely a peer of the United Kingdom"'.

Mrs Wells was goaded by her son, who found the upper servants at Uppark 'intolerably dull' with their 'fifteen remarks' that got them through each mealtime ('The days draw out nicely'; 'The frost continues'; 'The poor souls without coals must suffer') – and he told her so with teasing mimicry. She would invariably burst into 'agitated tears' at having this hollow charade – her life! – driven home. 'O God how dull I am!' cried Mrs Wells. 'O God how dull!'[10]

Young Bertie Wells was particularly needled by the absurd self-importance of the upper servants – and *Tono-Bungay* is deliciously, mordantly witty on this point. There come annually to 'Bladesover' three pensioned-off servants, invited as a reward (with pointed reference to the housekeeper and her cronies) for their years of loyal service. They sit about in the housekeeper's room in their 'black and shiny and flouncy clothing adorned with gimp and beads, eating great quantities of cake, drinking much tea in a stately manner and reverberating remarks'. Also at the housekeeper's table is Miss Fison (Miss Dyson was Miss Fetherstonhaugh's lady's maid at the time), and the butler 'Rabbits' (Mr Lambert?) – 'large, with side whiskers, even if his clean-shaven mouth was weak and little'. He has 'acquired from some clerical model a precise emphatic articulation without acquiring at the same time the aspirates that would have graced it'. For all his morning coat and black tie with blue spots, Rabbits drops his aitches.

H. G. Wells serves them up as a comic vignette, but there is also something pathetic about these people, aping their superiors but having nothing really to say; people ill at ease, as if wearing ill-fitting suits, grasping after the cadences of refined conversation.

Upstairs, Frances Fetherstonhaugh was equally obsessed with class and hierarchy. She must find an heir for Uppark before her death, and the estate dangled like a ripe peach before dozens of speculative friends and distant relatives. At lunch one day Lady Leconfield, of nearby Petworth, was asked what she would do with the silver, should she be given Uppark. Her reply did not please: 'Take it to Petworth, of course.'[11] She had become a genealogy bore, and spent time poring over the Fetherstonhaugh family tree in an attempt to discover an appropriate heir. In the basement, meanwhile, the housekeeper debated the fine degrees of precedence between visiting servants so that they should go into dinner in the right order. Both upstairs and downstairs were caught up in an elaborate charade with no true personal relevance. The only thing to give it sustenance, to make it real, was the house.

From the moment she put on her lace cap, lace apron and black silk dress, Mrs Wells reabsorbed the hierarchies of below stairs and became institutionalised. For her, the house was a kind of prison she must make the best of. Her life of apparent busyness was a vicious circle, a dead end. She was trapped. But for her son, Uppark was a springboard. H. G. Wells depicts George at Bladesover 'routing' among the books and treasures of the house while the rain beats down outside. 'Sitting under a dormer window on a shelf above great stores of tea and spices, I became familiar with much of Hogarth in a big portfolio . . . with Raphael . . . and with most of the capitals of Europe as they had looked about 1780, by means of several big iron-moulded books of views.'

Gravely ill, aged 21, Bertie spent four months convalescing at Uppark (an ill-tempered ban on the Wells offspring was temporarily lifted by Miss Fetherstonhaugh on hearing the dread word 'consumption'), and he worked his way through Shelley, Keats, Lamb and Hawthorne; books bound in leather and embossed in gold. At times he felt desperate, shut up 'in this accursed land of winds, wet ways and old women'.[12] But his sunny, chintz-decorated bedroom in the eaves and Uppark's 'beech-woods and bracken-dells' worked their cure. Bertie Wells absorbed the lesson that Uppark represented 'all that is distinctively British', and he took this nuanced, privileged knowledge out into the world, first as pupil, then teacher, then writer.

VIII

For Fear Of Spending It

How far should we trust H. G. Wells's portrait of his mother? He wrote An Experiment in Autobiography in 1934, nearly thirty years after her death. He tries, so he says, to see into her mind – 'I began to wonder what went on in her brain when I was in my early teens and I have wondered ever since.' But he can only guess, speculating that 'innocent reverie' takes up her rare moments of leisure, saving her from more acute unhappiness.

How far can a teenage boy, or young man, understand an older woman's inner life? 'Poor little woman!' is a typical exclamation. He pities her, 'dear little mother', but she seems, looking back, rather like a peg doll; a worn caricature in a black silk dress – 'the bothered little housekeeper in the white-panelled room below'. H. G. Wells's summing up of her time at Uppark – 'perhaps the worst housekeeper that was ever thought of' – has since become her public epitaph.

It is true that Sarah Wells was unprepared for the work involved, and the position did not seem to bring her satisfaction. According to her son she started off 'frightened, perhaps, but resolute', believing that 'with prayer and effort anything can be achieved'. But with an inexperienced and disinterested mistress there was no one to show the housekeeper how to do her work. She was expected to have absorbed it on her way up the ladder.

'She did not know how to plan work, control servants, buy stores or economise in any way', wrote her son. 'She did not know clearly what was wanted upstairs. She could not even add up her accounts with assurance and kept them for me to do for her.' (Though who would not encourage their clever, numerate son to have a stab at the housekeeping accounts on his rare visits? Mrs Wells was both intensely proud of, and anxious about, Bertie's on-off scholarship.)

Was she, perhaps, an adequate housekeeper, coping with unusually trying circumstances?

The surviving diaries of Mrs Wells document two phases of her life. First, her early years in service as lady's maid, then motherhood: twenty years of life (1848–68) squeezed into an old, 'extra enlarged edition' desk diary for 1835 (price 7s, half-bound).

Between 1868 and 1890 there is a gap, the diaries lost or destroyed. For her last decade of toil at Atlas House in Bromley, and first decade as housekeeper of Uppark, we have just her son's description to go by, served up both as autobiography and fiction. But a box of accounts survives for Mrs Wells's first few years at the big house, neatly folded lengthways into fortnightly bundles, tied tightly with string and sent off to Sir William King in Portsmouth, agent to Miss Fetherstonhaugh and architect of Uppark's great economy drive. There are also her mistress's banking books in which all payments are recorded (including £10 sent to one 'Bullock' – a poor relation? – every two months).[13]

In the year before Mrs Wells's arrival, somebody called 'Smith' received regular, hefty lumps of cash from Miss Fetherstonhaugh – up to £180 at a time. Smith, whatever his or her role, got through £350 to £400 a month (£17,000 to £22,000 in today's money). For the first five months of Mrs Wells's new job, Smith and the housekeeper overlapped, and Smith held the purse strings. Then from January 1881, 'Wells' was the only recipient of the cash handouts – and they were rather small in comparison.

She was not initially trusted with large sums of money; receiving £30 in January, £20 then £50 in February, and £50 then £80 in March. Soon, though, she was being handed £100 to £200 at a time (£5,000 to £10,000). These are phenomenal amounts of money for a woman who for thirteen years couldn't afford to replace her own bed linen, and it made Mrs Wells very anxious. She handled around £10,000 a year (£500,000 in today's money), her weekly accounts running along the lines of 'Coffee, lemons, sugar, pipkin & seeds, malt & hops' plus casual labour, as well as settling the various bills with tradesmen in Harting and Petersfield.[14]

The next chapter of Mrs Wells's diary keeping picks up her life ten years into her job at the big house. It was 1890: she was 67 years old, and money still made her nervous.

Went to Petersfield Miss F – Bank £150.

Sent Miss Pink the remainder of bills 9/ leaving only £1-00 in hand which is due to Joe!!!

Showery day sent to Petersfield £60-00. Put away £60-00. Put away £5-00 for fear of spending it.

Her mistress was by this stage 71 and her son Frank was 33, Freddy, 28 and Bertie, 24 (within a year to be married to his cousin, Isabel). Her husband Joseph Wells had given up the shop, and for the past three years had been living a couple of miles away in the tiny agricultural hamlet of Nyewood. She sent him regular if slightly reluctant payments that she recorded in her diary:

Sent JW £1-00.

Sent JW rent £2-00.

Paid JW £1-00. Very tired.

Joe's years on his own had not been spent entirely unhappily. At Atlas House 'My father camped, so to speak, amidst its disorder very comfortably', wrote H. G. Wells. 'He cooked very well, far better than my mother had ever done.' On moving close to Uppark he gave up all pretence at work and was kept by his wife, who he would see for the occasional afternoon tea, overnight stay in her rooms or walk in the woods. Mrs Wells felt both guilty and exasperated.

JW left after breakfast he sounded sadly depressed.
Sent JW £1·00 being the last. What will they do when I am gone.

This diary is a seven-inch Ferre's Twopenny Pocket Diary, one week to a page. Inside is an advertisement for 'The latest and most improved system of gas lighting, the Etoile Gas Lamp Regenerator'. Most country houses have by now succumbed to gaslighting; Chatsworth House in Derbyshire is at work on the water turbines that will shortly bring it electricity. But Uppark is not on the gas mains, so Mrs Wells does her work by oil lamp. In the back of the diary are advertisements for health supplements:

Beecham's Pills – for Bilious and NERVOUS DISORDERS, such as Wind and Pain in the Stomach, Sick Headache, Giddiness, Illness and Swelling after Meals, Dizziness, and Drowsiness, Cold Chills, Flushings of Heat, Loss of Appetite, Shortness of Breath, Costiveness, Scurvy, Blotches on the Skin, Disturbed Sleep, Frightful Dreams, and all the Nervous and Trembling Sensations, &c.

(Now in use for half a century, the secret ingredients in Beecham's Pills were aloes, a purgative and ginger soap.)

Her entries are no longer in ink but written with a soft stub of pencil, firmly pressed. The handwriting is now almost illegible: the hand of an old lady tremblingly filling in a mundane line a day. It is her bedtime ritual – what we might call today her therapy.

IX

Sadly Vexed

Sarah Wells's diaries are at first glimpse disappointingly mundane:
Busy this week with my black silk dress.
Called on Mrs Budd took dripping.

Went to Harting and paid folks.

Miss F had her first drive since Sept.

But read in context, from a Victorian housekeeper's room in the basement of a great house, they are revealing. They do not tell us too much about her thoughts, but it is possible to get a sense of what it was *like* to be down there, day after day: the frustrations, the consolations, the physical discomforts and the petty politics.

It was a startlingly unstable household. Written in the back of Mrs Wells's 1890 diary is a list of cooks:

Mrs Stewart came to Uppark August 5th 1880 left Sept 22nd 1881

Mrs Bartlett came some time left Aug 1882

Mrs Heard came 14th left April 1884

Mrs Francis came in June 7th 84 left April 1885

F. Gate came Jan 1886 left Nov 1887

Mrs Clements came May 90 left Jan 91

Mrs Cates came Jan 20th left Feb 8th 92

Mrs Holmes came Feb 92 left Aug 92

Mrs Keeble came Aug 17th left Sept 17th 92

Mrs Harrison came Sept 92 left Feb 93

In the twelve and a half years that Mrs Wells was housekeeper, from the age of 57 to 69, ten cooks came and went at Uppark. *Ten* cooks. This was a good job, relatively well paid, in a notoriously relaxed regime with a gloriously spacious, high-ceilinged kitchen overlooking the South Downs. The cook did not slave away in the basement. Early in the century the kitchens at Uppark had been moved outside to a handsome brick pavilion accessed by a service tunnel. The dank old kitchen became the housekeeper's still room for preparing breakfasts, sweets, preserves and tea. In these kitchens the cook, kitchen maids and 'casual friends' (according to Bertie) nattered away in the hot glow among bright copper pans in their own fiefdom. The workload was relatively slight: there were two bird-like old ladies to feed, who were often away, plus staff. House parties were rare; dinner parties unusual. Luncheon and tea were the usual hours for Miss Fetherstonhaugh's sporadic entertaining of military and clergy types. Why, then, was it so hard to keep a cook?

Traditionally, housekeeper and cook had a prickly relationship. The housekeeper deemed herself to be above the cook, but the cook (along with the lady's maid) was appointed by the mistress, not the housekeeper. Yet Miss Fetherstonhaugh gladly left the bother of recruitment to Mrs Wells, who was forever answering, or putting into the *West Sussex Gazette*, advertisements for servants. Perhaps she chose unwisely. Perhaps it was hard to find a cook for a big country house that had neither the excitement of gay house parties nor the labour-saving technology that professionals were coming to expect in the late nineteenth century.

Uppark was a mirror of the nation's servant problems at large: 'The servant who takes an interest in her work seems no longer to exist', complained an article in *The Sphere* at the turn of the century, 'and in return for high wages we get but superficial service. Where is the maid to be found who takes pride in the brilliance of the glass used upon the table or remembers of her own initiative to darn the damask? Every sort of contrivance now lessens labour – carpet sweepers, knife machines, bathrooms, lifts – in spite of these the life of a housewife is one long wrestle and failure to establish order.'[15]

For housewife, read housekeeper. With little or no support from above stairs, and none of the new Victorian technology, Mrs Wells was preoccupied constantly with staff spats in an era beginning to be known for 'the servant problem'. Domestic service was still the largest single female occupation in the country, but it was becoming unpopular. Shop work, factory work, any work other than service was now being sought by young girls – girls unwilling to subdue their spirits to the sort of crushing dictates enforced below stairs. The prolific servants' conduct books of the era strike a shrill, somewhat desperate note: 'Do not walk in the garden unless permitted or unless you know that all the family are out, and be careful to walk quietly when there, and on no account to be noisy.' 'Never sing or whistle at your work where the family would be likely to hear you.' 'When meeting any ladies or gentlemen about the house, stand back or move aside for them to pass.' These come from *A Few Rules for the Manners of Servants in Good Families*, published by the Ladies Sanitary Association in 1895 and again in 1901.

It was down to the housekeeper, of course, to try to instil these rules. Perhaps Mrs Wells was a bad manager of people. Perhaps, though, her raw material left much to be desired.

Wrote to Mrs Holmes hope she will come and help. What a worry this house is!!

Sadly vexed about Mrs Keeble not suiting.

Told Mrs Keeble about leaving what a miserable house this is!!

Worried with the Cook leaving how unsettled this house.

Mrs Keeble left. Mrs Harrison came. Miss Maxwell left.

Felt unsettled but hope it please God all will be ordered for the best.

The world was speeding on apace outside Uppark's walls. In 1887 the gramophone was invented; in 1888 the pneumatic tyre and the Kodak box camera. In 1890 London's first electric train made its journey underground, and by 1891 you could actually *telephone* through to Paris. Some innovations were welcome – there was now a treadle-operated Singer sewing machine in the housekeeper's room. Others were deeply troubling. Women were demanding the vote, divorce was more commonplace; there was even a 'Rational Dress' movement to liberate ladies from long, heavy skirts and tightly laced corsets. By the 1890s women were playing tennis and riding bicycles (even smoking cigarettes!) with a freedom Mrs Wells found faintly shocking. The comforting old hymns they sang at church were being edged out by strange, modern tunes – like that one they ploughed through last Sunday, 'What a Friend We have in Jesus'. Her old rural neighbourhood in Bromley, Joe told her, had grown into a noisy suburb of London. The 'brown and babbling' River Ravensbourne with its overhanging trees had been swallowed up by a new drainage system.

It was an era of furious, baffling change. In November 1892 Mrs Wells visited a young lady in the village and came away feeling horribly out of the swim of things: 'Felt very unsettled and seeing such altered ways makes one very dull', she wrote, sitting tight-lipped in the crepuscular gloom of the servants' basement.

Her son, making his way in this exciting new world, felt his mother's bafflement keenly as she got left behind. 'Vast unsuspected forces beyond her ken were steadily destroying the social order', wrote H. G. Wells:

the horse and sailing ship transport, the handicrafts and the tenant-farming social order, to which all her beliefs were attuned and on which all her confidence was based. To her these mighty changes in human life presented themselves as a series of perplexing frustrations and undeserved misfortunes, for which nothing or nobody was clearly to blame – unless it was my father and the disingenuous behaviour of people about her from whom she might have expected better things.

There is a photographic portrait of Mrs Wells taken in the 1880s, dressed in black silk and cap as a record for the great house. 'Mrs Wells, Housekeeper of Uppark' has a perplexed expression. She does not radiate confidence. She attempts to look dignified, but the eyes are tired and a little frightened, and the hand on her book is nervous.

X

Longing To Get Out

Mrs Wells clung to small routines and predictabilities to ward off those 'unsettled' feelings brought on by change. There is a sense that the very act of diary keeping soothed her with its repetitive nature; that every mundane entry had an incantatory effect. She had her rhythms, her routines and gripes. Staffing problems aside, there are, by and large, four types of entry. First, paying off the tradesmen who supply Uppark. She would walk or ride down Harting Hill every Monday and take a glass of sherry with each: 'Went to Harting and paid folks'.

Second, her sons. Sarah lived for letters and visits, and fretted in their absence: 'Bertie letter only a few words.'

Frank came to tea. I fear he never goes to Church. How altered. Sadly grieved about him.
Bertie exam – I trust my dearest one has got on well.
My poor old birthday. Not a word from my Boys.
Sent Bertie by Rail Brace of Pheasants. Wrote to Frank sent Leg of Mutton.

Third, church: 'What a comfort the blessed Sabbath day.' The South Harting Parish Church of St Mary and St Gabriel is an antique-feeling place of Elizabethan timber, narrow windows and sparsely spaced lamps. It was made darker still at the death of Lady Mary Ann Fetherstonhaugh in 1874 with a bequest of three piously illustrated stained-glass windows at the western end (Attending the Sick; Visiting the Prisoner, and so on), where light once streamed in to touch the far altar. Servants sat at the back, behind the gentry and village folk, and Mrs Wells kept a sharp eye on her maids during the lengthy sermons.

South Harting lies at the foot of Uppark's steep beech-wood territory: a vertiginous mile-long walk down a rough track, the maids' heavy skirts trailing in the mud. The walk back up to the big house would have made Mrs Wells's lungs wheeze in protest. When her mistress was in residence, and in a generous mood, she shared the carriage with her. The days Mrs Wells did not make it down Harting Hill to church (bad weather, ill health) were spent in glum resentment. Church was her respite. 'So thankful got to Church,' notes more than one entry.

Finally, and most interestingly, she writes regularly on the weather, and getting *out*. For someone who spent most of her life in the basement Mrs Wells was acutely sensitive to her environment, to the passing of the seasons and fine gradations of the weather. In just a line she economically – poetically, even – conjures the raw outdoors.

Boisterous winds did not go out.
Snow on the ground – came in the night but melting in the sun.
Rough day. Busy with elder wine.
Walked the garden. Cold winds.
Primroses.

Every day is weighed by whether she manages to breathe fresh air or not.

Showery day did not go out. Busy cleaning.
Feel very worn out. Tired. Busy all day. Showed house to servants.
    Longing to get out.

Her mood lifts as spring and summer come round; there is palpable joy as Mrs Wells feels the sun on her face, if only for half an hour.

Sat in the shrubbery read papers.
I walked after dinner yew tree field got primroses they are now lovely.
Short walk shrubbery. Sun shining all day, quite warm, such lovely
    spring days, how thankful I am my loved ones all well.
Got a few bluebells. Sent them to Bertie.

What were the consequences of confining servants to dark basement quarters, where the only windows were high and barred, the only exit through a long, dank tunnel?

In 1845 the Government commissioned a report on the condition of mental institutions throughout England, and its findings resonated with the below-stairs world of servants. Older asylums, which resembled dreary 'prisons or dungeons', were compared with the more 'modern establishments', designed with the well-being and comfort of patients as a priority. 'The patients ought to have the benefit of a cheerful look-out on a pleasing prospect', argued the Commissioners, concluding that the older asylums were not suitable for Victorian patients. Newly constructed asylums should 'avoid everything which might give to the patient the impression he is in prison.'[16]

Uppark was designed in the early eighteenth century in the old style: servants in the dark, gentry in the light. The kitchen was moved upstairs as entertaining got more lavish, but the rest of the staff remained below ground.

In the latter years of Queen Victoria's reign, drastic improvements were being made around Britain to the standards of living for servants. Enlightened country-house design did not favour troglodyte conditions, bringing them up instead into fresh air and daylight. Lanhydrock in Cornwall, a Jacobean mansion devastated by fire in 1881, was rebuilt according to the latest ideas in service design. Visitors today can see the ground-floor housekeeper's room with its large, light-flooded windows facing in two directions, while the next-door housemaids' sitting room is an airy, bright room where the girls would have entertained their friends.

In 1905 an article in the medical journal *The Lancet* claimed that the 'eminently depressing' living quarters for servants in poorly ventilated dark basements, where 'diffused light is but a matter of a few hours daily even in midsummer', accounted for the anaemic appearance of so many employed in affluent homes.[17] The body's need for Vitamin D made through exposure to sunlight was not known about at this time, though the health benefits of cod liver oil had been discovered. (H. G. Wells writes about his mother's 'fanatical belief' in the stuff to prevent the 'vitamin insufficiency that gave my brother a pigeon breast and a retarded growth'.) Mrs Wells recorded her bouts of ill health and self-medication in her diary: 'Very poorly took oil.' She noted this on 23 August of her last year at Uppark, twelve years of a largely underground existence. When the young Sarah Wells was lady's maid at Uppark, she spent her time mostly above stairs – stitching, dressing and hairdressing, helping Miss Frances with her ablutions in beautifully proportioned Georgian rooms looking out towards the South Downs. It was a house made for sunlight: all those windows facing east, south and west; all those tall, giltwood pier-glasses reflecting yet more light back into the rooms. From her mistress's quarters she could see the gardens, and perhaps imagine Joe at work down there in the fresh air. Now, as housekeeper, she was like a mole – 'busy all day in those vaulted passages,' as she wrote with resentment. Mrs Wells's mood darkened as summer passed. She dreaded the short days ahead.

18 July: 'Days already drawing in.' (Underlined three times.)

14 October: 'Rain & wind, dark dull day, winter coming on.'

27 October: 'Dull day foggy and wet, not so cold. No walk – how dark in these underground rooms.'

Seasonal Affective Disorder, or 'SAD', is a modern diagnosis of the suffering that can be brought on by shorter days and less sunlight. It is held that SAD sufferers are more likely to be women, and that they commonly start craving sugary foods: cakes, biscuits, chocolate. 'Fat little mother,' wrote H. G. Wells in a letter, under a sketch of a rotund little lady in a lace cap. The still room was a dangerous place for sugar addicts: all those cakes and scones, jellies and jams. More gravely, lack of exposure to natural sunlight is now known to induce depression, osteoporosis and breast cancer – even schizophrenia.

Victorians could only hypothesise at this time about the relationship between mind and body. It was understood that depression afflicted all classes – though the connection between lack of sunlight and symptoms of severe depression among the working classes had not properly been made. The terminology was still imprecise. Phrases such as 'nervous exhaustion' and 'nervous collapse' were used loosely for feelings of dullness, inertia, pessimism and deep unhappiness, where the victim was still able to function.[18] A nervous breakdown was vaguely described as 'shattered nerves' or 'broken health'; and a new label – 'neurasthenia' – was brandished towards the end of the century. Melancholy was another much-used term; or, more severe, 'falling into melancholia', which could be brought on by a trauma.

Hysteria was thought to be particularly the curse of women – and especially idle women.

But what about those under-stimulated, or frustrated, working women? Mrs Wells was the opposite of idle, but her vitality had been blunted and her mind shut down by the dull, repetitive nature of her job. Victorian psychiatrist Sir James Crichton-Browne, who devoted his life to the study of mental health, wrote in 1883 of the 'dreary, aimless vacuity of mind that is hysteria's favourite soil'.[19] As for the connection between mind and environment, this had barely been made. In 1885 Alexander Bain published his groundbreaking study *The Senses and the Intellect*, in which he argued that a new method of studying the mind was needed: one that took into account experience, the environment and physical actions. It was the advent of modern psychology.

Mrs Wells carried her personal tragedies closely within her: it wasn't done to rail against fate, and it was, after all, the Lord's will. But she had had more than her dose of sorrow. At the age of 26, she lost her sister. At 30, both her mother and father died within weeks of each other. Her black moods are recorded in her diary. 'Dull day spirits sadly depressed', she writes, with frequency. 'What a dream I seem in!!!' In 1864 her beloved nine-year-old daughter died suddenly. She recorded the anniversary of Fanny's death in every diary thereafter, along with her daughter's birthday (and burial) a few days later.

As a young mother, Sarah Wells visited relatives on a Sussex farm for a short summer holiday with babies Fanny and Frank. Her diary sings briefly with joy, against its more usual monotonous litany, for the green fields and wild flowers, the fresh air and sunshine. For most of her adult life this woman, so keenly alert to the natural world, was shut up in a dark basement. Eventually, her body and mind started to disintegrate.

XI

Queer How Altered

The final diary Mrs Wells kept at Uppark, covering 1892-3, is written in The Englishwoman's Pocket Diary. This book allows more room for her entries – a week over two pages – but still no space for Sunday. Down the right-hand side of each page is a ledger column for personal housekeeping, which Mrs Wells – not keeping her own house – ignores. She has her big black housekeeper's ledger, and this is enough.

It is written in ink this time, in a flowing but shaky hand, and the same well-worn phrases fill its pages. But this year something is different. There is a growing sense of claustrophobia; a certain desperation in her situation.

Oh! So tired. Longing to get out, how can people shut themselves up indoors.

Mr Thompson & wife with Mrs J Legge [the gamekeeper's wife] & Miss Tigg [the plumber, painter and glazier's wife] came to tea. Shut up all day waiting on them.

Physically, she is falling apart. Mrs Wells is now nearly seventy years old, with no prospect of retirement.

Began the [annual] house cleaning. My feet so tender what can it be? After tea my last poor old double tooth came out. Did not go out today. Suffering with pain and stiffness I fear it is rheumatism.

Her relationship with Miss Fetherstonhaugh is also degenerating. A new uneasiness is recorded – she even asks permission to go to church:

'Spoke to Miss F about the Evening service – gave her notice to leave.' It is hard, for this elderly woman, still to be owned by another and prey to capricious mood changes and querulous demands. 'Miss F more kind. I long to get away.' She feels increasingly ambivalent towards her employer – and the feeling is mutual.

'I think Miss Fetherstonhaugh was very forbearing that my mother held on so long,' H. G. Wells wrote in his autobiography.

Because among other things she grew deaf. She grew deafer and deafer and she would not admit her deafness, but guessed at what was said to her and made wild shots in reply. She was deteriorating mentally. Her religious consolations were becoming more and more trite and mechanical. Miss Fetherstonhaugh was a still older woman and evidently found dealing with her more and more tiresome. They were two deaf old women at cross purposes. The rather sentimental affection between them evaporated in mutual irritation and left not a rack behind.

There are hints in this diary that Mrs Wells's mind is indeed beginning to falter. These entries might be veiled references to staff spats, but she appears confused and paranoid.

26 March 1892: 'Busy all day as usual. I do not feel comfortable. Such strange things one hears and sees!!'

28 May: 'Unpleasant answer from the Cook who seems to act very queer.'

On 2 June she has a chat with 'dear Freddy', her eldest son, 'in my bedroom' – an odd place to receive guests, and perhaps significant enough to be noted. Is this the only safe place to talk? A fortnight later she is 'Greatly worried about servants'. By full summer comes a sense that the housekeeper of Uppark is finally reaching the end of her tether.

2 August: 'Numerous disagreeables, what I have to contend with.'

4 August: '12 years today I came here and left Bromley. What anxious years they have been to me. What rude insulting people I have had to live with and it is worse <u>now</u>.'

12 August: 'Worried with Head Dairy Maid's tales.'

13 August: 'Carried to Miss F the tales in circulation.'

On 22 August she sweeps her own bedroom (something was seriously amiss with the housemaids' regime if the housekeeper was reduced to cleaning her own room – but perhaps her growing paranoia insisted she do it herself), and the following day feels 'very poorly'. She doses herself with cod liver oil, but it's not enough to fortify her against Miss Fetherstonhaugh's bruising brush-off.

25 August: 'Miss F returned. Unpacked her boxes, but not required to dress her. Felt my deafness very much but I must be thankful for good health.'

As Mrs Wells's hearing gets worse, so her catalogue of staff upsets increases. By the summer's end she is permanently aggrieved. The girls are, no doubt, exasperated by their ailing, deaf housekeeper.

29 August: 'Cook as usual not a word that is kind.' (Mrs Keeble, barely there a fortnight, was a disaster. She was to leave in two weeks.)

2 September: 'That horrid woman upset me again. Oh how hard to be obliged to stay in such a place.'

27 September: 'Miss F – queer how altered! It must be my deafness.'

In November, Mrs Wells is told there is to be an important house party, the first in a very long time, and Miss Fetherstonhaugh (now 73) is in a terrible fret about it. She tries to impress upon her hapless, deaf housekeeper what is expected.

On 2 November Mrs Wells is found 'Busy airing sheets. I dread this party.' The dust! The bed making! The cleaning of all that silver! Three days later she is 'Busy writing for all the wants of the house' – as if the house were some voracious, potentially troublesome person. Two days later she is still 'Busy thinking of all I wanted.' The kitchen is in uproar, Mrs Harrison producing great wobbling jellies and syllabubs, pie crusts and consommés, her kitchen maids barred from false errands to the stables. Upstairs the dust sheets are being pulled off the furniture one by one, revealing the shrouded splendours of the grand Saloon and Red Drawing Room.

The guests arrive on Wednesday, 9 November: 'Got on better than I expected', writes Mrs Wells in her diary; 'so thankful. Miss F very quiet', which makes her uneasy. Has she pleased her mistress? All the 'folks' leave before lunch on Friday. 'Oh! So tired.'

But it is not over yet. A spate of pre-Christmas sociability leaves Mrs Wells peevish and exhausted. Her inbuilt reverence towards the aristocracy has, it seems, evaporated – even her feelings towards royalty. Their comings and goings are reduced to a fuss and a bother. Likewise, her deference towards Miss Fetherstonhaugh has soured. After a lifetime of putting herself second, suddenly she can take no more. On 21 November, the 83-year-old Lady Clanwilliam and her stout-waisted daughters come to lunch. Three days later the Duchess of Connaught (German-born wife of Prince Arthur, Queen Victoria's seventh child), icily correct, descends on Uppark for tea. With her is Lady Fitzwilliam of Wentworth Woodhouse in Yorkshire (Britain's largest country house). 'No time to go out', writes Mrs Wells.

After this marathon, there are no thanks from her mistress. Instead, 'Miss F always finding fault.' On Friday, 2 December, she unpacks a large delivery for the basement stores, sorting goods into the right cupboards, listing everything in her dog-eared housekeeping books. Her work, as ever, goes unnoticed: 'No thought of me if <u>tired</u> or not.' Instead, there is a distinct frostiness from upstairs.

3 December: 'Miss F very strange, resolved to have an understanding soon.'

On 6 December it's the turn of the Duke of Connaught (Prince Arthur) to arrive with his demanding retinue of valets and coachmen from Bagshot Park in Surrey. Mrs Wells is not impressed. 'Oh! Such fuss & work, how I wish I was out of it – what ignorant people as a rule servants are. Busy all day early & late. Poor Legge in disgrace.' (Legge was the head gamekeeper.) A couple of days later she is 'worn out with worry'. Worry has become a reflex, a modus vivendi. The worry makes her tired, and her tiredness makes her worry.

9 December: 'Miss F never asks if I am tired.'

Mid-December sees the annual ritual of handing over charitable Christmas gifts (cast-offs, in reality) to the poor of Harting village. It was a habit started by Frances's sister Mary Ann, and had been continued assiduously after her death in a custom shared by both mistress and housekeeper. One woman gets all the gratitude; the other sees to the detail. But this year things are altered.

14 December: 'Miss F refused my helping her with her charity clothes. What a comfort the blessed Sabbath day.'

Still, out they head in the chill of Friday, 19 December, distributing goods in the wagonette, and Mrs Wells succumbs to her usual knee-jerk subservience: 'How good Miss F is!!!' Two days later the reality sinks in when crowds of villagers are received at the house. Following in Miss Fetherstonhaugh's gracious wake is her housekeeper, dishing out tea and giving her ear to health and housing grumbles. 'Miss F gave her presents away to the poor people . . . I had to wait on them all.'

As the year draws to a close, Mrs Wells's diaries show her to be dog-tired. On Christmas Eve she sends up eight large mince pies; on Boxing Day she prepares for and waits on company while nursing a 'severe cold & cough'. On the twenty-eighth the water pipes at Uppark freeze solid. Two days later she travels seven miles by open trap with Mrs Harrison the cook to buy cough mixture in Petersfield. The journey, she writes, is 'very very cold'.

The year 1893 starts with no new diary. She crams her entries into the back of last year's: 'Slippery weather afraid to go out.' The elements conspire against her . . . and so does her mistress. Mrs Wells asks for a few days' leave in early January, catches the train to Clapham Junction and stays with her youngest son Bertie and his new wife Isabel, 'thankful to be at rest'. She sees the sights, spends time with her family and recovers her flagging spirits.

On her return she is summoned upstairs to the Little Parlour. Here the fire is lit and the dogs are slumbering, but today the mistress of Uppark is unusually stiff-backed and alert. Miss Fetherstonhaugh is glad of her companion Miss Sutherland's pale, sandy-lashed presence, as she has an invidious task on her hands. There is a hesitant knock at the door, and at once the dogs are brushed from black velvet laps. Her old friend Mrs Wells – cherished lady's maid, housekeeper at Uppark for twelve years – is given a month's notice to pack up her belongings and leave.

The coup de grâce from Miss Fetherstonhaugh is not written up in the housekeeper's diary. Just one line, bewildered and frightened: 'What shall we do for a living? Please God find me work to do. How cruel of that <u>woman</u>.' She cannot name her mistress, the friend who turned against her. But she need no longer celebrate her munificence, or bob her head and take orders. The social wrongs of the past twelve years are righted. Frances Fetherstonhaugh is merely, and rightly, reduced to 'that woman'.

XII

I May Still Earn A Trifle

Mrs Wells might reasonably have expected a pension, perhaps an estate cottage, after her time served at Uppark. Many housekeepers worked up to their death, but if they became frail were usually looked after by the family. Uppark, however, had a different regime, with no sense of noblesse oblige. To the socially insecure Frances Fetherstonhaugh, what mattered beyond all else was loyalty. In the end, she left the great house to a middle-aged colonel, the son of her friends the 4th Earl and Countess Winterton. To Mrs Wells she gave nothing. The housekeeper departed as she arrived, in a carriage bound for Petersfield station with her old travelling trunk.

'A poor little stunned woman she must have been then, on Petersfield platform', H. G. Wells imagined, long after the event:

a little black figure in a large black bonnet curiously suggestive now of Her Majesty Queen Victoria. I can imagine her as she wound mournfully down the Petersfield road looking back towards Harting Hill with tears in her blue eyes, not quite clear about why it had all occurred in this fashion, though no doubt God had arranged it 'for some good purpose.' Why had Miss F been so unkind?

Her fault, according to H. G. Wells, was that she gossiped about 'some imaginary incidents' in her mistress's former life, which had come back to Miss Fetherstonhaugh's ears. If this was true, it is revealing. It shows that Mrs Wells, the underdog, was increasingly beset with thoughts of injustice: slaving away for 'that woman' who was no more than the sister of a dairymaid. It also implies that Fanny Bullock/Fetherstonhaugh took to her grave a prickly sense of social alienation from the country-house world she inhabited. She carried a chip on her shoulder to the end.

In future decades, the injustice felt by Mrs Wells was gradually to consume the minds of household staff. 'Servants are looked upon as a part of the furniture of the house: live furniture, nothing more', wrote former butler Eric Horne in 1932, railing against the 'vast abyss' that separated master and servant. 'If the live furniture is in the town house and is wanted in the country house, or vice versa, it is simply moved there. If a piece of the live furniture gets broken in body and health, the gentry simply say: "chuck it out and get another".[20]

Most women in Mrs Wells's position would now have been in dire straits. How would she work again, given her age? Who would support her impecunious family? If the housekeeper was a spinster, who would look after *her*? Mrs Wells's savings were small: for the past decade she had been paying her husband's rent and bailing out three struggling boys. There passed some extremely anxious months (not helped by Bertie abandoning his wife and moving in with a student, Amy Catherine Robbins, in January 1893). Her deafness grew steadily worse; she could no longer hear the sermon in church. She wrote to an employment bureau and every contact she could muster after her years in service, but no one was interested in the elderly ex-housekeeper of Uppark.

Felt depressed. I hope soon to get employed.
Please God I could get some little house where I could be earning my living.
Miss Curtis called and said no replies. I fear I never shall get another situation.

She lived with her husband in the nearby hamlet of Nyewood, paying the rent out of her savings. It was not, in all likelihood, a harmonious time for husband and wife, reunited after a dozen years of separation. 'Wrote for £5 more of my hard-earned savings!!!' she records with agitation.

Meat went off quickly in the pantry, and her daily errand was no more exciting than 'Went to Rogate for Butter & biscuits', a hard hour's walk away. Shopping in Harting was demeaning – she was reduced to hunting for scraps and paying with coins, where once she ordered the best for the big house and handed out banknotes.

But Mrs Wells, devoted mother, was lucky with her sons. Freddy was now working in commerce in South Africa, and Bertie was beginning to make a decent living from his writing. The sons rallied round, stumping up a monthly sum to keep their parents. Middle brother Frank, a fledgling watchmaker, lived with his parents.

Initially Mrs Wells fretted. Two years into her retirement, she could not see it as such. She was still, at 72, fooling herself that she would find some work – 'I pray I may still earn a trifle.' The dismissal from her post rankled, its anniversary recorded in her diary.

16 February 1895: '2 years ago I left Uppark.'

The big house continued to exert a pull; it was still her compass point, and she was curious as to what was going on: 'Heard Mrs Legge was at Uppark' – the gamekeeper's wife. But did she dare show her face again, after her shaming departure?

On 8 March, two years after her fall from grace, Mrs Wells finally achieved a kind of closure. We learn this from an entry, sweet in its brevity, where she reduces her ex-mistress to her origins: 'Called on Miss Bullock.' Three months later Miss Fetherstonhaugh – or Fanny Bullock, dairymaid's sister, to some – died.

Sarah Wells went on to enjoy an Indian summer after her lifetime of toil. She was moved by Bertie to a 'pretty little house' at Liss, not ten miles from Uppark, with 'seven decent rooms and a garden'. Here she lived to the age of 83 with Joe and Frank. Money still preoccupied her, but things did not turn out so badly. In the back of her diary for 1899 she writes a tally of pounds received: Freddy sends £5 and Bertie £15 to £20 every two to three months. Her annual income for the year is £105, around £11,000 in today's money. 'The little old lady is rosy and active', wrote Bertie to Frank on New Year's Eve 1896, ' – fit for twenty years I shouldn't wonder.'

One century after Mrs Wells returned to Uppark to act as its house-keeper, a terrible fire broke out in the roof, consuming much of what Miss Fetherstonhaugh had striven to pass on. In 1989 the great house was gutted, the upper floors collapsing onto the ground floor with many archives and treasures damaged or destroyed. After long and painstaking repair, Uppark reopened to the public in 1995 – one of the most rigorous restoration projects ever undertaken by the National Trust. As for the servants' basement rooms, their dank, underground nature proved to be the perfect protection from the flames. They needed little renovation.

Mrs Wells's diaries – which travelled in her black trunk from Uppark to Nyewood, then from Nyewood to Liss – have ended up in the Rare Book and Special Collections Library of the University of Illinois, on loan from the National Trust. How this would have puzzled, not to say worried their author, had she been able to imagine such an end.

Part 3

Ellen Penketh

Erddig, North Wales 1902–1907

The princely salary of £45 a year.

Mr Artemus Jones,
barrister for defendant Ellen Penketh

Timeline

1901 – Life expectancy for men is 45; for women, 49.
First vacuum cleaner patented.
Heinz Baked Beans first sold by Fortnum & Mason for 9 pence a can.

1902 – Pharmacy Act: dangerous chemicals no longer sold in domestic-shaped bottles.

1903 – Mrs Emmeline Pankhurst and daughters start the Women's Social and Political Union to campaign for women's suffrage.
The Daily Mirror launched, initially as a woman's paper.

1909 – Lloyd George's 'People's Budget' speech, promising wealth redistribution.
Persil washing powder arrives in British shops.

1910 – London's Selfridges introduces a cosmetics counter, a year after the store opens.
Pond's Vanishing Cream and Cold Cream first marketed.

1911 – National Insurance Act: insures employees against ill health and provides some unemployment benefit.
1.4 million indoor servants working in Britain.

1912 – RMS *Titanic* sinks after striking an iceberg.
Hullo Rag-time! opens at London Hippodrome and runs for 451 performances.
Suffragettes resort to violence – 'deeds not words'.

1913 – Suffragette Emily Wilding Davison throws herself under the King's horse on Derby day.

The Corridor

This story starts, and ends, with a photograph.

It is the one true – straightforward, unbiased – record to survive. And it is such a handsome photograph: the oval, clear face; the slightly amused eyes. By Edwardian standards of beauty, Ellen Penketh has a certain allure. There is something of the Gibson girl in that longish face and 'sporty jaw', the hair piled up on her head in the contemporary pompadour style (but not too high: she was a servant, after all). Yet she lacks the haughty, slightly pitying look of those Belle Époque women drawn by Charles Dana Gibson. Ellen Penketh's expression is hopeful, like the posy of fake flowers she is holding. It is the sort of studio portrait a working-class girl might send to a fiancé – and it is in stark contrast to the photo gallery of stern-faced spinsters who line the basement corridor at Erddig Hall.

Servants who worked for the Yorke family in the early twentieth century tramped past these two dozen portraits daily on their way from laundry to scullery, butler's pantry to servants' hall. The passage is dark, as Erddig refused to succumb to the modern rage for electricity. It is also terribly cold, as the wind from the far Welsh hills lashes the west front with great determination, forcing leaves under ill-fitting doors and draughts through old sash windows.

The photographs are enlarged, retouched and boxed in by screeds of verse celebrating each individual's years of service, their dedication, their preference for life at the big house to any other sort of life at all. 'And for some thirty years and more/The cares of Office here she bore . . .'.

is typical. How did the Yorke servants feel, hemmed in by all these loyalty portraits? There is Harriet Rogers (heavy-lidded stare, thickly veined hands), forty-four years in service first as nurse, then lady's maid, then cook-housekeeper. There is gardener George Roberts posing with his wife, who holds in her lap a portrait of her mother, also in service at Erddig. John Jones (slightly boss-eyed, saw in hand) was photographed in 1911, thirty-three years after he entered service as a carpenter. The message is clear: stick with us and we'll look after you. Erddig – or 'Erthig,' to the Welsh – was an anchor in a fast-changing world.

Each poem, bashed out on a typewriter, is signed 'P.Y.' – Philip Yorke – and dated 1911 or 1912. What happened to make Squire Yorke abruptly start this celebratory exercise in verse? Many of these servants were long dead or departed when he began his task – why the need to backdate so assiduously? And why were so many new portraits of old servants taken at this time? They were done, ostensibly, for continuity's sake: the servants' hall at Erddig is famous for ten oil portraits of servants, complete with rhyming couplets, commissioned by his grandfather and great-grandfather. But in truth, it was more complex than this. The answer is hinted at in the verse Philip Yorke II wrote for Miss Brown, housekeeper at Erddig from 1907 to 1914.

Twelve years or more did intervene
Before Miss Brown came on the scene . . .
Of Housekeepers we estimate
We had in turn no less than eight . . .
But since Miss Brown her rule begun
Our lot has well and smoothly run,
And the result may now be class'd
As worth the 'fire' 'thro' which we passed.

P.Y. 1912

Five years previously the Yorkes had been caught up in a very public scandal – a scandal that did deep and profound damage to their patriarchal belief in staff loyalty. The woman at its centre worked at

Erddig as cook-housekeeper for five years, then was purged from the family narrative. The portrait of Ellen Penketh did *not* make it into the basement passage, and her letters were destroyed. Remembered only as 'the thief cook', she moves today like a ghost through Erddig and its otherwise copious archive collection. She leaves few footprints.

I found myself returning again and again to the portrait of Ellen Penketh, to try to work out who she really was. This is an attempt to piece together her story.

It is a tale of two women, both middle-aged, almost friends across the mistress–servant divide. One is plain, the other rather handsome. They are tacit companions on a joint and surprising new adventure: running a large country house in the unknown territory of the Welsh borders. Yet the adventure ends badly and bitterly in the courts, with an unexpected outcome. The case of Ellen Penketh reminds us starkly how the upper classes relied on the most impoverished and powerless people for the administration of their wealth. Mrs Penketh shouldered enormous financial responsibility in return for a very low wage, and when the family's impecunity was brought out into the open, she became the scapegoat. This is, essentially, a story about money.

We can follow both women's narratives through the prism of Louisa Yorke's Collins Pocket Diaries – forty-nine little leatherette volumes preserved to this day in the Erddig archive – and these diaries alone. The other woman, the housekeeper, remains resolutely silent. But there is enough information to extract a coherent and emotional account: one that closes with dramatic newspaper headlines and humiliation.

To understand the cook-housekeeper's part in the tale, we must first understand her mistress. Mrs Yorke was not the average Edwardian mistress – nor was Erddig the average country house. Ellen Penketh was appointed to the job in fairly extraordinary circumstances. She was interviewed by Louisa Yorke, new mistress of Erddig, from Mrs Yorke's sickbed in Clarence Lodge, a private nursing home on the outskirts of Manchester. It was November 1902 – a year of optimism for Britain.

The newly crowned King Edward VII was on the throne; the new Conservative premier, Arthur Balfour, was in office; and the bitter and interminable Boer War had finally ended. In the West End J. M. Barrie's *The Admirable Crichton* had just opened, titillating audiences with its story of a butler who assumes control of his useless upper-class employers while marooned on a desert island. The explorers Scott and Shackleton were inching through the Antarctic, through unimaginable scenery, towards the South Pole.

Four weeks before her meeting with Ellen Penketh, Louisa had gone under the surgeon's knife to have an ovarian cyst removed. It was a fraught operation, not least for a 39-year-old woman still hoping to have children, but it was successful, and in order to heal she had to stay motionless in bed with her knees strapped together. Louisa felt 'more dead than alive' as she lay recuperating. According to her daily diary entries she was lonely, cold and bored, and her mind was obsessed with the servant problems at Erddig.

Louisa was a doer. She could not bear to be laid up while chaos reportedly reigned fifty miles to the south. She drew up fidgety lists of what needed doing, while waiting for her husband of six months, 'My Philip', to visit by carriage. 'I have a great deal of business to talk over', she wrote impatiently to herself. Letters arrived from home that maddened her: 'Oh! The trouble of the servants at Erddig. It is sad to contemplate. The new Housekeeper Mrs Osmond is to leave at once. She will do no work except arrange flowers!' A friend came and told her (perhaps with some relish) 'all about the cook worries at the house. Oh! How I wish I could get settled.'

Louisa wanted very much to be 'settled', but the enormity of the task before her was daunting. In marrying Philip Yorke, a 53-year-old confirmed bachelor, she had also shackled herself to his inheritance, a once-great house currently run on a handful of disgruntled servants. 'I have, I think, undertaken more than I can accomplish', she wrote in her diary, one month into her tenure at Erddig. 'The management of this huge house with 6 female and 3 male servants is no joke.'

II

Unfashionable Creatures

Erddig is a dusky-orange slab of late seventeenth-century brickwork, aggrandised and lengthened in the eighteenth century by wealthy lawyer John Meller. It sits on an escarpment five miles into the Welsh border, every bit the imposing mansion house with its nineteen bays, three storeys, chapel and sweeping stone staircase. The house has two faces, and seemingly two personalities. Its west facade (austere, slightly forbidding, wind-harried) defensively fronts the bronze-tipped hills of North Wales. The sheltered, more kindly eastern face looks back towards England and all things soft and pastoral (pleached fruit trees, rose gardens, strutting peacocks, ornamental water features).

In Meller's time, fifteen maids in the attic rooms serviced 'Erthig' (as it is known locally), a house laden with increasingly lavish treasures. But there was no son to inherit this wealth. Meller died a bachelor, and Erddig passed to his nephew, Simon Yorke, in 1733. The Yorkes were the opposite of the mercenary, meticulous Meller. Ordinary, unambitious, content with their status as moderately prosperous Welsh squires, they thriftily eked out the coal riches of the estate for the next one hundred and fifty years. Male Yorkes were named either Simon or Philip, and their outlook on life was similarly stolid. Successive Yorke wives railed over their husbands' lack of elan, their dismal fashion sense or needless parsimony. As Elizabeth Yorke wrote to Philip Yorke I in 1770: 'You give a sad account of Bath but you are such an *unfashionable creature*.'

Fashion rarely came to Erddig, distant as it was from the metropolis. When Queen Victoria made a tour of Wales in 1889, the wife of Simon Yorke III – the Queen's god-daughter, no less – reasonably hoped to persuade the royal carriage procession at least to drive through Erddig

Park on its way from Ruabon station to Wrexham. Unaccountably snubbed, Mrs Yorke gave up her lingering interest in court affairs and referred ever after to the Queen as 'Old Mother Bunch.' Towards the end of the nineteenth century, she and her elderly husband scarcely left the house and its private grounds of 245 acres.

A strong sense of history, coupled with an obsession for cataloguing and hoarding, had by this time turned the house into something of a cluttered museum. To save Erddig and its contents for future generations, their son, Philip Yorke II, was required to make a financially advantageous marriage.

Philip's father fixed upon local heiress Annette Fountayne Puleston, but it was a short-lived and unhappy match. After enduring a watercolour holiday for a honeymoon, Annette and her maid escaped by hitching a ride on a milk wagon from a house party in Denbigh – 'without ever wishing me Adieu or any one else in the house', an anguished Philip wrote to a friend in 1877.[1]

It was, of course, a great scandal – not least for the rumour of an improper relationship between mistress and maid. The 28-year-old Philip left at once for the Continent and for the next sixteen years refused to come home, much to his parents' sorrow. He filled his time with travelling, painting, writing and photographing; a married man shackled to a missing wife. When his Victorian parents died in the last years of the nineteenth century, Philip inherited the house. He was the fifth generation of Yorkes to do so, but what a sorry heir he made – a fiftysomething bachelor in all but name.

Erddig sat shrouded and silent, its assets (coal and farming) dwindling steadily. Not quite empty, though – it housed various ageing and quarrelsome servants. An agent, Mr Hughes, looked after the estate in the absence of any master. Working for Mr Yorke was not, at that time, a job that brought much satisfaction. Weeds sprouted on the terracing; rainwater left brown stains on the ceilings. His parents' old cook-housekeeper Mrs Rogers left. Her replacement, Mrs Harrison, was often to be found in the kitchen 'the worse for Beer'. She lost her job when her sideline in selling pheasants was exposed, at which point a furious Philip Yorke gave the butler, Mr Jones, his marching orders too.

A plaintive letter from Jones reveals the acrimony of Erddig's basement life at this time. 'I could do very well with a good sensible woman', he writes in firm, indignant script to agent Hughes in 1897; 'I am sure the house should be one of the happiest in the land, but it is one of the most miserable all through one person' – cook-housekeeper Mrs Harrison.[2] Then the remaining laundry maid and housemaid gave notice. Who knew if Erddig would ever be inhabited again? For how could poor Mr Philip produce an heir?

His release came in the last year of the century with the news that Annette the bolter had died. Finally Philip was free to marry again – but the task was as much to find someone to take on Erddig as to take on himself, an ever more eccentric squire looking every bit his age.

An invitation to a house party at Erddig was tremendously exciting for Louisa Matilda Scott. The summons came from Mr Yorke in 1899, through mutual friends, when she was 36 years old and resigned to a life of good deeds and parsimony at her father's vicarage in Chilton Foliat, Wiltshire. Louisa's was a small, grey existence for an intelligent and sprightly woman. Entries in her Collins Pocket Diaries run along the lines of: 'I am very much excited now about our Easter jumble sale'; and 'Set to work and dusted hard til dinner'.

Red-haired Louisa was not a beauty, but she was one of life's enthusiasts: she played the piano, rang the bells at church, skated, cycled and sewed with determination. Yet her various talents were seemingly not enough to attract a husband, and she judged herself harshly – such as the day she forgot her lines at the Grand Cattle Show play, aged 33: 'I wish this day to be blotted out of my memory entirely . . I never felt more humiliated and disgusted with myself in all my life.' Louisa – Lulu to her family – was keenly aware of being ostracised by a younger, more eligible crowd: 'I hear there is to be a ball at Elcott on the 18th,' she wrote, aged 35. 'I wonder why I am not asked! No doubt for the same reason that I was not asked to Mrs Portal's Dance. I wish I knew the reason, but I must try not to care!'

She was born the second of five daughters to the Reverend T. J. Scott, a bearded Victorian who earned, in his prime, £500 a year (around £27,000 in today's money) and employed just one servant. (To put this in perspective, a carpenter at this time earned around £100, a doctor £350 and an upper-middle-class professional between £750 and £1,500.) Louisa's annual allowance of £20 (around £1,000 today) was supplemented with gifts and odd jobs, such as five shillings earned for mending a carpet. One diary entry notes that 'Mother gets up at 5 a.m. to open windows, etc.,' while she herself, with all her duties, would 'become a skilled parlour-maid in time. Plenty of practise.'

On 13 July 1899 Louisa packed her one pretty frock (a fashionable white) and travelled to Oxford to meet her chaperone, Aunt Julia. From here the ladies journeyed by train to Wrexham, in the old Welsh county of Denbighshire, where they were met by the Yorkes' quaint phaeton and driven the mile and a half to Erddig. There is a point on this journey, once the carriage swings in past the gate cottage and along the estate's winding track, that the big house is suddenly revealed to the visitor, sitting commandingly among mature beech trees in the far distance. Lulu and Aunt Julia might well have clutched each other's hands for courage.

The house party consisted of 'seven ladies, a young man and Mr Yorke'. Philip Yorke was wasting no time in trying to find a new wife, though so far his various proposals of marriage (written in rhyming couplets and neatly tied with a ribbon) had been politely rejected. Louisa saw past her host's eccentricities. He might be unconventional, teetotal and vegetarian, but Mr Yorke was also 'a paragon of goodness', she wrote in her diary. Finally, during this three-week summer house party, she coyly donned her white dress. 'How interesting!'

*

Theirs was a slow-burn courtship spun out over three more years, in which Philip's pointed beard became ever more silver and Louisa's eyes more deeply set. In January 1901, Queen Victoria died: her socially voracious son Bertie ('Tum Tum' or 'Edward the Caresser') became Edward VII. The first electric Christmas-tree lights went on sale; the first wireless signal was transmitted across the Atlantic (a thrilling, crackling exchange between Cornwall and Newfoundland). There was also the invention of the 'vacuum cleaner': too large for a normal house, but used most successfully the following year to suck up dirt at Westminster Abbey for King Edward's extravagant coronation.

In the bleak chill of a Welsh winter Louisa visited Erddig again with her parents. It was January 1902; there was a magic-lantern show with slides of Philip's travels; there was snow, and skating on the canal. When Louisa showed herself perfectly content to spend long hours 'sorting & tidying & writing poetry,' Philip must have inwardly rejoiced. Here she was at last: a wife-cum-curator. And so, at the close of Louisa's life, came the proposal that was to change Louisa's life. At 12.15 a.m., under an ancestral portrait by Gainsborough, Philip asked her to become his wife. 'It seems such a dream', wrote the 39-year-old Louisa in her diary. 'I can hardly believe it is true.' (Though she must, surely, have had an inkling.) The next day she was thrown into a panic. 'The sense of my coming duties & responsibilities almost frighten me, but I have Philip to help me in my difficulties.'

Duties? Responsibilities? Difficulties? Louisa's horror at what lay ahead might seem an odd reaction for a woman spectacularly rescued from spinsterhood. But as everybody knew, big houses were all about management – management of money, and management of servants. Louisa had experience of neither. They were married two months later, and set off on a cycling tour of Britain 'like two school children out for a holiday', returning to Erddig on 30 May 1902: 'Church bells cannoning, crowds of people cheering, two triumphal arches (made by workmen on the estate)', wrote the new Mrs Yorke in her diary. She felt 'like a Queen'.

III

Much Troubled About The Servants

Louisa set about the job of chatelaine as if she had spent her life waiting for the challenge. She pulled Erddig's old china out from the pantry, rearranged the furniture, rehung pictures and sorted 'My Philip's clothes' until she felt she could 'breathe better'. Then she turned her attentions to the servants.

This was not a straightforward matter. Since the first Simon Yorke, there had grown up a tradition of paternal benevolence towards servants. Generations of the same local families worked for successive Squire Yorkes; marriages were encouraged, even connived at by their employers. Contemporaries thought that the Yorkes were 'soft on the servants', and the fact that more portraits had been painted of them than of family members was seen as both eccentric and slightly distasteful. Like all Yorke wives before her, Louisa had to take on board the Erddig way of doing things. But as far as she could see, it wasn't working.

'I am much troubled about servants', she wrote just weeks into married life. 'I do not know of a housekeeper yet. Mrs Holm cannot come. I shall also want a laundry-maid, & kitchen-maid & house-maid. No "beer & skittles" for me, as Philip has often told me. I own I over-work, but what am I to do!' While it 'poured in torrents' outside – 'Wales is certainly a very rainy place' – she sat ensconced in the empty housekeeper's room, trying to make sense of how a big house should be run. 'I spent the greater part of the morning in the basement & giving orders all round.' When not downstairs, she was turning out the attics, battling dust and damp in a summer that proved to be 'as cold as November'.

The work sapped her. Six weeks after moving into Erddig Louisa took to her bed, doubled up with abdominal pains. She lay high in a threadbare chintz four-poster in the white-panelled bedroom she had picked as her own – much the cosiest, with views directly over the formal parterre gardens to the canal beyond – while her 'excellent' new head housemaid Martha Harvey stoked the coal fire. (Harvey doubled as Louisa's lady's maid, pinning up her hair and seeing to her clothes, just as Philip made do with help from butler and coachman instead of a valet: an economy which would not have done at all in grander households.)

One by one, servants old and new processed before Mrs Yorke to be interviewed. 'What a farce', she wrote, 'to be in bed.' Her new home had nine family bedrooms, two state bedrooms, a grand saloon, a music room, a tapestry room, drawing room, dining room, Chinese room, library, gallery and chapel. In Philip's parents' day it employed twelve indoor and thirty outdoor servants. If the house was to come to life once again, to receive guests and accommodate future children, it was going to need more than the current pared-back team. But as fast as Louisa hired them, so her problems seemed to escalate.

'I am having great trouble with the numerous servants', she wrote again on 17 July. 'Some are too noisy, some too grand, some find the work too much. I wonder if I shall ever be quite settled.' Men and women were appointed and sacked left and right. 'We are going to have many changes here. The groom is going, the housekeeper, the kitchen & scullery maids also the gardener & woodman. When shall we be settled!'

For the most part, Philip stood by and watched – though he was coerced into accompanying his wife into the laundry to give 'poor Annie, the laundry maid, notice. She is to leave on Saturday.' But he was unfortunately absent for Louisa's 'awful' two-and-a-half-hour interview with the agent Mr Hughes, who flatly refused to show her the estate and household expenditure books. How else would she learn how money was managed? 'I must have the accounts done differently', she wrote with vexation.

Gardener and bailiff Mr Ford was given notice after two years' service, turfed out of his rent-free berth at Erddig Lodge. 'He is sad at having to go', Louisa noted, 'but he is not man enough for the place.' Was anyone man enough for Louisa Yorke? Her married status seems to have empowered her, rendering her faintly terrifying – no longer the crushed spinster, mortified for forgetting her lines at the Cattle Show play. 'It is a great move to give up old customs of twenty years' standing,' she wrote in self-justification, 'but I feel that some reforms must be made at once.'

In many respects, Louisa was just the woman for the job. But she was also inexperienced, insecure and highly anxious about money. She knew that the key to getting the household running smoothly, and above all economically, was a good housekeeper. The retired Harriet Rogers, cook-housekeeper to Philip's parents until 1896 and Philip's nanny before this, hovered offstage as a daunting example of what Louisa had yet to find. Philip sent regular gifts of money to this Victorian paragon of self-sacrifice, who lived nearby and paid regular visits.

But where, in 1902, did you find a Victorian housekeeper? With the coronation of the new King, the dawn of a new century and the formation of the Labour Party in 1900, the British working classes were beginning to kick against the unquestioning hierarchical subjugation of the Victorian years. It was an era of growing tensions – between the extravagant, frivolous lives of the rich and smart, and the narrow, hard existence of the working classes. Domestic service was still the largest single female occupation, but there was a distinct shortage of younger women for the bottom rungs of the ladder. Between 1901 and 1911, the number of maids aged 14-plus willing to go into service dropped by over 62 per cent.[3] The Harriet Rogers type of housekeeper – self-sacrificing, dutiful, identifying closely with the family – was a dying breed. Her replacements were a mixed bunch.

On 12 August, Miss Mackreth arrived at Erddig, a middle-aged lady of refined manner who requested the title 'Lady Housekeeper' in deference to her alleged past connections. 'Lady Helps' were a short-lived vogue of the era, a solution to the new shortage of suitable candidates: gentlewomen who had fallen on hard times and who could be turned into upper servants. But in practice, it rarely worked out. Like the governess, she was neither in one world nor the other, and in a house with several servants she was inevitably a source of friction.[4] Still, Louisa was hopeful. ''Tis such a comfort', she wrote, 'to have Miss Mackreth here, a lady, who will help us to economise . . . I fear [she] will find it very hard work to cut down expenses but she will have a good try to do so.'

The two, briefly in league, travelled into Wrexham by pony and trap 'to interview Miss Whiting about servants'. Miss Mackreth told the employment agency exactly what she was after – but then found *herself* without a job after just two months. 'I am going to have a cook-housekeeper again', wrote Louisa – someone who would both put in the hours and, in this combined role, save the Yorkes money. On 7 October – the day Louisa was examined by her doctor and diagnosed as having an ovarian cyst – she and Philip went 'by train to look for a housekeeper. Capital woman, but she will not come so far as Erddig.' One week later she got up from her sickbed again 'to interview Mrs Jonathan . . . She is a nice & very sensible woman.'

The robustly down-to-earth Welshwoman Mrs Jonathan started work as cook-housekeeper on 18 October, the day that Mrs Williams, 'the poor old cook', was shown the door. Louisa had 'a long talk' with Mrs Jonathan, knowing that in a week she would have to leave home for some time. She was to be operated on, in Manchester. She would have to let go of the reins, which was not a comfortable thought for the formidable Mrs Yorke.

IV

A Very Capable Little Body

1

Mrs McTaggart, the matron, tut-tuts when she hears of the troubles of poor Mrs Yorke, not six months married. Nurse Crighton shakes her head in sympathy as she straps Louisa into the hated tight belt she must wear 'for a year and a day' to help her heal. There is also Dr Sinclair, who visits and examines and would rather talk of the servant problem than his patient's reproductive system. He promises to mention her plight to some of his respectable clients in large houses around Manchester. The whole of Clarence Lodge, upstairs and downstairs, is keenly aware that Mrs Yorke of Erddig Hall is in want of a cook and a housekeeper, or possibly a cook-housekeeper.

Word spreads. It travels around the sedate, walled suburb of Victoria Park, with its gabled family houses and maids in neat print dresses scrubbing down front doorsteps (home to the suffragette Emmeline Pankhurst and her young daughters; also to the late Pre-Raphaelite artist Ford Madox Brown). It passes through the knotty heart of Manchester to the smoke stacks of Pendleton in the north-west, where cotton mills and factories for dyeing, printing and bleaching judder and clang.

Word of Mrs Yorke's predicament passes around the cramped slums and filthy ginnels, entering the servants' hall of a wealthy industrialist's modern mansion, Chaseley Field. Here the widowed Mrs Hannah Armitage lives in some splendour, ministered to by twelve female servants. Her late husband Joseph John Armitage commissioned this sumptuous Victorian house of encaustic tiled floors, vaulted ceilings, elaborate fireplaces and heavily panelled doors. It was built with new money, and everything, from the electric light bulbs to the plumbed-in closets, is top of the range.

Ellen Penketh, 32, is second in command in the kitchen. For a working-class woman born in the industrial north-west, this is a prestigious job. The Armitages are like royalty in Pendleton. Her old master's father, Sir Elkanah Armitage, went into the cotton industry aged eight and died £200,000 the richer (£14 million in today's money). But Ellen is anxious about her future, as it's known among the servants that Mr Armitage has bequeathed the house in his last will and testament that Chaseley Field is to become Pendleton High School for Girls – and where will this leave the servants?

Ellen's mother, Mrs Lucy Penketh, also lives in Pendleton. Single-handedly she runs a grocer's and off-licence at 37 Buxton Street, a store (or 'badger's shop' as it's called in these parts) sitting between a saddler and a calico printer's. I imagine Ellen visiting her mother to discuss this latest work possibility. Wrexham – that's Wales, i'n't it? How big is Erddig Hall? How many mouths to feed? Her father Thomas Penketh, a wheelwright, is not at home to give his opinion: he lives and works thirty miles to the west in Liverpool. Above the shop live Ellen's younger sister Mary, 29, blind and a remarkable dressmaker; her 23-year-old brother William, a butcher; and Percy, baby of this family of ten children, now 22 and a clerk for a colliery. There's also ten-year-old granddaughter Lucy, born in Liverpool to eldest son Haugh.

On Thursday, 20 November, Ellen Penketh asks the cook for a few hours' leave. She travels by the new electric tramcar into Manchester Central, changing lines to journey south-east to Victoria Park. The fare is two pennies. She has on her large black Sunday hat, skewered to the front of her head with two hatpins, and a dark shawl crossed tightly around her body. Underneath is her one smart white blouse with wire-stiffened collar and a full-hemmed heavy skirt falling to just above the ankle.

Mrs Yorke receives Ellen in her bed-sitting room at Clarence House. She is pale and drawn after four weeks spent convalescing and her long, red, frizzy hair is loose since she has stopped pinning it up. The unconventional nature of this interview is perhaps remarked on and lightly laughed off by Louisa, encouraging a peculiar intimacy between these two women not so far apart in age. Mrs Yorke runs through the recent troubles at Erddig. She does not see that each candidate's unsuitability speaks of her own inexperience.

Ellen listens deferentially, warming to this lady so unlike Mrs Armitage. Mrs Yorke seems almost sisterly, conspiratorial. By the end of their meeting she wants this job very badly, even if the pay at £45 a year – £2,500 in today's money – is less than she had hoped for. (Country-house housekeepers might now expect to earn around £65; cooks £50 to £60.) Louisa, in her turn, is rather pleased with the way things have turned out. She likes the fact that Ellen Penketh is an outsider, removed from Wrexham and from Wales, from basement politics and decades of tradition. She is satisfied to have found her herself. Every new mistress likes to appoint her own deputy, and here in Manchester Louisa feels she has gained some perspective on the situation and finally chosen well.

Her diary entry for that night is positive: 'After tea Mrs Penketh who wishes to come to Erddig as cook, came to interview me. She seems a very capable little body & most anxious to come. She also knows of a kitchen maid.' Two days later she writes to Mrs Armitage of Chaseley Field for a 'character' – Ellen Penketh's all-important reference. The response is positive, for the next time we hear of Ellen she has the courtesy title of Mrs Penketh, and is installed as cook-housekeeper of Erddig Hall.

With Louisa's return a month later, a golden era was to begin at Erddig. She had departed a sick woman, leaving a malfunctioning big house. She came back on 28 November 1902 healed, doubly determined and with a key new member of staff to help her succeed. There was a certain amount of jostling and repositioning, naturally, on her return, but she would have none of it: 'A great many things went wrong and I scolded right and left.' Mrs Yorke's scolding was becoming quite a feature of basement life at Erddig. But one thing was different: 'Mrs Penketh, the new cook is going in most splendidly', she wrote on 12 December. Three days later the new head gardener Mr Brown arrived, together with a new butler, Mr Wakefield – 'very large but very active'. Her team was finally in place. Mrs Yorke had now only to focus on her husband, suffering from 'the most awful rheumatism & lumbago. He can hardly stand upright.'

Louisa's own health worries seemed too insignificant to mention, but they were most peculiar. Her diary notes a near-constant feeling of indigestion and sickness. On Boxing Day Mrs Penketh pulled off a triumphant 'huge lunch party of 11', after which Louisa felt 'rather bad & went to bed early. Queer malady I am suffering from.' Meanwhile Nurse Crighton's detested belt was cutting into her waist most painfully, and her green satin dress had got so tight across the chest that she had to have a humiliating false front of four inches let into it. 'All my clothes are getting tight', she wrote, 'though there is no cause for it!'

The fashion for ladies at the time was for a flattened, low 'monobosom', a tiny waist and a jutting behind – achieved by tight lacing into the uncomfortable 'swan bill' or 'S-bend' corset. Queen Alexandra carried off this look with great elegance despite her advancing years (she was now 57), but it was an impossible fashion for anyone wishing to move freely, as Louisa certainly did. Her expanding shape flummoxed the local doctor, Dr Williams. 'I think he is inclined to give me up as a "bad job"', she wrote. 'I still feel so dreadfully fat.' He did have a possible theory, but this was surely so unlikely that Louisa could not yet bring herself to write it in her diary. Dr Sinclair, her Manchester surgeon, was called to give a second opinion. He pronounced that she 'had gout and gout only & must have abdominal massage and the Baths in Bath'.

V

Put To Work

There is an imbalance in this story, which up until now is all Louisa's – her wooing, her wedding, her moving like a hurricane through Erddig Hall. Now that her mistress is finally 'settled', we can turn to the story of Ellen Penketh.

Ellen was born in 1870, the third of ten children, in Sutton Heath – a district of St Helens, Lancashire, which during Ellen's childhood exploded in size. There were over a dozen working mineshafts with their attendant iron winding houses and pithead gear. There were brick factories and potteries with towering chimneys and foul-smelling waste. There was a thriving industry in clock- and watchmaking, and plenty of wheelwrights, such as her father, to service the carriages and omnibuses that competed alongside train and canal transport between the two great industrial hubs of Liverpool and Manchester.

It was a harsh, noisy, polluted place to be a child, where the maiming and death of working men was a fact of daily life; but it was a vigorous, thrusting environment for all that, and a close-knit community. Many Penketh lived in Sutton Heath; a good number still do. Married at 23, Mrs Lucy Penketh was either expecting or nursing a child (and sometimes both) for the next thirteen years. Three died; seven survived. The National Census tells us that the family moved around the area in search of work: from Sutton to nearby Rainford; to Melling on the Leeds and Liverpool Canal in Merseyside; to Pendleton in Salford, crowded suburb of Manchester. Like her siblings, Ellen went to school, which from 1880 was compulsory up to the age of ten, learning to write in curling italic letters and to calculate in pounds, shillings and pence. Then she did what many Lancastrian girls ended up doing. Rather than work in a factory, she chose to go into service.

The 1891 census finds Ellen, aged 21, working as a 'waitress' in the home of William Saxon, a solicitor in Altrincham on the outskirts of Manchester. A waitress was employed by middle-class families to receive visitors, open doors and wait at table. The upper classes had footmen. Working as a servant was then seen as the more respectable or 'refined' choice, with more chance for advancement and self-betterment. Domestics looked down on 'factory girls', but both worlds could be terribly harsh. In 1881, when Ellen was 11 years old, a third of the inmates at Pendleton Workhouse, Manchester were former domestic servants – including three housekeepers, all widowed. The professions of other female inmates (fustian cutter, flax tenter, cop reeler, throstle spinner) conjure vividly the thundering machinery and complex enormity of the Industrial Revolution. Ultimately both professions sucked women up and spat them out.

On entering Erddig Park and its silent green acres, Ellen Penketh might well have felt she had been cut loose from all that was familiar. What was one to do here on an afternoon off? How would she get into town? Wrexham was an unrefined market town with three dozen breweries and a large mining industry. Who would her suppliers be, and wouldn't she spend half her time getting fagged walking to and fro the great Park? Did Mrs Yorke really think she'd get Ellen on a bicycle, like her own and Mr Yorke's?

December was a bitter month to start work in the basement of a great house, but it was also a sociable, merry time of year. Marriage had turned the Yorkes into a gregarious couple, and their entertaining in this first year reached a climax over Christmas and New Year. Louisa's visitors' book records eight to dinner on Christmas Eve, eleven to lunch on Boxing Day, fourteen to lunch on 29 December, ten to tea on 14 January, twelve for 'luncheon, tea & acting' on the fifteenth, twelve to dinner on the twenty-second for 'music & glee singing' . . . and so it went on. Mrs Penketh was thrown in at the deep end.

We can hold up a mirror, as it were, to Louisa's diaries for clues of what was going on below stairs while she and Philip socialised and played the piano upstairs. But we can also reimagine it vividly, thanks to the near-untouched servants' quarters still in existence at Erddig today. Ellen Penketh entered the house on her first day in much the same way that the modern visitor does – through the outer yard, its central midden then heaped with straw and dung from the stables. Here she dismounted from the trap and was helped with her trunk – her worldly possessions – by Thomas Goulding, the 17-year-old groom. There might well have been more than one man pressing to help, for the 32-year-old Mrs Penketh was unusually attractive for a cook-housekeeper.

I can see her looking around, taking in the pleasant cluster of out-buildings in warm red brick and the series of yards made for gossip, with runs and warrens perfect for errands and flirtations. (Groom Thomas Goulding was to marry laundry maid Edith Fairman; groom Ernest Jones married head nanny Lucy Hitchman; while head housemaid Martha Harvey snared the estate foreman, widower William Gittins.) A small door over a worn flagstone step took Ellen Penketh from the inner stable yard to the female preserve of bakehouse, laundry and scullery, huddled conspiratorially around a small, sunny brick yard.

So, with some raising of eyebrows, the new cook-housekeeper was welcomed – the eighth in as many years since the sainted Mrs Rogers's departure. Ellen was led past an excessively dingy scullery and meat pantry on either side of a mean corridor (a vision of Mrs Armitage's servant quarters at Chaseley Field might have sprung to mind, all fresh paintwork and electric lighting), and she was brought to a halt outside the kitchen door. Maids must have enjoyed watching the reaction of each new cook to the kitchen. Open that door, and you enter a different dimension. No doubt Ellen Penketh gratified the girls with a Lancastrian expletive as she took in the soaring ceiling and the large Venetian window looking on to the garden outside. Three great, rusticated arches housed a brand-new coal-fired range and an enormous hotplate with a surround of glazed white tiles. Above the arches was painted the slightly forbidding Victorian adage 'WASTE NOT, WANT NOT'.

It is still an impressive room today, with its long, scrubbed, central table, the hanging hams above, the ranks of dressers and mahogany cabinets filled with the copper batterie de cuisine – jelly moulds, sauté pans, stock pans, fish kettles . . . But despite it being at ground level and not (like so many kitchens) underground, the room is strangely gloomy. The window is generous but it faces east, the view hemmed in by a cedar and a Scots pine. The walls back then were painted a depressing combination of beige and dark brown. It was a place of work rather than pleasure. A grandfather clock next to the far door ticked loudly. Ellen Penketh was led through this door and up a short flight of stairs to her accommodation.

It was certainly a step up in the world of service, once you'd added a 'housekeeper' to the title of 'cook'. There were all manner of extra privileges which Ellen – never having worked in a house big enough to warrant a housekeeper – had only half guessed at. The cook's bedroom at Erddig was a poky, oddly shaped room opposite the kitchen, its window half obscured by a lean-to shed. The housekeeper's quarters above, on the other hand, comprised a delightfully airy bedroom and adjoining sitting room with views both to the east and west, each with a marble fireplace. You might well get ideas above your station in a set of rooms like this. The views to the front of the house were tremendous: the sweep of green escarpment, the far Denbighshire hills (with the iron winding gear of Bersham Colliery's pithead to the fore), the setting sun and a crow's-nest view of visitors arriving and departing. To the back, the servant runways could be spied upon, the tradesman's bell observed and maids let in after dark by lowering a key in a basket attached to a string.[5]

The housekeeper's suite occupied the short brick link built between house and kitchen in the nineteenth century. Its position was symbolic: she *was* the link, the conduit between servants and mistress.

VI

Quite Equal To It

In most big Edwardian country houses, upper servants were still fastidious about maintaining their dignity and superiority. They ate apart, they socialised apart and they issued orders, ringing their bells to be waited on. But life in the smaller country houses, especially those some way from London, did not slavishly follow these examples. The Yorkes were not titled aristocracy, and the atmosphere at Erddig was different. Ellen Penketh might have expected intimidating new rituals, isolating deference from lower servants, icy silences over dinner (not talking at meals being one of the edicts of servant conduct manuals). She might well have dreaded her first month, inexperienced as she was. But the Yorkes' benevolent treatment of staff over generations had fostered a more intimate, informal atmosphere. It was Christmas, and talk was all of the servants' ball.

On New Year's Eve Ellen and her girls stuffed, trussed and roasted a goose for the Yorkes' house party while plotting and preparing for their own evening in high spirits. Every hotplate on the hob held a simmering pan, filling the room with steam (two hours to cook carrots, recommended Mrs Beeton; just twelve minutes for Brussels sprouts).[6] Later the big table was pushed against the wall, the gramophone was installed with Mr Yorke's permission and best dresses altered with sashes and corsages for dancing – the military two-step, the waltz, the 'circle and chain mixer' with men and women grasping alternate hands, skipping down a long chain to a couple of fiddles. The Christmas Ball was a long-standing tradition for the servants at Erddig, with forty heads recorded in 1904, rising to sixty in 1905.

This was all new to Louisa Yorke, too – finally asked to the ball aged

39, now chatelaine of the big house. Her diary entry for New Year's Eve reads: 'We had goose for lunch & the servants had a regular jollification downstairs. Most of the day was spent in preparations & at 9pm they gave a Ball in the kitchen. We went to look in at 9.30 & much enjoyed it. They danced til 3am.'

Did Ellen expect such 'regular jollifications' as she found at Erddig? She would have written long letters home describing her change in circumstances. Glimpsed obliquely through Louisa's diary, we can see her settling in to her new life. On Saturday, 21 February 1903 there was an outing for the upper servants: 'Brown, the gardener, Wakefield, the butler, Mrs Penketh, housekeeper, & Harvey, head housemaid went to the dance at Rhos last night and much enjoyed it.' In May, much of the household, led by the Yorkes, travelled five miles in convoy to Ruabon to see 'Buffalo Bill and his Wild West Show'. 'Many of the servants went & enjoyed it immensely.' This was the last such outing for Brown the gardener, sacked a fortnight later for a night 'out on the spice with Wakefield'. 'Philip will not stand drunken-ness', wrote Louisa. 'This is the second time.' There were lines that could not be crossed. But the Yorkes would look after you. On 8 January, 'Mrs Penketh fell down & hurt her cheek & nurse took her to the Surgery.' They also looked after their servants' souls. Daily prayers were led by Philip in the chapel at 9 a.m., with hymns from the two dozen Erddig favourites ('Loving Shepherd of Thy Sheep'; 'Fight the Good Fight with All Thy Might'). On Sundays, servants were encouraged to go by dog cart, if not raining, to their preferred local church or chapel, and so achieved something of a life apart from the big house.

In March that year Philip and Louisa departed for a three-month tour of friends and relations, leaving the servants to get on with the annual spring clean. Had Ellen Penketh ever been left unsupervised for so long? Together with Hughes the agent, she and Wakefield were effectively mistress and master in absentia while complex and chaotic renovations were carried out at Erddig. The entrance hall was to be papered 'with very thick paper (embossed) at 1/- a yard', Louisa noted a month before her departure; 'The Library ceiling is also to be done, also the State bedroom & landing ceiling & the Chapel lobby & landing above are to be papered & the ceilings done also.' This, together with painting work, was to cost 'not more than £50' (£3,000 today).

Just two months into her new job, an immense amount of trust had been placed on the shoulders of Mrs Penketh. It is important to register this, because when Louisa turned against her cook-housekeeper, she did it so viciously that it is tempting to presume the seeds of disenchantment were already there. But I have mined Louisa's collection of Collins Pocket Diaries for clues that might tell against Mrs Penketh. There are none to be found.

Wakefield the butler, on the other hand, did not distinguish himself. While the Yorkes were away they received 'the most terrible news from home.' The exquisite crystal chandelier in the saloon had fallen down and smashed into tiny pieces. 'Wakefield was cleaning it & evidently twisted it round to the left & the whole thing fell down. Such a lot has been broken: it is too sad to think of.' Louisa privately thought the 'top heavy' butler had been drinking. When she returned to Erddig and discovered he was not managing his 'boys' properly, Wakefield's career was in jeopardy. His dispatch is not mentioned in her diary, but records show that William Monk Wootton joined as butler this same year, moving with his family into Erddig Lodge on £55 a year (£10 more than Mrs Penketh's wages), his 18-year-old son Sydney taken on as hall boy. Wootton was to stay with the family for a decade.

Louisa's mood was quite the reverse with Ellen Penketh. The new cook-housekeeper seems to have been her mistress's most intimate confidante, being the first at Erddig to hear of Mrs Yorke's extraordinary news. Louisa was not fat – she was pregnant. She could now let out her dresses with impunity. On 16 April she wrote in her diary; 'I have written to tell Mrs Penketh of my good news to come.' On 22 May the Yorkes finally returned, catching the train to Wrexham. 'It was so delightful to be met by the new India-rubber tyred carriage', wrote Louisa, now eight months pregnant, but still anxious to walk the grounds of Erddig the moment she got home. Later she 'went with Mrs Penketh to see all her little chickens and ducks'.

The scene as described by Louisa seems idyllic and joyful. It is also illuminating: Ellen had taken on the working-class women's tradition of keeping poultry in the back yard for pin money now that she had some space (and, apparently, freedom) to do so. She was showing herself to be practical, resourceful . . . even maternal. She was also ensuring a supply of fresh eggs for Erddig. On all accounts, Louisa – accustomed as she was to doing odd jobs for odd shillings – must have applauded her cook-housekeeper.

Ellen Penketh is not mentioned again by name in her mistress's diary for four years.

With the birth of the red-headed little Simon Yorke IV, Louisa's focus shifted upstairs. 'I love the nursery better than any other room in the house', she wrote in July 1903. Having waited forty years for this moment, she couldn't stop 'baby worshipping', despite the new nanny hovering in the wings, soon to be joined by a nursery maid to help keep the baby's meringue-like frilly bonnets goffered and beribboned, as was the fashion.

Nanny Lucy Hitchman, 26, was a butler's daughter who had heard about the vacancy at Erddig on the servants' grapevine, having previously worked with head housemaid Martha Harvey at Henley Hall in Ludlow, Shropshire. The following year Sarah Rudge, 33, also arrived from Henley Hall, taking up the post of head laundry maid: three old friends, each now at the top of her field.

One can easily imagine a clique forming, with the inevitable in-house politics. But if it was a clique, it may have been a happy one. From their almost constant appearance in Louisa's diaries, servants are abruptly dropped as a topic because, presumably, all was well below stairs. There is just the odd predatory male servant who gives trouble. ('Footman left for impudence' . . . 'The groom is a worry but I will make him leave the house at 10 p.m.')[7]

While Louisa stalks the nanny and the 'blue carriage' out in the gardens, it is time to return to the basement, to try to piece together the texture of Ellen Penketh's life. A cook-housekeeper was essentially a cook, but with extra responsibilities and double the dose of in-house politics. Dovetailing the two jobs together was a way of smaller houses saving money, but in a large house such as Erddig, trying to exist thriftily on decreasing sources of income, it was a difficult role to pull off – especially with a master and mistress bent on both economising *and* entertaining.

The ritual went thus: all week, Louisa and Philip would cycle or trot around Wrexham in the carriage paying visits and leaving visiting cards. On Saturday they sat at home in the grand saloon, coal fires blazing, waiting for visitors (and sometimes none came, as the Welsh rain poured down). They would also receive guests, without warning, on any day of the week. In the back of the Erddig visitors' books is a running tally of calls received and calls made, trapping the socially incontinent Yorkes into a cycle from which there was no escape. They received, on average, seven or eight visitors a day.

'Tea' for an Edwardian country house was a set ritual: small cakes, biscuits, one large cake on a stand (fruit, caraway seed or Madeira), hot teacakes and thin sandwiches, laid out in the drawing room by the fire. Butler or footmen hovered throughout. Downstairs in the kitchen, baking for their lives, were cook-housekeeper Mrs Penketh, kitchen maid Lizzie Copestake and scullery maid Annie Parry. While kitchens elsewhere were now widely using gas ranges (some even the new electric ovens), Erddig had a coal-fired range – stoked, naturally, with coal from its own estate.

A kitchen range was a temperamental monster to control. With every new posting cooks had to learn how to master their monster, playing the damper controls to get the right results. If the wrong dampers were left out, the firebox might melt and the boiler crack. Each cook had her own methods of testing the heat with flour or paper. Mrs Black's *Household Cookery and Laundry Work* of 1882 gives the following guidelines:

1. If a sheet of paper burns when thrown in, the oven is too hot.
2. When the paper becomes dark brown, it is suitable for pastry.
3. When light brown, it does pies.
4. When dark yellow, for cakes.
5. When light yellow, for puddings, biscuits and small pastries.

Ellen Penketh had most probably used a gas-fired range at the suave Chaseley Field in Manchester. It was also unlikely that she had worked with a wood-fired bakehouse, such as Erddig boasted, dedicated to daily bread making. Unlikely, too, that she had catered for such numbers as regularly descended on the big house.

Take, for example, the summer of 1905. 'There are to be 4 big parties on one week', Louisa noted in her diary on 11 June. 'I hope I shall survive' – but she is confident that 'Our Cook & Butler are quite equal to it'.

20 June: 60 to tea, for the Meeting of the Society for Prevention of Cruelty to Animals.

21 June: 66 to tea, Chester National Science Society.

23 June: party for the 'out-door work people' and their wives. A 'meat tea' and a band.

24 June: 71 estate children to tea, 50 adults; races and games.

6 July: Roman Catholic 'Treat', 430 guests.

15 July: Garden party and band for 50 people.

That is around 750 people over six days. The baking done, Mrs Penketh, her girls and the young footmen would carry cakes, biscuits and sandwiches outside and arrange the tea on long tables in the garden, squinting up at the grey clouds and calculating how long they might have before it all had to be carried inside again. For baby Simon's first birthday on 24 June 1904 – 'One of the most important days of the year', wrote Louisa – 'We had 250 people to his party. A thunderstorm came on & spoilt a lot of the cakes. I had to have the tea indoors . . . It all went off splendidly.'

VII

The High-Water Mark

Mrs Yorke – newly pregnant with her second child – was a transformed woman. Becoming a mother seems to have emboldened her, and she ran the house almost single-handedly, bolstered by her second in command, Ellen Penketh. As far as Louisa Yorke was concerned, the cook-housekeeper was keeping her end up admirably.

This being the case, there is one thing I find puzzling. Mrs Yorke held an account with Duttons the grocers at 1 High Street, Wrexham. Her account book lists every purchase made, and it makes interesting reading – for there among the macaroni and split peas, the honey and arrowroot, the Worcester Sauce and Bovril, are items that any self-respecting cook-housekeeper would surely be making herself: Genoa cake. Cherry cake. Seed cake. Macaroons. There are also regular purchases of Cooper's marmalade, bramble jelly, strawberry and raspberry jam.

Might this be read as a clue that Ellen Penketh was perhaps overworked, or understaffed, or simply a bad planner? Clearly, she could not cook. Perhaps, shopkeeper's daughter that she was, she found herself unable to resist the bright packaging of the brand names and convenience foods of the era. Maybe it was Louisa's doing, indulging an appetite for luxurious little treats she never knew she had until she came to be mistress of Erddig. Turkish Delights, for example, are ordered once a week. Either way, the family's annual spend was escalating. In 1903, Ellen's first year, Louisa totted it up in her accounts book as £694 (around £40,000 in today's money). In 1904 it doubled, to £1,284. In 1905 it was £1,356, and in 1906, £1,544 (£88,500 today). The reason is obvious. The Yorkes loved entertaining, and as Louisa grew in confidence, so did their numbers of guests. She kept a list of all house-party guests in Erddig's visitors' book:

1902 – 32
1903 – 68
1904 – 90
1905 – 86
1906 – 120
1907 – 113

These visitors might stay for one or two nights, but many stayed for two weeks or more, all requiring elaborate meals, clean linen, coal fires and extra laundry. It was like running a hotel. Servicing all this were fourteen hard-pressed indoor servants, costing in all around £22 a month. Compared to most big houses at the time, Erddig's entertaining was relatively modest (and certainly more strait-laced; Louisa would never have facilitated bed-hopping in the manner of those upper-class hostesses). Elsewhere in Britain the Edwardian house party was reaching its apogee – the 'Saturday-to-Monday', where one arrived with several trunks of clothing and a lady's maid; where gargantuan meals were consumed at least four times a day; where champagne was served 'at moments when a glass of barley-water might have been acceptable'.[8] The Yorkes' gesture to the era was to throw a really big dinner party, in the pillared dining room hung with ancestors, about four times a year. The table laden with heavily decorated Victorian dishes was now a thing of the past. These days it was all about originality, sleight of hand, little amuse-bouches; the wow factor, if you like.

Louisa was initially an insecure hostess, recording slights and successes in her diary. But she soon got into her stride, clocking up 'great' successes and 'fair' successes, invariably involving music and games after dinner – and one lampshade going up in flames, extinguished by Wootton and the footman.

It was considered 'modern' to be in revolt against extravagance and outdated Victorian customs, a fashion that suited the straightforward

Louisa and her teetotal husband. To have just eight dishes served at dinner – soup, fish, entrée, joint, game, sweet, hors d'oeuvre and perhaps an ice – was considered modern.[9] Great importance was attached to the entrée, known as the 'cook's high-water mark', because it gave scope to the cook's talent in preparing and decorating 'made dishes' served in decorated shapes and moulds. At Erddig, Mrs Penketh's high-water mark included her Vol-au-Vent of Chicken; her 'Chicken Shape' and Oyster Patties (turned out and plated up on the long kitchen table by paraffin lamplight) Dozens of these copper entrée moulds still sit today in the mahogany kitchen cabinets, waiting their turn: little prawns, lobsters, tomatoes; fish shaped as a child might draw them.

Louisa reached her own high-water mark in 1906 when she began recording her table plans, decorations and menus in the back of the visitors' book. She was developing a confident artistic eye, revelling in the modern 'rage' for table decorations. On 30 October, when twelve came to dinner, the long, polished table was decorated with Erddig's prize-winning chrysanthemums, Gloire de la Reine roses and long boughs of red Virginia creeper, an autumn feature of the house's west face. Daringly there was no starched white tablecloth. The guests ate turtle soup, turbot in lobster sauce and 'artistic vegetarian entrée' (Mrs Penketh's chance to show off), followed by saddle of mutton, pheasant, Charlotte russe, fruit salad, cheese capons, roast chestnuts, pears, grapes and apples. (Charlotte russe – a dessert of Bavarian cream set in a mould of sponge fingers – seems to have been one of Mrs Penketh's specialities.)

Conversation, as the guests sipped their 'sun-dried' turtle soup, might have touched on the many welfare reforms under way following the Liberal Party's landslide victory that year: free school meals for children, pensions for the elderly, labour exchanges for the unemployed . . . Brave ideas, certainly, but who was going to foot the bill?

One month later twelve more came to dinner, entering the dining room to admire the great Gainsborough portrait of Philip Yorke I, the new oil portrait of Mrs Yorke in her amethyst choker, the magical effect of the pier-glass mirrors throwing back the flickering candlelight, and the table piece – single white chrysanthemums and plumbago cardinals ('the most lovely', noted Louisa). They ate Palestine soup (made with Jerusalem artichoke), whitebait, sweetbread, boned turkey, partridge, jelly, chocolate mould and cheese capons, rounded off with home-grown apples and pears, Erddig's prize-winners at the recent Chester show.

These menus are today on display in the dining room at Erddig. I quote them in full because it seems important to remember who *created* rather than wrote them; who stirred the lobster sauce, whipped the egg whites, decorated the vegetarian savouries so as to make the guests gasp with pleasure. Important, not least because the cook-housekeeper of these years has since been denied a part in the Erddig narrative. Ellen Penketh, kitchen maid Lizzie Copestake and scullery maid Annie Parry must have felt a keen share of the hostess's triumph as the heaped and elaborately garnished serving dishes were borne upstairs by the young footmen.

On a day such as this the kitchen team would also have cooked a large breakfast, provided lunch for guests (cold cuts, savouries crafted from last night's leftovers, rissoles, salads) along with the usual vegetarian dish for Mr Yorke (savoury rice, macaroni cheese, stuffed eggs), lunch for the servants' hall (thirteen mouths including their own, plus up to twenty outdoor servants and any visiting lady's maids and valets), lunch for the nursery upstairs, all puréed and crust-free according to Lucy Hitchman's specifications for Master Simon and little Phil. And by the time poor Annie Parry had finished washing it all up in the dank scullery, standing on duckboards at a low sink, rubbing at the copper pans with turpentine and fine brick dust, it was time to start baking again for that afternoon's tea.

It was hard, hard work. On top of this, at the end of the day the accounts had to be done by the cook-housekeeper. Ellen Penketh would wipe her hands on her apron and make her way heavily down the long green basement corridor to the housekeeper's sitting room.

VIII

Overspent

A large mirror foxed with age hangs between the windows in the little wood-panelled lair of Erddig's housekeeper. It rests on the mahogany work table, and anyone entering is immediately drawn to study their reflection in a way that would surely incense the writers of those Victorian servants' manuals. But this wasn't an instrument of vanity; rather, it was a classic piece of Erddig parsimony. By placing a mirror behind the single lamp on the table, you double the light source.

And so Ellen Penketh, paraffin lamp in hand, enters her snug berth from the dark corridor and sets the light down on the table. There *is* double the light, yes. But also double the damage. She looks at her tired eyes and drawn face, once so pert and hopeful. The house has taken her youth. She was 32 years old on arrival. She is now 37, and comfortably into middle age. Her feet ache, her hands are hardened and the gleam is fading from her eyes.

Two oval portraits of the Yorke children hang on the wall by her glowing coal fire. Master Simon, bonny in sailor outfit and hat with ribbons; little Phil, swamped in a white bonnet that frames his deliciously chubby face like a sunflower's petals. Ellen has been intimate witness to her mistress's blossoming with the fulfilment of late motherhood. She has cosseted those children as if they were her own – dressing their dollies in little outfits made by blind Mary, her seamstress sister up in Pendleton – how Mary *lived* to please those boys with gifts.[10] And she would be a saint if she did not occasionally resent Louisa Yorke's good fortune.

She had been Mrs Yorke's accomplice for every exhausting household plan, from the repainting of the kitchen walls (deep blue, to set off the copper pans), to the incessant rearrangement of the Erddig china and silver treasures, to the plotting in detail of every ambitious dinner party. Ellen Penketh had seen, to be blunt, an anxious, frumpy woman transformed by marriage, motherhood and the luxury of not having to work for a living. Mrs Yorke was a kind-hearted woman, but she was also, by now, a bit of a tartar.

It all boiled down to the question of money. Erddig, with its reputation for generous hospitality, was floating on a raft of debt. In marrying a poor curate's daughter instead of an heiress, Philip Yorke had sealed the estate's downward slide. Erddig's annual income of less than £5,000 (£290,000 in today's money) came from the farms on the 2,500-acre estate, and the Hafod and Bersham coal pits, but it was being fast eroded by falling income from tenants and high taxation. Philip was also prone to extravagant (if much needed) estate improvements. Louisa, no stranger to money worries, was shocked to find out the extent of their debt. On 2 October 1903 she wrote in her diary, 'Bank account is overdrawn to the amount of £1,500 which worries me very much indeed.' This is around £86,000 in today's money.

The cook-housekeeper was key in driving down costs. Every month, Mrs Penketh was obliged to tot up her spending with Wrexham's various tradesmen and hand her account book to Louisa, who would sign it off and ask Philip to write out a cheque to pay the bills. Mrs Penketh would then take the cheque to the National and Provincial Bank in Wrexham, cash it and do the rounds with a chinking weight of money in her bag. On her return she would hand to Louisa the cash needed to pay the servants their total wages of around £22 a month (£1,300 today), plus their £3 'beer money'. Handling sums of £60, £100, even £180 were normal (from £3,500 to £10,300 today).

When the expenses tipped over her self-imposed budget, Louisa would write 'Overspent' at the bottom of the page and take out her guilt and anxiety on the cook-housekeeper. Regular 'scoldings' had become part of Ellen Penketh's life, and she began to dread them. The other prong of this pincer movement upon Mrs Penketh was the new agent, whose study adjoined the housekeeper's sitting room. The Victorian-minded Mr Hughes – he who had refused to let Mrs Yorke see the estate account books – had been dispatched. In the autumn of 1905 William Capper, 43, started work at Erddig. The heavy, leather-bound estate ledgers began to be filled in meticulously, inviting Louisa's approval. 'I interviewed Mr Capper the Agent for an hour. He seems a splendid agent & takes a great interest in everything.' She was not a woman given to gushing – 'I wish the lawyer Mr James were a little more expeditious with his work,' she adds in the next breath.

Capper was soon all over the place like a rash. Overtly helpful, covertly watchful, he poked his nose into the doings of the cook-housekeeper, the work of head housemaid Matilda Boulter, the cellar of William Wootton the butler. He was not your usual Chester man, having done a long stint in the cattle auctions and stockyards of Bakersfield, California where he earned enough money to set himself up as an auctioneer and valuer on his return. Married to Clara, father to young Eric, Doris, Alicia and Donald, he lived in a large detached Victorian house in Wrexham with one maid-of-all-work.

Capper's presence made Erddig's servants twitchy. A letter from head housemaid Matilda (Tilly) Boulter to Mrs Yorke during the annual spring clean of 1907 hints at the tensions below stairs.

2 June: 'Everything is going on quite alright & we are getting on . . . Mr Capper is often up so he can see how we are getting on & he knows there is a great deal to do.'

29 June: 'I think we have done all that was on my list . . . Mr Capper was here this morning. I dare say Mr Capper tells you all about everything. He knows we have been busy. Now I expect Mrs Penketh & Mr Wootton writes to you about their part of their dutys.' There is a sense of self-justification in her tone: she is getting her side of the story in first.

But the assiduous Mr Capper came at a price, and in order to cut more corners Louisa decided to take the household accounts away from the agent and give them instead to her capable cook-housekeeper. What effect did this have on the relationship of these two upper servants, side by side in the green basement corridor? A clue to their characters might be found in their signatures. Capper writes his very large, with scrolling flourishes, at the top of each page of the estate ledger. He is, at a guess, a dapper little man of unshakeable self-belief. Mrs Penketh's is found in the 'Time Book' that records the servants' monthly wages, each name signed off under her or her mistress's eye. It is careful yet flamboyant, with more than the usual curls and whorls of the Victorian schoolroom. There is something devil-may-care in that sweeping kick of the *k*'s downward stroke.

This is, of course, pure speculation. As is this: did Mr Capper pop next door rather too regularly to give unwelcome help with the accounts? Did Ellen Penketh feel spied on and undermined? Did a faintly flirtatious friendship turn sour? Something happened – of this I am sure.

IX

The Thief Cook

Twenty-two guests stayed at Erddig during the month of August 1907. On Monday 'the glorious twelfth' – the start of the grouse-shooting season for most country houses in Britain, but not for Erddig and its vegetarian squire – Ellen Penketh cooked her last dinner party.

It was, Louisa concluded, a triumph: ten guests on either side of the long dinner table with host and hostess at opposite curved ends, facing each other over vases of pink and white sweet peas and maidenhair fern. Louisa ignored Mrs Beeton's rule that 'no strongly scented flowers' should be used as table decorations – Erddig's sweet peas made one perfectly giddy with their summer perfume. The china she chose was Blue Spode. Footmen Arthur Barker and Fred Jones carried dish after dish from the fug and bustle of the kitchen up the short flight of stairs to the dining room: julienne soup, salmon, sweetbread, saddle of mutton, velvet cream, marble jelly, cheese straws and dessert apples. After dinner there was music and song by 'Dr da Cumbra & Miss Sturkey' in the Chinese room, lit by the eighteenth-century French ormolu and crystal chandelier.

There was nowhere better than Erddig in the summer, Louisa had long thought. The estate was an idyll where the world was kept at bay – and the world was more than usually intrusive that year. There was much worrying talk of a war with Germany. On 31 August the new Liberal Prime Minister Sir Henry Campbell-Bannerman brokered the 'Triple Entente' between Britain, France and Russia to counter the sinister triple alliance of Germany, Austria-Hungary and Italy. Closer to home, the suffrage movement kept up its shrill protests in public places, capitalising on February's morale-raising 'Mud March' in which three thousand women – Marchionesses, maids, textile workers, factory girls – had trudged in the rain from Hyde Park to Exeter Hall in London to plead the cause for women's suffrage.

Louisa floated around the rectangular canal on Sunday 8 September with her boys, now aged four and two: 'I took the chaps in the punt & again used my new Punt Pole which is a beauty.' She had no premonition of the bomb that was about to explode in her and Philip's lives – and neither, perhaps, did Ellen Penketh. When it came, it came out of the blue.

Monday, 9 September 1907: 'Mrs Penketh who has been cook here for 5 years is a regular professional thief. She has stolen & robbed goods & money to the amount of £500. Mr Capper & I interviewed her.'

Hyperbole. Repetition. Louisa is in a fury, writing in a tone not previously seen in her diary. Her very language seems to have changed, or coarsened: are these the choice phrases of Mr Capper? Most awkwardly the Yorkes have guests staying, Gwen Darley and Stephen Donne, who are of course avid to hear more, servant stories being the bread and butter of polite conversation. The following day

Mr Capper is invited (or invites himself) to lunch. With two extra pairs of ears in his audience he waxes lyrical, puffed up with the drama of the whole outrageous story. Downstairs in the gloomy blue kitchen Lizzie and Annie garnish cold cuts and fry up rissoles as best they can, for Ellen has disappeared, leaving her work undone and the basement in uproar.

'Mr Capper came to lunch and told more & more tales of Mrs Penketh's misdeeds', writes Louisa. 'Mrs Penketh is gone off for the day. We had not much heart to do anything so we sat & bemoaned our fate.' What Capper had discovered, as he began to ask questions one day in Wrexham, was that the Yorkes owed vast amounts of money all over town. Their account with Henry Woollam the butcher was unpaid. Pritchard & Co., the general drapers, was unpaid. Dutton & Co., the grocers, had not been paid since November 1906, and the amount owing had grown to £200 4s 10d (an astonishing £11,500 in today's money). In all, £361 12s was owing on the Yorke account books – while a further £142 19s 7d was owing *off* the books, for bills which had been quietly suppressed with the suppliers' collusion. It was a huge amount of money: £500 (around £28,700). So what, he demanded to know, had Mrs Penketh been doing with the money Mrs Yorke had been giving her? The cheques had been cashed, and the Erddig account book marked 'paid' against each supplier. But they had *not* been paid. It was all in all a blistering vindication of Mr Capper's original contention: if the household accounts had been kept under his control, none of this would have happened.

The next day Philip Yorke, who usually avoided unpleasantness or confrontation of any kind, cycled to Wrexham to see the family lawyer, Mr James. He returned with James, who interviewed the woman Louisa was now calling 'the thief cook'. Her anger was unabated. 'She is thoroughly frightened & a good thing too', she wrote that night in her diary. 'She was told she must leave today. She left at 7.15 wringing her hands.' What Mrs Yorke didn't know was that the servants had quickly pooled together what little money they had – £2 (£100 today) – to save Ellen Penketh from destitution, as she had nothing to her name. Whether through pity or affection we don't know, but they also worked out a place for her to stay the night, late as it was: she could go to Mrs Edwards, who kept a corner shop in Wrexham. Mrs Edwards, who did much upholstery work for Erddig, had a daughter who was engaged to a Gittins – a family of long association with the servants' hall. Gussie, the 16-year-old nursery maid, was a Gittins. Perhaps it was her suggestion.

And so Ellen Penketh, shopkeeper's daughter, half walked, half ran in the luminous twilight of a September evening, to 68 Poyser Street, where she was taken in by another shopkeeper. Frightened and dishevelled, the ex-cook-housekeeper of Erddig Hall had little more than the clothes she was dressed in.

On Friday the thirteenth, another long house party regretfully kicked off, despite the absence of the woman who normally drove Erddig's engine below stairs. Nervous housemaids Jinnie Fairman and Edith Haycock showed Mrs Beryl Binning to her room and brought up hot water and afternoon tea. The next day Mr Yeates was welcomed, and on the Monday Mr Browne arrived. The talk of the drawing room (and of the servants' hall below) was all of Mrs Penketh. Louisa told the dreadful story so many times her own diary began to sound repetitive. 14 September: 'Busy morning with Mr Capper. Alas! The Cook, Mrs Penketh, in whom I had so much trust, has robbed us of £500. She done it [sic] so very cleverly that hardly anyone could have found her out. Mr James came to talk about it but Mr Capper is the most practical. I fear we shall get no redress.'

The Yorkes were not given to talking ill of their servants; quite the opposite. Their very tolerance had earned them, over generations, a reputation for being over-lenient. But in the company of their house guests, all with a view to express and a horror story to impart (not least the well-connected and forthright Beryl Binning), Louisa began to mouth the platitudes of the era. Vita Sackville-West parodied such conversations in her novel *The Edwardians*, based on her childhood at

Knole in Kent. "Servants are so unscrupulous, one can't trust them a yard", Lucy, Duchess of Chevron says to her friend Lady Roehampton. "However long they have been with one, – even if one looks on them as old friends, – one never knows when they will turn nasty."[11]

On 16 September, Louisa wrote in her diary that 'Mrs Binning has had to part with her housemaid as I have parted with the Cook. It is sad to think how I have been cheated through thick & thin.' The whole scenario touched a raw nerve for Louisa, just six years ago a spinster eking out an allowance of £20. Her social insecurity, her occasional heavy-handedness, her poor judgement when recruiting servants, her mismanagement of money . . . these things Louisa was aware of, and ashamed of, and her bubbling fury was as much directed at herself as at 'the thief cook'. How could she have been so naïve, so trusting? It was ruining the house party.

17 September: 'I spent most of the day looking for bills & cheques. Mrs Penketh is I believe at Mrs Edwards. She will, I expect, unless she pays the money, be in prison before long. Her systematic cheating is almost incredible after all our kindness to her.'

The worst episode for the Yorkes was yet to come.

Perhaps it was Louisa pushing for vengeance; wanting her pound of flesh. Or perhaps it was the massed outrage of their guests and social callers that drove the Yorkes into a corner. Either way, they decided to press criminal charges against Ellen Penketh. This catapulted the case into quite a different arena – one that the very private, mild-mannered Philip Yorke may not have reckoned on. By pressing charges, the serene, closed world of Erddig would be prised open, laid bare and judged. Philip (now a white-bearded 58) had intimate experience of the courtroom. As Squire Yorke, a gentleman with a reputation for philanthropy, he sat at Wrexham Magistrate's Court as a Justice of the Peace. He was also twice yearly summoned by the High Sheriff of Denbighshire to sit on the jury at the Courts of Assize at Ruthin, the Welsh market town twenty miles to the north-west. He knew, therefore, of the trauma of the witness box, the tricks of the barristers and the brutality of those Victorian gaols. He knew, too, about the press.

But Philip felt ill used, and he was a man who could not let a slight go unpaid for. Louisa's diary indignantly recorded any knock to his reputation; any 'insulting letters or 'unfeeling remarks'. On 24 February 1905 she wrote that 'Philip read to me some old letters of his past life. It is quite wonderful that all who tried to do him some injury came to grief.' And now his trusting, good-hearted wife had been gulled by Mrs Penketh. Such was Philip's anger at anyone laying a trap for his Lulu that he reached for the proverbial sledgehammer to crack the nut.

At seven o'clock on the evening of 19 September, Inspector Tippett of the Denbighshire Constabulary walked purposefully down Victoria Road, left into Poyser Street and stopped at the doorway of number 68. He cast his eye over the corner shop's tin advertisement boards – Zebra Grate Polish; Birds Custard Powder (No Eggs! No Risk! No Trouble!). He lifted his hand and rapped three times. By now curious faces were watching from windows and a crowd of children had gathered. 'Ellen Penketh,' said Inspector Tippett, 'I hereby do arrest you on a warrant under the Larceny Act of 1901.' She was handcuffed and propelled at a smart pace the half-mile to the police station on Regent Street. Here he read over the warrant. 'Prisoner made no reply,' Inspector Tippett wrote in his ledger. She was shown into a brick-vaulted cell – one of five – and locked up for the night. If Ellen Penketh could not find bail for £50 (around £3,000 in today's money), she would be taken straight to Shrewsbury Gaol until the hearing at the magistrate's court in Wrexham in a week's time.

The 'worry' of what they had set in motion was 'too awful' for Louisa and Philip. Still – that night they ventured out locally to dine at Lady Egerton's, transfixing the table with their shocking tale. 'We opened our hearts to Major Leadbetter who has advised us to prosecute her.' Did Louisa's liberal conscience give her pause to consider the predicament of Ellen Penketh? If so, she did not record this in her diary. Or else she let Philip voice it for her: he was from this point on 'kept awake at night' by thoughts of Mrs Penketh's 'foolishness'. Two days later, he rose from his bed having had second thoughts: perhaps out of clemency, or through fear of scandal, or the dawning realisation of what his wife would be put through as primary witness – Louisa didn't record her husband's motive. Simply that, 'He is going to try & withdraw the prosecution'.

But it was too late.

X

Won't You Help Me?

Before her arrest, Ellen Penketh did not sit it out mutely above the corner shop at Poyser Street, waiting for the policeman's knock at the door. She moved fast to try to set things right. What happened after her eviction from Erddig was told in court by Mr Davies, elderly clerk of solicitors James & James.[12] It is fascinating for the glimpse it gives us of her background (all fear, mistrust and accusation), and the unique chance to hear her faint voice. The day she left Erddig Ellen bumped into, or sought out, old Mr Davies and told him what had happened. 'He was rather interested in the matter,' the court was told, 'because he knew Miss Penketh, and he was also a tenant on Mr Yorke's estate.' Belonging to Erddig clearly inspired a kind of group loyalty – among tenants as well as servants.

Ellen begged him to go with her to Manchester to see her family and ask what they might do to help. 'She said she was rather afraid of facing her people herself.' Mr Davies was a friend and he thought of her reputation, for she was kept company that evening by one Mr Wright, a storekeeper for the Corporation Electricity Department and a keen sympathiser in her plight (later to offer £50 bail). Mr Davies suggested she spend the night with his own daughter, Mrs Woollam, before journeying together to the train station the next day.

I imagine this incongruous couple boarding the train for Chester and thence to Manchester: an elderly legal clerk, a terrified domestic servant. At Manchester station they board a double-decker electric tram bound for the western industrial suburb of Pendleton and its slums, and the shop of Mrs Penketh. 'Go and see thy old mistress, Mrs Armitage,' says Ellen's mother. 'She knows you wouldn't be plutcherin owt, God help us. She'll see thi' right.' So they walk, Mr Davies and Ellen Penketh, along the dirty road to more prosperous streets and hence to Chaseley Field – but the big house has now become Pendleton High School for Girls, a place of chalk dust and algebra. 'Mrs Armitage has gone,' says the housekeeper, 'long gone. No, we don't know where.'

Ellen is desperate; this was her last hope. She walks back home in tears – who else is there left to help her? 'Your father,' says her mother. 'See what he can do to keep you out of trouble. Tell him you'll happen go to gaol if not.' And so Mr Davies, his confidence ebbing, takes the train west with Ellen the next day to Liverpool, to seek out Thomas Penketh the wheelwright. Ellen hangs back, nervous of her father's reaction. 'I dare na',' she says. 'You talk to him first. Then I'll come in.'

Thomas is immediately suspicious. Here's this man of the law, coming on behalf of his feckless daughter. 'I'm not going to sign any paper,' he says, backing off.

'I have no paper for you to sign,' says the mild Mr Davies, who later reconstructs the scene in court. 'Miss Penketh wants to know if you can do anything for her, as her father.'

Mr Davies explains that if a sum of £200 (£11,500) could be raised, then proceedings against his daughter might be dropped.

'You might as well ask me to raise a million pounds,' says Thomas Penketh. 'I shall do nothing. She's already tried to rob me often pounds.' Ellen is in the doorway, nervous. 'Won't you help me, Father?'

'No, not in the least,' he replies.

On entering Shrewsbury Gaol, prisoners pass beneath a keep-like portcullis that separates them from the world outside; in particular from the neighbouring train station and all its bustle of departure. It is a Victorian gaol, known then and now as 'the Dana' after the medieval lock-up it came to replace. Until its closure in 2013, it had a reputation as one of Britain's most overcrowded prisons. In 1907 it still had a gibbet for hangings. Ellen had not yet been convicted and her stay was short, but her treatment would have been no different to any other woman arriving in handcuffs. Female prisoners were met by a wardress, taken into a room and demanded their particulars, all entered in a ledger known as the 'female nominal roll'. Today this massive tome is kept by Shropshire Archives – and there I found her committal, written over two pages in copperplate ink:

Number 115: Name, Ellen Penketh

Date & place of committal: 20.9.07 Wrexham Co.

Offence: fraudulent use of cheques to the value of £210 12s. 1d.

(larceny as servant)

Committed to Denbighshire Assizes Ruthin Prison

Education: 3

Age, height and colour of hair: 37; 5ft; brn.

Occupation: Cook

Religion and place of birth: C of E; Rainford

No previous convictions.

Ellen was then told to undress, was relieved of hairpins and any jewellery and marched to a grimy bath of hot water. From this she was dressed in coarse prison garb and led to a numbered cell, not unlike a small pantry in a country house, where she was given a coloured, numbered medal to wear. The door clanged shut. No further instructions were given to 'first-nighters' such as Ellen.[13] Instead, a printed tract on the wall listed the punishments for crimes such as 'Not folding a bed in the proper manner. Not folding up clothes in the proper manner. Not washing feet twice a week, prior to using water to clean the cell.'

It had come to this: the worst. Ellen Penketh had one week to wait for her court hearing at Wrexham and possible release, but how optimistic was she? She had written a desperate apology to Mr Yorke, but here he was, still pressing charges. She would at least have a chance to put *her* side of the story to impartial ears, but the money was – apparently – gone. Every day, every hour, every minute of that week, her mind must have worked over the details of what had happened. The tangled knots. The half-truths. The muddle well meant, but now gone poisonous. The missing sovereigns. There was also, perhaps, a mounting sense of fury.

'After all our kindness to her,' the outraged Louisa had written in her diary. But what of the many kindnesses of Ellen Penketh? All done in the line of duty, maybe, but delivered sincerely nonetheless. It was as if she had never existed in their lives; never cooked Louisa a Charlotte russe, never taken little Phil to see the chickens and collect the eggs, never collaborated with her mistress in each triumphant bout of entertaining. If you were a titled or upper-class lady and you ended up in prison – as so many well-heeled suffragettes resorting to violent tactics now did – you were set free pretty smartly, thanks to your connections. But if you were unknown and friendless, you would end up getting prosecuted and thrown in gaol. Ellen Penketh was probably under no illusions as to what would happen next.

'This was a terrible day,' wrote Louisa on Thursday, 26 September. 'At 10 we went off in the carriage to appear in the Courts against Mrs Penketh.' Wrexham Magistrate's Court dealt with dozens of small cases monthly, and its judgements were in keeping with the times. Crimes that autumn ranged from the theft of thirty-four rabbit skins (for which one boy of 13 got seven days in Shrewsbury Gaol followed by four years in a reformatory, his 12-year-old accomplice six strokes with a birch rod); to the theft of chickens (two months' imprisonment and hard labour); to the theft of two pairs of corduroy trousers and a waistcoat from the Workhouse (seven days' imprisonment). Ellen Penketh was collected at dawn from Shrewsbury Gaol by a police officer, driven by horse and closed carriage the thirty miles to the courthouse on Wrexham's

Regent Street and led to the dock. Here, standing between two warders, she faced her employers once again.

But to surprised muttering, Mr Churton (acting for James & James) announced to the magistrate that in the light of Mrs Penketh's 'very repentant letter', and the fact that she had been in prison now seven days, Mr Yorke wished to apply to Their Worships for consent to withdraw the prosecution. Mr Yorke believed the prisoner 'had been led away by some person whom he need not mention, and who practically had been at the bottom of the whole mischief'. There was murmured consultation on the bench, then, 'Silence,' called the Chairman. 'Pray silence in court.'

An expectant hush: the blood sings in Ellen Penketh's ears. Louisa looks mutely at her gloved hands, clutched together. The Chairman clears his throat. 'While appreciating Mr Yorke's kindness and goodness of heart,' he pronounces, 'we are of the opinion that, in duty to the public, the case should be proceeded with. Please to call the first witness.'

Louisa was to find herself in the dock giving evidence while Ellen Penketh sat and listened. The tables were spectacularly turned – and Erddig's informal accounts-keeping system was laid bare. 'Prisoner was housekeeper in her employ for five years all but two months. It was part of her duty to keep a rough book containing tradesmen's accounts,' began Mr Churton. He went on to list the cheques cashed by Mrs Penketh and the accounts left unpaid with tradesmen. It looked, on the surface, baldly incriminating. Then it was the turn of Mr Downes Powell, defending. Finally, we come to the nub of Ellen's predicament: 'Did the prisoner ever tell you when you interviewed her that she had kept some of the accounts back?'

'Yes,' answered Louisa.

'Did she tell you why?'

'She said she did this because she did not wish the bills to appear too high.'

'Had you been grumbling at her?'

'Yes, for her extravagance.'

Extravagance. This was a sin to Louisa, curate's daughter – yet her conscience was troubled and guilty. To avoid her mistress's anger, Ellen Penketh had deliberately begun to lower the accounts, suppressing bills with a nod here and a pleading word there, among her very understanding suppliers, who perhaps couldn't resist the charm of Erddig's personable cook-housekeeper. She would, she told them, make it up over the next few months.

This was fine, if messy, until Ellen Penketh apparently lost a large sum of money.

'Did she then tell you how she had lost it?' asked Mr Downes Powell.

'She said she found her bag open, and that she had lost a hundred and thirty pounds,' responded Louisa (this is around £7,500 in today's money).

'Did you not ask her why she had not told you about the loss?'

'Yes.'

'Did she say where?'

'No . . . She said that [it was] after she had cashed the cheque for two hundred pounds, and was on the way home.'

'What was her reply?'

'That she was afraid to let me know.'

If this was true, it was entirely plausible that a servant would be terrified of confessing to such an enormous loss. Ellen Penketh was then forced to try to pay back the amounts owing to suppliers out of her own meagre savings: accounts that had been suppressed over twelve months by a total of £142 19s 7d (around £8,200 today). This was clearly impossible on a salary of £45 a year.

'Do you know that when she left Erddig she had no money?' the barrister persisted.

'Yes,' replied Louisa, ever more faintly. She would not look at the prisoner.

'And that the servants made a collection for her in the house?'

'Yes.'

'Now, during the time she has been in your service,' he asked, 'have you noticed her dressing extravagantly or making a big show or anything of that sort?'

'No.'

And now came that technique beloved of all barristers: a meaningful pause.

Mr Bevis, manager to grocers Messrs Dutton & Co., was called to the witness box. The teetotal Philip Yorke suspected that Mrs Penketh had abused an account for wines and spirits in his name – in other words, that she was not only a thief but a drunkard too. This was swiftly demolished in court, with proof that the sum owing on this account – £27 18s 7½d (around £1,600 today) – was a reasonable bill for the cook of a busy country-house kitchen. Next came Woollam the butcher and Pritchard the draper, each with stories of Mrs Penketh's attempts to pay back the money owed, followed by two cashiers from the National and Provincial Bank. Then it was the turn of Erddig's agent, Mr Capper. He pointed out that Mrs Penketh's story about losing the money after leaving the bank 'couldn't be very true, or it would have been heard about in the town'. When Mrs Yorke asked the accused why she hadn't mentioned the loss before, Capper informed the court, Mrs Penketh answered that she 'had often wanted to do so, but had not the courage.'

What had seemed a straightforward, even banal case (servant steals money) was, it turned out, not at all straightforward. It touched on incendiary issues in the relationship between mistress and servant, even between the upper and lower classes. There was a suggestion of bullying, and real fear. There was collusion between suppliers and cook-housekeeper: a favoured relationship which finally went awry. There was the peculiar matter of the gold sovereigns disappearing from the bag, which did not quite ring true, and the suggestion that someone else had 'been at the bottom of the whole mischief' – yet the 'destitute' Mrs Penketh was clearly not spending the money on herself. And there was the odd retraction of punishment from Squire Yorke, who managed suddenly to transform his vendetta into an act of mercy.

After a brief retirement, the magistrates returned to the court. They had considered the case, said the Chairman. It was to go for trial to the Assizes. Bail was offered on a surety of £100, which, to applause, Mr Yorke agreed to provide, presumably through gritted teeth (it is around £5,700 in today's money). For him, this was the worst-case scenario.

'She is at large', wrote Louisa the next day.

As soon as she was released from Wrexham Magistrate's Court Ellen Penketh travelled by train back to Manchester, to her mother's shop, where she was compelled to stay until the trial. But to Louisa, the genie was out of the bottle. That day Mr Wootton the butler delivered to Mr Yorke his copy of the *Wrexham Advertiser* with a more than usually mask-like face. The paper served Wrexham and all its surrounding towns as far as Chester and Ruthin, and was much read by the middle classes. On that day, stories ranged from the Welsh-language movement gaining momentum, to Stoke-on-Trent workhouse paupers refusing to eat their Monday mutton broth, to the regular column by Miss Ida Meller, 'Fashion and Things Feminine'.

There it was, on page seven, in large font:

The Serious Charge Against an Erddig Housekeeper.
Extraordinary Proceedings. Prosecutor Wishes to Withdraw. Accused Sent to the Assizes.

The article took up a good half-page. Louisa and Philip bravely went visiting on their bicycles. 'The great topic of conversation is the 9 days wonder of Wrexham, namely the misdoings of our former cook', she wrote that night. Now that the stakes were so much higher, she had to maintain her dogged conviction of Ellen Penketh's guilt – and her friends were quick to support her, rounding on the 'thief cook' where previously they had praised the lightness of her drop scones and moistness of her Madeira cake.

Plump, beribboned and complacent, 'The Housekeeper' as caricatured in *Heads of the People*, 1840. Her badge of office is her bunch of keys; the sherry glasses hint at a gathering of upper servants. This was the stereotype – the reality was rather different. © *Time & Life Pictures/Getty Images*

...entham Hall, ...affordshire, in the 1820s. ...r all its splendour, the ...per servants took their ...er-dinner brandy in ... outbuilding squeezed ...tween a washhouse ...d a chicken run. *British Library/Robana/REX*

In her youth the Duchess of Sutherland (Lady Stafford) was a celebrated beauty – but by the 1830s she had 'all the appearance of a wicked old woman', according to diarist Thomas Creevey. © Copyright 2014 Bridgeman Art Library

By the early 1900s the lake at Trentham Hall was so foully polluted by waste from the Potteries that the Sutherlands stopped visiting. In 1912 the house was knocked down; all that survives are the gardens.
Trentham Gardens

Dorothy Doar's letter to agent James Loch, 3 April 1832, begging for six weeks leave to have her baby and send it out to nurse. It was highly unusual for a housekeeper to be married, or to have a child. *Reproduced with permission of Staffordshire Record Office D593/K/1/3/20*

Sarah Wells, High Victorian housekeeper of Uppark, photographed in her sixties for the house records. © *National Trust*

Uppark, West Sussex: where the servant-master relationship was irrevocably undermined when the master married a dairymaid in 1825. The dairymaid's sister later inherited the estate. © *National Trust*

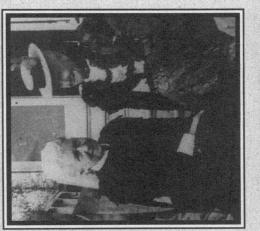

Miss Frances Fetherstonhaugh (left), plain 'Fanny Bullock' before she inherited her sister's title and the estate in 1874. © *National Trust*

The service tunnels at Uppark, connecting stables, dairy, kitchen and laundry with the great house. Mrs Wells spent much of her working life underground in these passageways. *National Trust*

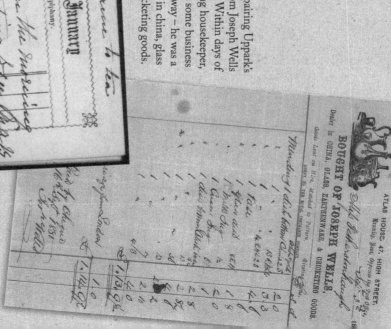

A bill for repairing Uppark's crockery from Joseph Wells of Bromley. Within days of becoming housekeeper, Mrs Wells put some business her husband's way – he was a struggling dealer in china, glass and cricketing goods.

Sarah Wells's diary, 1892: downstairs politics between female servants fill its pages. Ten cooks come and go in as many years.

Courtesy of The Rare Book & Manuscript Library of the University of Illinois at Urbana-Champaign

Ellen Penketh, cook housekeeper at Erddig. Her mistress was to take her to court for allegedly stealing £500 – and yet, surprisingly, kept this portrait of 'the thief cook' in the back of a family album. © *National Trust*

The Yorkes of Erddig Hall, North Wales: Louisa, Philip and their children 'Little Phil' and Simon. Louisa, rescued from spinsterhood at 39, had no experience of running a large house.
Reproduced with permission of Flintshire Record Office

Erddig Hall: 'I have, I think, undertaken more than I can accomplish,' wrote Louisa Yorke in her diary, one month into her marriage. 'The management of this huge house with 6 female and 3 male servants is no joke.' © *National Trust*

The Charge against a Wrexham Housekeeper.

Ellen Penketh (37) formerly housekeeper in the employ of Mr. Yorke, of Erddig, was charged with having fraudulently converted the sum of £201 12s 1d, the monies of Mr. Yorke, to her own use.

Mr. Ellis Jones Griffith, M.P. prosecuted, and Mr. Artemus Jones defended the case.

Mr. Griffith said that the prisoner had been housekeeper to Mr. and Mrs. Yorke at Erddig, and in the course of her duties she kept a book in which were entered the house-keeping expenses and a list of the tradesmen's accounts for monthly supplies. These entries were copied by Mrs. Yorke in her own book and certain payments in respect of .... up the petty cash .... they were not .... of November 1906, the prisoner used to keep the .... could not be found. From that date the bookkeeping .... were forthcoming, and up to the 1st Oct. 1906, missing from them. The housekeeping book kept by Mrs. Yorke contained the total for each month, and from the first Oct. 1906, to the 1st July 1907, tradesmen's bills and petty cash for the ten months amounted to £1295. A number of cheques were given to the prisoner by Mrs. Yorke to that same aggregate. These cheques the prisoner took to the bank and received cash for. In the ordinary course of events she would pay the tradesmen's bills, enter the payments in a book and submit it to Mrs. Yorke. The charge against the prisoner was that she had misappropriated the amount mentioned in the course of cashing these cheques. There were respect of Messrs. Duttons, grocers, the prisoner had received £110 13s 11d, in respect of Messrs. Woollam, butchers, £46 1s 10d; in respect of Messrs. Pritchard, drapers £44 17s 2d. None of these amounts had been paid by the prisoner.

Mrs. Yorke bore out Counsel's statement. Since the prisoner had left other bills had come in which brought the total deficiency to £500. When accused the prisoner said she had lost £130 whilst coming from the bank.

Mr. Artemus Jones (cross-examining): Should you be wrong in saying to the jury that you did not know very much about housekeeping accounts?— May I hand my book to the jury so that they may be able to see?

Thank you: I should like to see it too. The housekeeping accounts, to put it mildly, are rather confused?—Not my book, no, not at all. They were in an unset state?—Yes.

Then may I take it that the housekeeper's book was in an unset state?—Yes.

In point of fact, am I not right in stating that you didn't know the state of the accounts until your solicitor helped you?—I gave prisoner money to pay bills, but later I found that the bills had not been paid.

I am not asking you that; is it not a fact that you have had several conversations with your solicitor because you were not able to understand your housekeeping accounts?—No.

eft: Louisa Yorke's accounts book from 1907, evidence in the court *ase* she brought against her *housekeeper*. Her bookkeeping *was* ridiculed by Ellen Penketh's *barrister* as 'rather confused'.

On the right-hand page she lists *the* departure of later housekeepers: *Miss* Brown and Miss Hitchman.

Reproduced with permission of Flintshire Record Office

ight: After two months in Ruthin *Gaol*, Ellen Penketh faced her *employers* from the dock. The *case* was widely reported in the *local* press, much to the Yorkes' *mortification. Reproduced with permission of Flintshire Record Office*

Wrest Park in the early 1900s: an 18th-century-style chateau – and a millstone inheritance to the young Lord Lucas. © *Country Life*

Housekeeper Hannah Mackenzie (seated) and Cook, Hetty Geyton, both hired in 1914 when the house became a war hospital. *Private collection*

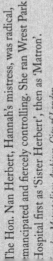

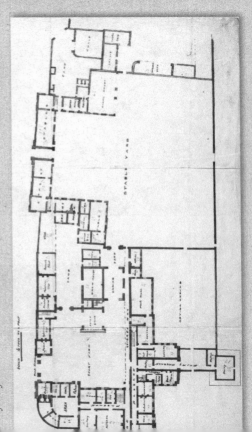

Cecil Argles, land agent for Wrest Park: a 'sedately married man' who fell violently in love with Hannah Mackenzie.

© Estate of Martin Argles

The Hon. Nan Herbert, Hannah's mistress, was radical, emancipated and fiercely controlling. She ran Wrest Park Hospital first as 'Sister Herbert', then as 'Matron'.

London Metropolitan Archives, City of London

Wrest Park floor plan, early 1900s. The service wing to the east was transformed to receive soldiers straight from the Front, with bathing house and 'louse house'.

© Holfords of Westonbirt Trust

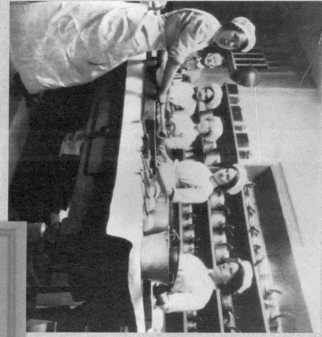

A studio portrait of Hannah Mackenzie in New York, by then housekeeper to Grace Vanderbilt, the 'Queen of Fifth Avenue'.

© Ross Mackenzie

Cook Hetty Geyton (right) and her girls in Wrest Park's kitchen.

Private collection

Hannah celebrates her hundredth birthday. 'She enjoys a glass of whisky and a cigarette', reported the Northampton Chronicle & Echo, 1981. © Ross Mackenzie

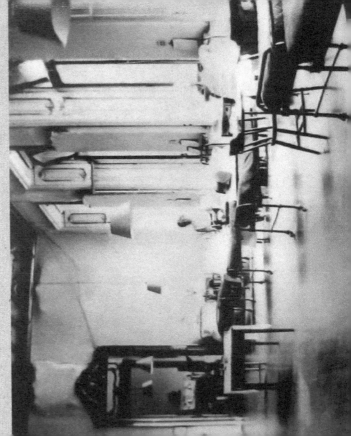

Wrest Park library: before and after its transformation into a hospital ward, freshly wired for electricity. *Both private collection*

Grace, aged nineteen, in 1922: already a beauty. 'Mr Bell came to lunch, & as usual said some very idiotic remarks, making me feel very uncomfortable.' © *The British Library Board (Add 83246 A 1 f3)*

Charleston Farmhouse as it is today. Cook-housekeeper Grace Higgens was not allowed to walk in front of the house when guests were dining. © *Paul Cox/Alamy*

'Bloomsbury' in Sussex: the extraordinary ménage that Grace entered as a 16-year-old housemaid. Vanessa Bell cuts Lytton Strachey's hair while (left to right) Roger Fry, Clive Bell, Duncan Grant and guest look on. © *The Granger Collection/TopFoto*

Grace in the garden at Charleston, 1920s. Vanessa Bell thought her bone structure 'unusually aristocratic' for a working class girl. © *The British Library Board (Add 83246A 1:f9)*

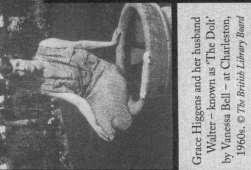

Grace Higgens and her husband Walter – known as 'The Dolt' by Vanessa Bell – at Charleston, 1960s. © *The British Library Board (Add 83246A 8:f103)*

Holkham Hall, Norfolk: the imposing sight that greets housekeeper Nicky Garner when she drives to work every morning. *By kind permission of Viscount Coke and the Trustees of the Holkham Esta...*

Nicky (centre) and her 'girls', 2012. 'Nicky is not at all the stereotype,' says Lady Coke. 'She's the sort of woman you might go and have a beer with.' © *Magnum Photos*

'We hear so much against the woman', Louisa wrote, 'that Philip is going to withdraw the bail.' Gossip had come to their ears that Mrs Penketh – rather than turning up at court and surrendering bail – was simply going to disappear. Manchester would swallow her up and she would never be heard of again. The careful and precise Philip Yorke was enraged. And so, five days after her reprieve, Ellen was without warning rearrested at her mother's shop, handcuffed and transported fifty miles south to face her former master in Wrexham Magistrate's Court again on Tuesday, 1 October. Here, bail was formally withdrawn. 'The prisoner will be only too glad to release Mr Yorke from his surety,' snapped her barrister, Mr Downes Powell, incensed by such unwarranted shilly-shallying. He had an alternative: Mr Willis Sterrett (a blacksmith) and Mr Wright (a storekeeper) would become surety for £50 each. Mrs Penketh was not without friends.

As the *Wrexham Advertiser* reported the following Friday ('Mr Yorke withdraws his Recognizances'). 'Mr Sterret was accepted, but Mr Wright was not, and the prisoner, therefore, left the court in custody.'

XI

You Scolded Her

The road from Wrexham to Ruthin Gaol rises then drops into classic northern Welsh scenery – all high hills, brown-purple slopes and sheep, everywhere, grazing on the intensely vivid green of the fields. Ellen Penketh would have seen none of this from her closed police carriage. This upper servant was about to enter her second gaol in twelve days.

Ruthin is a prosperous little market town with exhilarating views of the Clwydian Hills – and of the shingled roof and bell tower of its Pentonville-style prison, which lies at the bottom of steep Clwyd Street.

There is no mistaking the purpose of this building, with its sheer stone facade, small, square windows and a doorway halfway up the wall in the courtyard for access directly onto a gallows platform. Ruthin's most recent (and only) execution was in 1903. It was to be the last, for the Victorian prison of one hundred cells was closed in 1916 and merged with Shrewsbury Gaol.

The drill here was much the same as at Shrewsbury on entering: a 'vigorous medical check and regular bath against fleas, lice and mites'. The earthenware bath was reached by mounting three stone steps – at the top of which Ellen Penketh might have hesitated, seeing the scum of others clouding the surface. She was issued with the drab prison uniform and taken to her cell, four paces long by three wide, and the heavy door was bolted shut.

Most female prisoners – nationally a thousand admitted every week by 1895 – were there for drink or prostitution offences. There were just six cells for women at Ruthin, two to a floor of a three-storey wing that looked west on to the laundry room below and the meandering River Clwyd. Here Ellen and her cohorts were put to work. Reporters Mayhew and Binny described such labour in *The Criminal Prisons of London, and Scenes of Prison Life* in 1862: the 'bare red arms working the soddened flannels against a wooden grooved board', and 'turning the handles of the wringing machine', all glimpsed through a 'dense white mist of steam'.[14] 'They worked in silence. 'No singing, no whistling, no attempts to communicate by signs or writing. No unnecessary looking around,' read the rules framed on Ellen's wall. In the exercise yard, men wore peaked caps that covered their faces entirely, like sinister masks with eyeholes. By eight o'clock, after an unvarying supper of oatmeal gruel, she was back in her gaslit cell in the twilight: put to work sewing, knitting or weaving, and counting the days.

'I do not like motors and I think I never shall,' Louisa had pronounced, but on Monday, 2 December she overcame her aversion in order to travel to Ruthin for the trial of Ellen Penketh.

The Yorkes were lent a chauffeur-driven car by their friends the Frazers, which was able to halve the three-hour carriage journey as they sat in the back on upholstered leather. As they puttered deeper into Denbighshire at twenty miles an hour, the place names became stranger: Coedpoeth, Bwlchgwyn, Llanfair Dyffryn Clwyd. They were entering a foreign country. Louisa bore her carsickness bravely. It was nothing, after all, as to what was about to happen. She had thought of little else over the past weeks, to the extent that she was sick of the whole subject. 'I meet with so much sympathy on all sides & so many letters come on the subject of the cook that it is getting rather wearisome', she had written on 2 October. She left Erddig in the care of a new housekeeper, the 60-year-old chapel-going Miss Brown, who would do no cooking, merely 'superintend'. Kitchen maid Lizzie Copestake had been promoted to the post of cook.

The Yorkes checked into the Castle Hotel in Market Square, a 'high-class family and commercial hotel' with Puginesque tiled floors, panelled walls and an excellent view of H. M. Prison directly below. They had stayed here before – 'three days of worry and expense' – talking to their barrister before the case was then postponed.

Ellen Penketh had, by now, spent two months in Ruthin Gaol waiting to be called to trial. Today she was handed back her creased civilian clothes and led, probably on foot, the back route to the Ruthin Assizes (thus avoiding Market Square and the eyes of the breakfasting Yorkes). Philip and Louisa might not have had much appetite for an Edwardian breakfast anyway. They put on hats and heavy coats and left the hotel, turning left down steep Well Street and into the blinding morning sun. Past a Methodist chapel, right along Record Street, past the County Constabulary to the imposing classical portico of the Ruthin Assizes. Up five steps, through four stone pillars: by now Louisa's heart was thudding, as she knew what was coming.

'What brutes Barristers can be', she wrote with feeling that night. 'How can anyone respect them.' Mrs Yorke had again been summoned to the witness box – this time for two hours. The Ruthin Assizes was imposing, with its gaslit brass candelabra, spectators' gallery and glass-domed ceiling shedding light on the accused. Where Wrexham County Court's inquisitors were pedantic, the barristers at the trial today were flamboyant, cunning, bullying. Mr Artemus Jones, assigned to defend Ellen Penketh, was a barrister well known on the North Wales circuit, and he used every well-worn trick in his repertoire.[15] First he tried to expose Louisa as a silly, feather-brained woman, a period cliché that would have infuriated her.

'Should you be wrong in saying to the jury that you did not know very much about housekeeping accounts?' asked Mr Jones. 'The housekeeping accounts, to put it mildly, are rather confused?'

'Not my book, no,' replied Louisa firmly; 'not at all.'

'Then I may take it that the housekeeper's book was in an upset state?'

'Yes,' she answered.

'In point of fact, am I not right in stating that you didn't know the state of the accounts until your solicitor helped you?'

'I gave the prisoner money to pay bills,' said Louisa, doggedly sticking to the essence of the case, 'but later I found that the bills had not been paid.'

'I am not asking you that,' retorted Mr Jones. 'Is it not a fact that you have had several conversations with your solicitor because you were not able to understand your housekeeping accounts?'

This was not true, she told him. Mr Artemus Jones then moved on to the need for economy at Erddig.

'In getting the prisoner to keep the accounts instead of the expert agent you were economising, were you not?'

'We tried to,' replied Louisa. 'How she must have hated this line of attack.

'Because your family was a growing one, and your expenses were going up?'

'Yes.'

Jones asked her if she ever complained to the prisoner about the rising expenses. 'And – I am not suggesting that you are a severe person – you scolded her?'

'Yes.'

'And because you did so she kept back some of the accounts?'

Again and again, Louisa Yorke was led down the barrister's blind alleys until Mrs Penketh's villainy looked either improbable or entirely justified, given the apparent heartlessness of her master and mistress. First, Mr Jones pointed out, Philip Yorke offered bail. 'And then after two or three days your husband changed his mind?'

'Yes.'

'And without a word of warning this woman was dragged handcuffed from Manchester to Wrexham.'

'I didn't know she was handcuffed,' said Louisa, perhaps with a fleeting memory of Ellen Penketh the person, the friend.

'Did you know she was dragged from Manchester to Wrexham by the police?' persisted the barrister.

'Dragged!' protested his counterpart, Mr Ellis Jones Griffith, prosecuting.

'Brought or taken, I suppose Mr Jones means,' came the dry voice of the judge.

'A pictorial phrase, which you should be able to appreciate, Mr Griffith,' hit back Mr Artemus Jones with customary brio. As the men in court laughed knowingly, Louisa braced herself, wondering what was to come next.

'Do you tell the jury that you think this woman pocketed the amounts which are missing?'

'I don't know at all,' came her faint reply.

The first day's hearing ended on a salacious note. Under cross-examination, the Yorkes' solicitor Mr James admitted that enquiries had been made 'as to whether the prisoner was in *a certain condition*', his justification being that this would have had a bearing on whether she was likely to surrender bail. 'A mysterious detective from Salford' had been used by James & James to make these enquiries as Mrs Penketh 'lay at home' in Manchester.

'This was a most malicious slander on the woman,' cried Mr Artemus Jones. 'What grounds had you for circulating it?'

Mr James retorted that he had not circulated it; he had merely heard that the woman was 'unwell'.

'From whom did you hear about this woman's condition?'

'Mr Capper told me.'

But the story, evidently, was untrue.

Louisa and Philip spent a sleepless night at the Castle Hotel. The day had not gone well. Tuesday could not be expected to go much better, as Mr Jones Griffith had to attend a funeral and so 'an underling' would take the case for the Yorkes. 'Oh, what worry for us!' Louisa was doubly disadvantaged because Ellen Penketh did not appear as a witness, so she had to bear the brunt of the cross-examination herself – and it was of such a *personal* nature. Her battered little dark green cash book with burgundy spine and edges, combed through by both barristers, contained all the private excitement and extravagance of newly married life and motherhood – things such as 'baby's 1st bonnet, 9s' and 'ribbons for him, 2s/10'. Then there was the 'portrait of myself in black dress with amethyst necklet' paid for in August 1906 (£5 10s), along with £5 spent on a portrait of Simon Yorke, then aged two (£5 is around £300 in today's money).

Why wasn't Ellen Penketh called to the witness box? We are by now longing to hear her voice – for her to stand up in court and say her piece. There are big unanswered questions, side-stepped in court, which tantalise. Who was Mr Yorke alluding to as being 'at the bottom of the whole mischief', leading the cook-housekeeper astray? How had Ellen tried to rob her father of £10 (around £600 today)? Had she dosed herself with one of the lead-based 'abortifacients' women could buy for a few pennies at a chemist's shop – or was her 'condition' a malicious rumour of Mr Capper's? And what was it really like to work for Louisa

Yorke? Ellen remains a potent silent witness to the story. A defendant only became competent as a witness in 1899, and many didn't take this option. Perhaps Mr Artemus Jones knew that the 37-year-old Lancastrian cook-housekeeper would not perform well under pressure; that she would instinctively crumple before the Yorkes. Perhaps the story of the missing gold sovereigns did not quite stack up.

At the close of proceedings Jones addressed the all-male jury, drawn from various property-owning locals. He asked the men to consider one question, and one question only: had the prisoner 'fraudulently converted the money to her own use'? There was, he said, no evidence to suggest this. In summing up, he contended that Mrs Penketh had done 'the most natural thing in the world' in asking the tradesmen to 'keep over' accounts until the following month, in the face of Mrs Yorke's grumblings. When the prisoner lost the money, he said, she did not like to speak of it, and hoped gradually to make it up. Indeed, how would she dare speak of it? It was 'quite natural' that she would tell her mistress nothing of this loss.

'She was a poor woman,' Mr Artemus Jones reminded the jury; 'not like her employers and others, idlers on the great highway of life, whose actions would be entirely different.' I imagine the eyes of the male jury sliding from Louisa Yorke (reddish hair, large hat, stout figure encased in black), to Ellen Penketh (slight, handsome, her face a picture of remorse). The final twist of the knife, for the Yorkes, was Mr Jones's reiteration of the cook-housekeeper's wages – the 'princely salary of £45 a year', given to a woman who handled 'hundreds of pounds a month and thousands of pounds in the course of a year. If any woman ever had a chance of fraudulently converting money to her own use,' Mr Artemus Jones concluded, 'it was the prisoner.'

The judge, it appeared, had already made up his mind and he directed the jury thus. From her attitude in the box, he said, Mrs Yorke 'did not seem to be a hard woman, but a kind lady'. He commented on the improbability of the story about the loss of money near the bank at Wrexham. It was not every day, His Lordship remarked drily, that £130 in gold 'rolled about the streets of Wrexham without the police hearing about it.' He also commented on the absence of Ellen Penketh as a witness (which was not strictly correct conduct for a judge): 'If there was any doubt about it, the jury would probably have liked to have seen the prisoner in the box,' he said; 'but for some reason she had not been brought forward as a witness.'

Ellen sat with her eyes cast down. The two warders rested impassively on either side, waiting for the sign to escort her back to prison. The jury retired to deliberate.

XII

'White-Washed By Un-Civil Law'

'The whole affair is scandalous,' wrote Louisa that night. 'All the evidence was against the prisoner, also the Judge, but the Welsh jury said she was *not guilty*.' What rankled most for the Yorkes was the barrister's summing up: *'Idlers on the pathway of life'*, as Louisa recorded it – a phrase never to be forgotten. She was forced to stay in bed until 11.30 a.m. the next day to recover from 'all the worry'. What had gone wrong for them? It had seemed such a black-and-white case: Mrs Penketh 'stole the amount of £500, yet she was let off free, by a Welsh jury. There is no justice at all.' Licking their wounds, the couple left deepest North Wales for the sanctuary of Erddig and the outraged support of their friends. As the *North Wales Guardian* and *Wrexham Advertiser* were trawled for juicy details of the trial (almost a full page in each), there was much muttering about all things Welsh.

'There is a rumour that the jury were bribed at Ruthin,' wrote Louisa, still consumed by the trial four days later. 'There can be no other way of accounting for the miscarriage of justice. We had many visitors and all were very sympathetic.' But the wheels of the big house had to keep on turning. There was a new housekeeper at the helm, a slew of female staff about to leave the following year (perhaps out of sympathy for Ellen, or tarred by association with her), and the difficult matter of a pay rise for staff following the impertinent insinuations of Mr Artemus Jones. The old worry of unsettled servants reared its head again, distracting Louisa from the Penketh saga: 'There is great excitement in the house with regard to precedence among the Servants. I wish these things could be settled without my being worried.'

But for Philip, who had only his charitable institutions, his cataloguing of papers and minimal contact with his two young sons to keep him distracted, the court case bit deep. Not only had their financial difficulties been exposed in public, but to be slandered as 'Idlers on the pathway of life'! The Penketh episode scarred him. He sacked his lawyer, stopped his payments to charities and unsuccessfully tried to close a public footpath through the estate. He became obsessed with setting the record straight. 'Philip is still dreadfully worried about the Ruthin affair and is trying to vent his rage in the newspapers, but none of the Editors care to take it up', wrote Louisa a week after the trial. There was an unsettling liberal wind blowing through society, and an increasingly militant atmosphere between 'bosses' and 'workers'. Tales of outrageous slights against the upper classes were no longer the stuff that sold newspapers.

And so Philip Yorke had to content himself, slightly pathetically, with his great verse marathon in the servants' basement corridor. Perhaps, after all, what mattered most was that the remaining servants took his side and believed in his munificence. Five years later, when the gossiping girls from Ellen Penketh's day had moved on, her epitaph was typed up for all to read, framed within housekeeper Miss Brown's eulogy – whose

. . . coming we may here remark
Brought to a close a period dark,
For long on us did Fortune frown

Until we welcomed good Miss Brown,
One whom this latter did replace
Did for five years our substance waste,
As foul a thief as e'er we saw,
Tho' white-washed by Un-Civil Law.

And what of Ellen Penketh? The trail from here goes cold. 'The accused was discharged', ends the report in the *Wrexham Advertiser*. Discharged to scenes of jubilation and support from her Wrexham friends, it would be nice to think – though it is unlikely they would have managed to make the long journey, let alone the stay overnight. Perhaps Mr Artemus Jones stood her a glass of port wine at the bar of the Wynnstay Arms, as he basked in the familiar glow of another court victory. She won no damages; her reward was her liberty.

Ellen would never work as a housekeeper again – her notoriety, and lack of a character reference from the Yorkes, would surely see to that. She returned to Manchester, to her family, and is found by the 1911 census living at home above the Pendleton shop with her mother and blind sister Mary, listed as a 'Domestic Cook' aged 41. The appalling death toll of the First World War probably robbed her of any last chance at marriage – but it also provided an opportunity for women like Mrs Penketh to break free from domestic service. According to her death certificate she found work as a cook in a Manchester hotel, dying of a stroke at 63 in a state-run old people's home of a thousand beds next to Hope Hospital – the site of the old Salford Workhouse. She died in 1932: four years after women got the vote on the same terms as men.

Louisa Yorke lived through two world wars to die, aged 87, in 1951. At some point she made the very surprising decision to *keep* the small portrait of Ellen Penketh, tucking it into an oval frame on the back page of a family portrait album. Perhaps she buckled before the Yorke family tradition of documentation. Perhaps, with Philip's death (aged 73) in 1922 and the passing of time, she remembered those first five happy years of her married life with more fondness. Mrs Penketh was, after all, a significant part of this era. Maybe the evident unsuitability of her peculiar bachelor sons for the inheritance of Erddig made her wistful for its heyday.

So there it rests, with Louisa's firm hand underneath in ink: 'Mrs Penketh. Cook at Erthig from 1903 to 1907'. The story of her misdeeds passed into family legend, warping with the years until she was recalled by upstairs *and* downstairs as not only 'the thief cook' but the drunkard, too – tales which became the National Trust's official version when Erddig, in parlous decay, was transferred to the Trust by ageing bachelor Philip Yorke III in 1973.[16]

Part 4

Hannah Mackenzie

Wrest Park, Bedfordshire 1914–1915

It wasn't so much her looks – it was her character.

ROSS MACKENZIE, GREAT-NEPHEW OF
HANNAH MACKENZIE

Timeline

1914– The Great War. Some 400,000 servants leave to help the war effort.

1916 The Tango and Foxtrot are the latest dance rage.

1917 'Separate Fastener' or Zipper patented. Cutex introduces liquid nail polish.

1918 Representation of the People Act: all men and property owning women over 30 get the vote.

1922 AGA cooker patented. BBC Radio launched: concerts and news from 6–10pm. First domestic refrigerator by Electrolux.

1923 First fridge freezer by Frigidaire.

1924 The Vac-Tric vacuum cleaner launched.

1926 Toastmaster on sale – first fully automatic pop-up toaster.

1927 The first talking picture, *The Jazz Singer* with Al Jolson.

1928 Women get equal voting rights.

1929 General Election results broadcast on the wireless for the first time (Ramsay MacDonald becomes Labour prime minister).

1930s Corsets and bras transformed by elastic thread, or 'Lastex'.

I

Not A Normal Auntie

In old age, Hannah Mackenzie was remembered for the nicotine stain in her shock of white hair and her fondness for shouting out, in a throaty American accent, 'Now look here, sister!' and 'You bunch of bums!' She was forceful, irreverent, a practical joker and a flirt. In her retirement she consumed one hundred Chesterfield cigarettes and a bottle of Scotch a day – delivered by relatives to her hospital bed in Northampton even as dementia set in. She also, evidently, had great charm.

Her career in domestic service spanned the Victorian industrialist middle classes, the Edwardian conservative nouveau riche, the liberal aristocracy during the Great War and the American super-rich of the Roaring Twenties. She went into service at the turn of the century, when whalebone corsets and gaslighting were the norm. She reached her prime twenty-five years later in a New York palazzo working as head housekeeper to the Vanderbilts, with shingled hair, silk stockings and a six-line telephone system. By any standards of domestic service, this was an unimaginable career for a working-class woman from Inverness.

This story shines a spotlight on one year of Hannah's career – August 1914 to August 1915. It is a snapshot of a great house at an extraordinary moment in time: a critical juncture in British social history. Wrest Park in Bedfordshire was the first country-house war hospital to receive wounded soldiers from the Great War. It was one of many such hospitals, but an exemplary one, and the two women who ran it were among the first in the country to experience what the war actually meant in all its horror. Amputations, gas poisoning, shell shock, shrapnel wounds . . . the Honourable Nan Herbert and her housekeeper Mrs Mackenzie were witness to it all – and it changed them, perhaps fundamentally.

One year after her appointment, with Wrest Park Hospital at the peak of its efficiency, Hannah was forced to resign. 'Downstairs' had become 'dangerous and disorderly', an unhappy place for domestic staff to work – all, allegedly, her doing. What is more, the public-school-educated land agent Cecil Argles had fallen 'violently' in love with her. Housekeeper Hannah Mackenzie was the only thing, Mr Argles confessed, that stopped him from going mad.

In researching Hannah's story I had no idea what, or how much, I would find. Many housekeepers typically left no trail behind them, especially when a great house such as Wrest Park changed hands after the First World War. All I had was one photograph – a formal portrait of two upper servants taken in 1914. The woman with a red cross on her implacable bosom looks at some imaginary point in the sky: this is the cook, Hetty Geyton. The younger, seated woman has an air of poise and composure: so much so, you might mistake her for the lady of the house, were it not for the bunch of keys in her lap. She is, for a servant, remarkably comfortable with the camera.

The Honourable Nan Ino Herbert kept a detailed diary of Wrest Park's role in the Great War, probably with an eye to posterity. Today an annotated version survives with the family, typed out and pasted into a series of scrapbooks first by Nan, then by her daughter in the 1950s. This has since become the official version of events at Wrest Park: a remarkable unpublished archive crammed with small black-and-white photographs. Domestic servants form just a footnote to the narrative, but it's clear that they were a source of upset and constant anxiety to Nan. The real business to her was the war, the wounded soldiers and the smooth running of the hospital. Domestic spats were not meant to be a part of this heroic story. Yet Hannah Mackenzie jumps off the pages of Nan's diary – feisty and strong-willed, a manipulative charmer, attractive to men. What the mistress wrote about the housekeeper is scant, but it is also telling. Here, clearly, was a 'character'. Hannah's audacious story seemed to capture the texture of domestic service during the Great War: uneasy, complicated, explosive.

Piecing together the fragments of her life involved much patient detective work. Biographies, letters, notebooks, census returns, shipping records, dusty archives – I trawled through them all. Once I had narrowed down the census returns to the right woman and sent off for her death certificate, I was astonished to find that Hannah had a living relative in Northampton with a clear memory of her.

Ross Mackenzie, her great-nephew, was born in 1947; Hannah was his favourite great-aunt from a large family clan now split between Inverness, Northampton and Australia. One snowy afternoon, over champagne, Benson & Hedges and egg mayonnaise bridge rolls, Ross told me all he could remember of Hannah, filling in the gaps in her story. It emerged that she went on to work as housekeeper to the greatest American socialite of them all – Mrs Grace Vanderbilt. Wrest Park was just one episode in a colourful career, imparted to the young Ross through well-oiled anecdotes. He remembered her fondness for practical jokes, and the way she 'trotted round London with her handbag' (crocodile skin; a gift from Jackie Kennedy). She smoked Cuban cigars. She could drink a man under the table. She was, in later life, deeply into séances and spirit friends. At her funeral in 1985, two brigadiers were among the congregation. Hannah, in the eyes of her great-nephew, was 'such good *fun* – not like a normal auntie'.

I set out to re-examine Hannah Mackenzie's mysterious disgrace at Wrest Park Hospital during this febrile era for domestic service. 'Settled Hannah's "holiday"', wrote her mistress disingenuously on the last day of August 1915. The house had become 'dangerous and disorderly': what exactly did this mean? Was Mrs Mackenzie a troublemaker? Or was she working in an impossible situation? Hannah's experience and her disgrace were perhaps indicative of an old order crumbling. Up until now, the role of housekeeper had been straightforward, even prescriptive. From the Great War onwards it was not at all so. The war acted as a leveller of hierarchies, and with their collapse the function of domestic staff was no longer so clear-cut – nor did the old servile reflexes come so easily. When a great house changed its use as dramatically as Wrest Park, from indulgent weekend chateau to war hospital, the role of the upper servants became still more unfamiliar and insecure. Mistress vied with matron, who jostled with cook and housekeeper for ascendancy. The kitchen was renamed the 'Commissariat Department'; military men attempted to take over the managerial role of the housekeeper. There was all to play for.

Wrest gained a reputation as the War Office's best country-house base hospital. It patched up the bodies of some two thousand men, sending them back to the Front to fight again until a fire led to its premature closure in September 1916. It was a shipshape place of ruthless efficiency: of timetables, mass catering, delousing and rehousing. It ran like a machine. But it was also a place of knotty and impenetrable human relations. There was passion and hatred in play here at Wrest; chaos and disorder, along with the raw realities of war. At the heart of this tale are our housekeeper, Hannah Mackenzie, the maverick spinster aristocrat she served and the land agent who fell for her. It is also a story about Scots in exile. Intriguingly, the most famous writer of his time, J. M. Barrie (creator of *Peter Pan*), was a benefactor and regular guest at Wrest. He was a friend of the family; was he also captivated by the housekeeper? Everything we know about Barrie and Hannah Mackenzie suggests that this was almost certainly the case.

II

All Expenses Will Be Borne By

Lord Lucas

It is important, first of all, to explain the kind of household that Hannah Mackenzie was about to join, and the unusual brother and sister at its heart. Bron and Nan Herbert were not interested in running Wrest Park as their country seat. They were two young liberals, radical thinkers (albeit with large private incomes), uninterested in a life of idle privilege. Nor had they any interest in beautiful objects, social rituals or domestic hierarchies. Bron Herbert inherited the house in 1905 at the age of 29, along with the title 9th Baron Lucas and 5th Lord Dingwall, on the death of an effete maternal uncle. It was a house he didn't want, and initially he didn't know what to do with it.

There is an air of unreality to Wrest Park, an eighteenth-century-style French chateau built in the 1830s, marooned in the flat farmland of Bedfordshire some forty miles north of London. Built as a pleasure palace, occupied intermittently, the house and all its trappings seemed to belong to another era. Bron was looking forward; Wrest – beautiful, graceful, enchanted – was resolutely of the past. The new Lord Lucas dealt with his inheritance by loaning the pick of its art treasures to the National Gallery and leasing the house to the US Ambassador, who triumphed by enticing King Edward VII to stay in July 1909.

'Down to Wrest', wrote Lord Lucas's sister Nan in her diary in August 1909,

where we wandered about the incomparable gardens and through the empty house, which is filled with all the knick-knacks and little personal belongings and ghosts of two generations ago. How gloriously and selfishly absorbed our grandparents were in their possessions – and what would they have said could they have seen us – Bron a Radical and I a 'Swabby' (as he calls me!) – as their heirs!

(A swabby was a sailor.) When the US Ambassador Whitelaw Reid died in 1912, Wrest Park lay empty, apart from the odd 'gay weekend' for brother, sister and their witty, smart, bohemian circle, 'taking the chef and extra staff with us'.

What was the *point* of these huge houses and their estates? Nan and Bron were no longer sure. Britain was changing. In 1909 the Liberal Chancellor Lloyd George proposed his 'People's Budget' with the express intent of redistributing wealth. There was to be a supertax for the wealthy, increased land tax and inheritance tax – which would in part fund unemployment benefit, pensions and health insurance. The latter reached an unwelcome tentacle into the private world of mistress and servant. Out of the ninepence per week this insurance would cost, the employer would pay twopence and the employee twopence.

Then came the war. 'It is a terrible catastrophe but it is not our fault,' wrote the new King George V in his diary on the night of 4 August 1914. 'Please God it may soon be over & that He will protect dear Bertie's life.'[1] Bertie was the Duke of York, a teenaged midshipman in the navy. 'First and foremost – keep your heads,' advised *The Times* two days later. 'Be calm. Go about your ordinary business quietly and soberly. Do not indulge in excitement or foolish demonstrations.' Finally, 'Explain to the young and ignorant what war is, and why we have been forced to wage it.' This, presumably, included one's servants.

The outbreak of war, as experienced through the newspapers by those who lived 'in the securities of England,' seemed 'immeasurably remote from the real green turf on which one walked,' wrote housekeeper's son H. G. Wells, now 47 and the literary celebrity of his day. His novel *Mr Britling Sees it Through* (1916) tells us how the first two years *felt* for an upper-middle-class household in rural Essex. It became one of the most popular novels of the Great War. Britain had not been at war like this for three hundred years, Wells reminds the reader. War was a thing altogether outside English experience and the scope of the British imagination.'[2] For the first two months Mr Britling was like an 'excited spectator at a show, a show like a baseball match'. It was as if these large estates throughout Britain had been waiting for this awful, yet rather wonderful moment. At last they could prove their usefulness. When Germany invaded Belgium, the gentry rushed to offer their houses to refugees. 'There was something like competition among the would-be hosts', writes Wells; 'everybody was glad of the chance of "doing something", and anxious to show these Belgians what England thought of their plucky little country.'

On the day Britain declared war on Germany, the 5th Duke of Sutherland launched an appeal for country houses where wounded soldiers could convalesce. Two hundred and fifty homes were offered almost immediately, among them some of the country's greatest landmarks – Dunrobin Castle in Scotland, Highclere Castle in Hampshire, Harewood House and Carlton Towers in Yorkshire, Leeds Castle in Kent, Hatfield House in Hertfordshire. It was brilliantly obvious to Bron what he should do: Wrest Park was to become a hospital. With this masterstroke he was able to transform his millstone inheritance into something active and useful. His energetic sister Nan would run it for him; their great friend J. M. Barrie wanted to be involved, too.

Three days after war was declared, Wrest Park was accepted by the Admiralty 'for the use of men (not Officers)'. On 6 August Nan made the two-and-a-half-hour journey by steam train up to Ampthill, Bedfordshire, then was driven by motor car to Wrest where she 'outlined everything' to the outdoor staff and land agent Argles. 'The furniture was being cleared before we left the house. On Friday Barrie gave us £1,000 for the hospital, and I spent the day struggling to form our list of nurses and procure dressings in the face of a thousand other people doing the same!' Writing to a Miss Constance C. Bloomfield at the War Office one week later, Nan informs her that the house is being equipped with 130 beds, 'but 70 more could be procured on a few days' notice, making in all 200 beds. A matron and staff of certified nurses have been engaged, and all expenses of upkeep will be borne by Lord Lucas.' She adds, in deference to Bron's natural reticence and his job as President of the Board of Agriculture: 'We are anxious to keep this offer out of the papers if it can be so arranged.'

This simply was not possible. The story was irresistible: a great country house, a Liberal Cabinet Minister and the involvement of playwright J. M. Barrie. Wrest Park and its war efforts were very much in the papers from that moment on.

III

Apply To Mrs Mackenzie

'They've all gone,' Nan wrote in her diary on 10 August, 1914. All the young officers had quietly vanished to France with their regiments. 'One is talking with a man one day; by the next he has disappeared.' Not Bron, now 38, who was held down by his job in the Cabinet. 'It's ghastly for Bron,' wrote Nan, 'but he is working 15 hours a day, which helps him.' Really, though, it was ghastly for her. 'No news,' but many apprehensions and [at the back] of all the sickening gnawing sense of being left behind.'

Nan was not one to be left behind. She was a restless, independent, fearless young woman in search of a big project. In her twenties she had rejected the Church of England and embraced Theosophy, the alternative religion of the day with headquarters in California. She then served as a 'directress' of a Theosophic school in Cuba, before following the anthropologist, and Balkan expert, Edith Durham to

Montenegro, acting as 'bottle washer' to the Red Cross unit during the Balkan Crisis. At 34, she was still addicted to travel and adventure. The sudden imperative to turn Wrest Park into a hospital was both a gift to a hungry woman like Nan, but also an inhibition. It meant she could no longer keep moving at whim.

Her great friend Angy Manners was busy organising her own nursing party, shortly setting off for Belgium to tend to the wounded. All Nan could do was 'give' Angy a couple of her nurses recruited for Wrest Park. 'I feel disgruntled with everything,' she wrote, 'but perhaps by waiting one will get the real job.'

If Wrest Park Hospital did not feel like the 'real job' to Nan, might this have affected the way she went about recruiting staff? She had little experience of hiring or managing servants. While her cousin Ettie, Lady Desborough, kept fifteen domestic servants (including two footmen) at their London house alone, Nan and Bron had made do with a cook and parlourmaid in Pimlico. Equipping and staffing a great house like Wrest for a speculative future had an air of fantasy about it. Nobody knew how long this war was going to last, or if the country house hospitals were going to be needed at all.

How did the Honourable Nan Herbet find her housekeeper? By the 1911 census Hannah Mackenzie can be found working, aged 29, as housekeeper of a newly built Lutyens mansion in the village of Overstrand on the north Norfolk coast. Overstrand was known as 'the village of millionaires' for its concentration of large new houses and moneyed types who descended during the summer months. The house was designed at the turn of the century for the 2nd Baron Hillingdon, a retired banker and Conservative politician who wanted to make a great statement. Overstrand Hall is impressive, with that Lutyens-esque air of having always been there – all Jacobean timbers, flint and stone facings, brick and tile inner courtyards. It was a house where the social season *mattered*. Queen Alexandra was a visitor to the Hillingdon family, and there were frequent house parties that attracted actors, authors and poets.

Hannah was 32 years old when she arrived at Wrest, either from Overstrand Hall (which was to transform itself into a 'luxurious' nursing home for officers), or from closer to hand; she had family connections in Bedford. It was in some respects a strange job for an upper servant to jump at, since it came with no future guaranteed; but perhaps it appeared as a way of doing *something* in August 1914.

In those first few months of war there was feverish activity among those who were left behind. Women everywhere tried to 'do their bit'. All the women on the Isle of Wight were busy making soldiers' pyjamas. The women of Bedford were stitching hundreds of 'special slippers'. Nan's cousin Ettie set up a work party at Taplow Court in Buckinghamshire: by 11 December, 995 garments had been sent to hospitals and soldiers abroad.[3] Nurses were everywhere in short supply. Thousands of women joined the VADs (Voluntary Aid Detachment), received basic medical training and went to the war zone as unpaid nurses, cooks, clerks, housemaids, laundresses and drivers. Or there were the less glamorous FANYs (First Aid Nursing Yeomanry): women who drove ambulances, scrubbed and disinfected wards, ran soup kitchens and hot baths for dirty soldiers.

The war demanded manpower. A leader in *The Times* called on those employing 'men in unproductive domestic occupations, both in and out of doors' to encourage them to join up – footmen, valets, butlers, boot boys, grooms, gamekeepers. By the spring of 1915 women began to be recruited for the munitions factories; they were not paid the same as the men, but they earned substantially more than they did as maids. In all, between 1914 and 1918 almost four hundred thousand male and female servants left domestic work for positions in the armed forces or to do war-related work.

Loyal old retainers, who couldn't imagine another world or social order, stayed on at most estates. But at Wrest Park there were no loyal retainers, save for head gardener William Mackinlay. He and his team of a dozen old-timers stayed put throughout the war, clipping the verges and pruning the roses of the handsome formal gardens; leading the carefully booted horse and its mower over the acres of lawn, earning 18s, 19s and 20s a week (around £39 to £43 in today's money). There was also irascible old John Land in the gamekeeper's cottage; and in the Lodge, land agent Cecil Argles, 42, who had worked for Bron these past nine years.

There was, however, no resident female staff. Nan Herbert had to start from scratch, recruiting not only housemaids and kitchen staff but nurses too. The most obvious first appointment was the housekeeper, who could then be relied upon to recruit the young girls herself. Within days Hannah was procured, swiftly installed and was placing advertisements in *The Times*: 'Wanted, Scullerymaid. 6 in kitchen: wages £20. Apply to Mrs Mackenzie, Wrest Park Hospital, Ampthill', reads one. Another in the same column seeks a 'Third Parlourmaid, to wait on doctors' and nurses' dining room: wages £20'. Their wages are equivalent to around £860 today, per annum.

There is a wartime photograph of Nan, snatched off guard in crumpled nurse's apron, cigarette in hand, face split by a gap-toothed grin. She does not look like the chatelaine of a country house. Nan saw Hannah as a kindred spirit: someone her age, not over-serious or pompous. Hannah had, so they say, a refreshing (and sometimes devastating) directness of manner. To Nan – uncomfortable with unctuousness and subservience – this felt like an advantage. Certainly Hannah felt the same about her new mistress, who seemed, at this stage, bracingly liberal. No obsequious bowing and scraping required; no head butler to cramp her style. This was going to be a house run entirely by women.

In her diary Nan refers to her housekeeper simply as 'Hannah', rather than the conventional courtesy title of 'Mrs Mackenzie', and is a keen, not unaffectionate, observer of her foibles. (In contrast, Hetty the cook is always 'Mrs Geyton'.) Hannah was Nan's right hand, her lieutenant, in that first frantic month of setting up.

IV

Transformation

The visitor to Wrest Park walks up six stone steps into an elegant, marble-floored oval hall with wood panelling and, above, cavorting white putti. From here, double doors open on to a further, stirringly theatrical double-staircase hall, big enough to hold fabulous receptions, flooded with light from a lantern roof above and hung all around with gold-framed portraits of family and royalty. This hall – the centrepiece of Wrest Park – did not change. Everything beyond it did. Hannah's first job was to oversee the transformation of the house. Ante-library, drawing room, library and print room were to be turned into hospital wards. A team of ageing gardeners and odd-job men rolled up and dragged the fine old Turkish carpets down to the cellars below, along with all of the paintings, eighteenth-century furniture, Beauvais tapestries, swagged velvet curtains and Fabergé eggs. All that the housekeeper was supposed to cherish and conserve as part of her job was gone.

The crystal chandeliers were bagged in white sheets. Wooden ladders went up and walls were covered with yards of pale calico, nailed into place over flock wallpaper and gilded mouldings. Electricity was temporarily installed, lamps dangling the length of each ward. Fireplaces were partially bricked up – much more fuel-efficient (and kept like that to this day). Each of these great rooms opened up one on to the other in an enfilade – an unbroken chain of high-ceilinged space running almost the length of Wrest Park. Twenty tall windows looked southwards on to the elevated terrace, the immaculate French parterre below and eighty acres of eighteenth-century landscaped gardens. The ground floor was to be known as 'A Ward.' The mistresses of other country-house hospitals were more fanciful in their naming of wards ('Cuckoo', 'Nightingale', 'Forget-me-not'). At Highclere Castle Lady Almina insisted that each wounded officer had his own room, down pillows, linen sheets and silver-service dinners. But Nan was an 'A Ward' sort of woman: no-nonsense, pared back, direct.

Using her friend J. M. Barrie's gift of £1,000 (about £43,000 in today's money), Nan set about procuring 130 standard-issue hospital beds (narrow, iron, with wheeled legs) and vast amounts of bed linen and blankets, along with a team of laundrywomen equal to the task. The old Wrest laundry cupboards would not suffice: this required organisation on an institutional scale.

The first-floor bedrooms were converted into 'B Ward'. Four-poster beds, mahogany dressing tables and mirrors spotted with age were carried down the great curving staircases to the basement. In their place, rows of iron beds were arranged to face the windows, creating 'quiet, homely and comfortable' wards with other-worldly, distant views of the dome-topped Pavilion reflected in the still surface of the Long Water canal. The top floor of Wrest Park, up in the eaves, traditionally housed the housekeeper's bed-sitting room and the maids' dormitory. This is where the nurses were now to sleep – but did they require better furniture and effects than domestic servants? These rooms were last furnished in the early Victorian era: they were spartan and of their time (threadbare squares of carpet, beds 2ft 6in. wide instead of the standard 3ft). Yet this was a war, and the nurses were there to serve the soldiers.

This muddying of hierarchies was already throwing up awkward questions for the housekeeper. Should the nurses' beds be less or more comfortable than those of the soldiers? Should they be allowed more, or less privacy than the housemaids? And where did all this leave Hannah Mackenzie vis-à-vis her mistress, who was to work simply as Nurse Herbert – or indeed vis-à-vis Miss Martin of the Metropolitan Hospital, who was soon to be Sister in Command of Wrest Park? There was no precedent for this new order; Mrs Mackenzie was required to muddle through. Nan showed the real order of things by appropriating for herself the sunny, spacious housekeeper's bedroom and sitting room at the west end of the attic corridor. These rooms she filled with precious furniture (including 'the Seaweed Cabinet') and valuable oil paintings (one Claude). 'My jolly sitting room on the top floor' became her lair, her place of retreat from the intensity of hospital life.

Domestic servants were now to sleep in the service wing to the east of the house, a small townscape of buildings twice as long as the chateau itself grouped around a central square. This was the domain of coach boys, grooms, valets and gardeners. Now scullery maids, housemaids, parlourmaids and laundry maids would invade the men's realm – an apt metaphor for what happened on the Home Front during the Great War. For the first time since the wing was built, women would sleep in close proximity to men. The traditional role of housekeeper as moral guardian was going to be impossible to maintain. But, as Nan shrugged, it was wartime. There were different priorities now.

The service wing was also to serve the soldiers as they arrived, shunted by train and motor ambulance straight from the trenches. Nan put the estate carpenters to work converting the stable block into a bathing house and stripping room. All this meant that the maids' bedrooms, the laundry rooms, kitchen and housekeeper's room would be placed very much at the heart of the drama. Those wounded 'Tommies' – their people, after all; the working classes – would enter Wrest Park by way of the servants' quarters.

'A week of unceasing scrimmage of work over Wrest', wrote Nan in her diary on Sunday, 16 August,

with the result that we have the entire place stripped – beds in, walls covered, 20 nurses on the list, extra milk, eggs, vegetables arranged for, sewing organized in the village, cook engaged and stores arriving, and everything so near completion that we could start work on Tuesday or Wednesday, if necessary. Miss Bennett, the matron of the Metropolitan Hospital, arrived yesterday and was ravished by it, as we indeed intended she should be.

There is something of the capable commanding officer in Nan's summary. Might it have dawned on Hannah, at this early stage, that her mistress had not only taken over the housekeeper's private rooms but also her role in management? Equally impressed by Wrest Park Hospital was Dr Beauchamp, friend and doctor to the aristocracy. Sydney Beauchamp had been greatly involved in the setting up of the hospital, and he found it hard to let go. On Monday, 17 August 'he was so carried away by enthusiasm, that he undertook to see Wrest inaugurated himself'. The stage was set – yet Wrest's future still hung in the balance. It had been offered as a naval hospital, but now it did not look as if it would be needed. The Allies were increasingly mired in the bloody business of halting Germany's advance through Belgium and into north-eastern France.

No one quite knew what was going to happen next.

V

Anything To Make The Boys Happy

Wrest Park's call to action came three weeks later. On 5 September Lord Knutsford, chairman of the London Hospital, telephoned Bron at his Commons office and asked if Wrest might be used as a convalescent home for his wounded soldiers. Two days later, sixty-six men were moved from their beds in Whitechapel and sent to Bedfordshire. These were the very first of Britain's war wounded to leave hospital, and the newspapers were quick to put a positive, patriotic spin on the story: 'A party of sixty-six British soldiers, delighted that they were taking another stage in the journey back to the Front, left London Hospital yesterday afternoon for a convalescent home', reported the *Daily News*.

They will be cared for at Wrest, the fine mansion near Luton which Lord Lucas has placed at the disposal of the War Office. In all probability they will be the first batch to face the enemy a second time. As they clambered into the motor-cars lent by members of the Royal Automobile Club they were confidently asserting that in a week at most they would be starting back for France.

The villagers of Silsoe waited all afternoon to see these 'Heroes of Mons'. As the motor cars finally drove past the thatched and terraced cottages, they stared hard at this first physical proof of battle. For them, this was where the war really began. Here were British men with bandaged heads, men with crutches – just one month after their flag-waving departure. It had been hard to take in, this past month of banner newspaper headlines, that Britain was really at war; that 'destruction, and agony on a scale monstrous beyond precedent was going on in the same world as that which slumbered outside the black ivy and silver shining window-sill', wrote H. G. Wells in *Mr Britling*.[4]

After the initial panic buying of food, 'the vast inertia of everyday life in England asserted itself'. 'Business as Usual' became the slogan of the moment, along with 'Leave things to Kitchener'. But here it now was: the proof. The crowds at the estate gates – mostly women and children – waved their Union Jacks and 'cheered lustily', coaxing a smile from the 'dust-stained, khaki-clad visitors.' Their tunics, noted the greedy-eyed reporter from the *Bedfordshire Times*, were 'more or less stained, and bore evident marks of conflict'.[5]

The motor cars purred through Wrest's black and gold gateway, flanked by French-style lodges, along a tree-lined avenue towards the mellow eighteenth-century-style chateau. It was early September and the estate was green, fruit-heavy, hushed. A Red Cross flag floated lazily from the roof. As the soldiers stiffly unfolded themselves from back seats, organised their slings and crutches and limped towards the front entrance, they might well have thought themselves to be arriving at Louis XIV's Versailles.

Perhaps, for these first brave arrivals, the steps were lined with uniformed maids, headed by housekeeper Hannah Mackenzie. More likely, though, the girls were supplanted or obscured by twenty nurses in snowy aprons, collars and cuffs, headed by Miss Martin and Nurse Herbert. And so from the initial, excited anticipation and massed endeavour of all those women at Wrest, the faintest of battle lines began to be drawn. There were the nurses . . . and there were the domestic servants.

The month of September 1914 was to be remembered as 'among the happiest weeks' of Dr Beauchamp's life. It was, in retrospect, a soft beginning for Wrest; a sort of prelude before the ghastly business of war surgery began in earnest. There was a delightful novelty to having working-class Tommies in one's home. The day after the men's arrival, Bron posted a rubber stamp and ink pad for the hospital chequebook, along with some Virginia cigarettes and twelve fishing rods and tackle (a 'source of untold happiness and innumerable wiles', according to Nan). The men, Bron wrote to his cousin Ettie, were said to be 'extremely happy and very jolly'. In the midst of this determinedly upbeat letter he added that his cousin Aubrey Herbert was reported 'wounded and missing'.

There was competition among every woman in the house for 'the boys" approval. These were women who had no children. They were women whose sweethearts were away at war: women far from their families, whose brothers and brothers-in-law were at the Front. They had been working in female domains for longer than they cared to remember. Nurse Piper, Nurse Simpson, Nurse Warner, Nurse Mandler, Nurse Camm, Nurse Riley, Nurse Burdon, Sister Rogers and Sister Martin: all had their own stories. The maids too, those unnamed young girls photographed in kitchen and dining room; all carried private anxieties.

Hannah Mackenzie was one of twelve children, of which there were three brothers. To begin with, first- and second-born William and James, at 40 and 39, were too old to be called up. But 26-year-old Alick, her favourite brother, was sent off to the Front with the Cameron

Highlanders 2nd Battalion after a military career in India. Her older sister Jessie had two sons, both of which were to leave for France: 19-year-old Samuel and William, who signed up in Glasgow just 16 – one of the many thousands of Kitchener's 'boy soldiers' who lied about their age. Her younger sister Nellie, newly married to Lance Corporal Hugh Munro of the Cameron Highlanders, had recently bid goodbye to her husband, like thousands of other women. So Hannah had enough to occupy her mind and was, in the words of her mistress, 'thankful to be engrossed in work'.

The influx of these boisterous soldiers gave Wrest's women an unexpected blast of light relief. You could not go for a walk around the grounds (and there might, these days, be any number of hollow excuses to do so) without coming across a dozen men in khaki or blue sitting along the canals that encircled the gardens. Here, on grassy banks under weeping willows, these young men tried to forget what they had seen in France. A pet swan drifted curiously from fishing rod to fishing rod – and Nan was everywhere with her Kodak box camera (slogan, 'You press the button, we do the rest'), recording Wrest's 'brilliant career as a Convalescent Home'. Dozens of small black-and-white photographs pasted into the scrapbooks show soldiers posing beneath classical Roman statuary; soldiers sitting thigh to thigh with brilliant-white-clad nurses on the steps; soldiers holding up their fishing catches, eels included.

'The astonishing assortment of fish were then carried off to the kitchen,' wrote Nan, 'as old Mrs Geyton could always be prevailed upon to fry them for the men's supper.' Mrs Geyton, she adds, was a 'great character' who (as in most upper-class descriptions of their cooks) 'flung saucepans about when angry, and was inordinately extravagant'. She was also profoundly maternal, doing anything 'to make the boys happy'.

There was fishing, and there was dressing up. No country house was complete without its fancy-dress box; the rage for dressing up among the aristocracy reached a kind of frenzied peak in the pre-war years. Wrest Park's Victorian costume box was unearthed by the 'little cockney', Private Summers – and from that time on evening concerts were 'in steady demand, especially as extra beer was served', wrote Nan, herself a veteran of fancy dress and witty skits. 'We nurses sat on the stairs, the convalescents in the hall singing, reciting and dancing.' And the maids? I imagine them peeping through half-open doors, or craning down from the balcony up high.

During the American Ambassador's time the great Italian tenor Caruso had sung for guests in the grand Staircase Hall. Now, 'Paddy, dressed in a tabard of the de Grey coat of arms, danced Irish jigs in a corner, and Private Whalley in a very décolleté dress with bulging front, pursued Dr Beauchamp to ask him in ringing whispers "about the baby"'.

Hannah loved all this tomfoolery and high jinks. She is remembered by her great-nephew as a lover of practical jokes; a fan of the whoopee cushion, the little packet of itching powder, the stink bomb. When housekeeper to the Vanderbilts in 1920s New York, she would fill the fountains with spent champagne corks just for the wicked pleasure of seeing the butler jump with fright when he turned on the jets of water in the morning and the corks bounced down the marble staircase, *bang bang bang!* (this became one of Hannah's favourite anecdotes). But where, in the new hospital hierarchy, would she have sat? Nan writes of the nurses' inhibitions, 'torn between extreme conventionality and a desire to follow the ways of Mount Olympus (the front seats where Bron, guests and I were sitting), uncertain whether to look embarrassed or to applaud'.

Throughout Britain, working-class soldiers were at that moment infiltrating wealthy homes, chipping away at deeply ingrained social structures. How it must have perturbed the girls' Victorian parents. 'Whatever you do', cautioned one upper-middle-class mother to VAD hopeful Sybil Warren, 'you are not going to nurse. You can go [to the war] as a pantry maid, but not as a nurse.' She did not want her daughter

THE HOUSEKEEPER'S TALE

dealing with the 'lower classes – Tommies'.[6] These boys had shaken up
sedate, provincial England. On Sunday, 16 August 1914 the population
of Bedford doubled when 17,000 Highland Territorials arrived in
town, after an exhausting journey on no fewer than sixty-seven troop
trains. The young men were billeted with Bedford's unsuspecting
citizens (payment 3s for officers, 9d for soldiers, per day). The 'bare-
kneed clansmen' with their pipes and drums shook Bedford 'out of the
doldrums', according to the local paper. The town's young women were
so smitten by these 'strapping, brawny visitors' that there were many
marriages (and babies conceived) before the troops' departure nine
months later. A columnist for the *Bedfordshire Times* – a 'bitter kiltless
civilian' – writes disapprovingly of certain 'things happening in the
dusk' along the riverbanks of the Ouse.[7]

For all that Wrest was a closed world, Hannah Mackenzie was able to
read about the Highlanders in the paper. Their arrival in Bedford was a
huge event – so huge that King George V visited the town that October
to view the Territorials parading en masse with pipes and drums. There
would be a full-blown Highland Games held the following Easter on
the sports fields of Bedford Grammar School, Bron's alma mater. It's
hard to appreciate today, but these were *foreigners*, to those southerners
in a pre-television age, with strange accents and even stranger dress:
sporrans, kilts, spats, hose tops, glengarry bonnets. There was a
continuing obsession with bagpipes in the local press: a total of twelve
pipe bands had arrived in town along with the troops.

Hannah was a Highlander, yet she had spent many years working
in England, seldom making the long journey back home. I can picture
her, seized with a longing to hear the pipes and the drums again,
making her excuses for far-flung shopping expeditions by motor
omnibus to Bedford (a twenty-mile round trip). The occasional scenes
of 'disgraceful conduct' outside the pubs would have transported
Hannah to the mean streets of Inverness and her youth. The rugged
accents of those Seaforths and Argyll and Sutherland laddies made
her realise just how far she had travelled in her thirty-two years. And

yet, at the sound of the bagpipes, an instant lump might have formed in her throat. She was so far from home.

The thin-faced marching men in diamond-patterned hose tops and navy glengarry bonnets brought to mind her favourite brother, young Alick, whose battalion was sent to the Western Front that December. He must have heard good things about Bedford from his countrymen, for he moved there after the war, got married and set up a business selling pianos. Many Highlanders returned to see the women who had looked after them like foster-mothers before their tearful departure by train for the Front. Bedford was the furthest most of them had ever travelled in their young lives.

VI

It Was Her Character

There were the 'boys' – and there were the men.

Hannah Mackenzie enjoyed the company of Tommies as much as any woman, but her eyes were on those who mattered. Lord Lucas was a remote figure in London. Far more important in her day-to-day life was Dr Beauchamp. Sydney Beauchamp, 53, was the darling of private practice: 'his character was one of singular beauty', wrote a friend, remembering how at Caius College Beauchamp was known as 'the Lovely B'.[8] Nan observed her housekeeper's machinations. 'Hannah handled any man of importance with supreme skill', she noted. 'She studied Dr Beauchamp and attended to his needs until she had him tied to her little finger.' Later, when the clipped and precise Major Churton arrived from the War Office as resident surgeon, 'Hannah flew straight to him like a bird.' I look again at that wartime portrait of Hannah Mackenzie and imagine the full force of her charm: the directness of her grey-eyed gaze, the amused yet firm mouth. 'She was attractive to men,' her great-nephew Ross told me; 'it wasn't so much her looks – it was her character.'

There was one other man who demanded very special attention. Nan's diary makes no overt mention of Hannah and J. M. Barrie, but the evidence suggests a keen sympathy, even close friendship between the two. Barrie was the literary and theatrical giant of his day. Aged 54, the previous June he had been made a baronet by King George V (having refused a knighthood in 1909). This same year he made £45,000 (around two million pounds today) from a mixture of plays, revues, sales of books and investments. His name was rarely out of the West End or off Broadway – four one-act plays ran in London during 1914. He was, back then, so much *more* than *Peter Pan* (now in its tenth year and a Christmas fixture), but for all his towering success and wealth he was a very private man.

Barrie was small – just over five feet, with sunken blue eyes, a huge domed forehead and a deep, mournful voice. He was a compulsive storyteller, with his distinctive Scottish accent, beginning his tales with 'I always remember . .' He disliked small talk, preferring to get straight to the nub of the matter. When Barrie went up to Wrest from London for the weekend, the fun began in earnest: cricket, croquet, billiards, theatrical revue, fancy dress – yet there was an intensity about him that could go either way. Biographers describe him as entertaining, charming and immensely generous. He could also be selfish, moody, and proprietorial. He had a habit of planting postage stamps on new friends' ceilings by flicking them up on a coin: there they stayed as badges of ownership. This was very likely his first action on meeting the men of Ward A, because Barrie felt unambiguously possessive of Wrest Park Hospital – just as he felt a fierce affection for Nan and Bron Herbert, friends of just two years. 'I'm hoping, if you have time, to hear from "our" hospital', he wrote to Nan that September.

And then he was among them, shaking the slim hand of housekeeper Hannah Mackenzie, complimenting her on arranging his room in the

'Bachelor Wing' so finely when most of the house had been so very thoroughly institutionalised. 'Ah, a fellow Scot!' I imagine him saying. 'From Inverness, you say? We must talk, Mrs Mackenzie, we must talk. I was in the Highlands myself just this last August, when war broke out you know. Odd to be fishing in the glens at that time …'

Would Hannah have been overawed by him? I don't think so. I see our housekeeper, pink faced, strut back to her office in the basement to tell head housemaid Maggie and Hetty the cook about her new friend Mr Barrie. 'Something special for dinner tonight I think, Mrs Geyton. And a drop of our best Scotch from the cellars.' This is not so very fanciful. Compare the early stories of James Matthew Barrie and Hannah Mackenzie.

Barrie was born in a cramped cottage in Kirriemuir, Angus in 1860, the ninth of ten children. His father David was a handloom weaver, and the family – though upwardly mobile and with a great belief in education – were poor. Barrie was plucked from Kirriemuir by his ambitious eldest brother Alexander and educated in Glasgow, then Dumfries and finally Edinburgh University. After a spell on *The Nottingham Journal*, he caught the train south to London to try his luck.

'There are few more impressive sights in the world than a Scotsman on the make', he once wrote.[9] And of Scottish people who share a home: 'the affection existing between them is almost painful in its intensity'. By 1914, J. M. Barrie could count among his friends some of the greatest talents of Edwardian England: the architect Edwin Lutyens, artist William Nicholson, writers Thomas Hardy, H. G. Wells, Bernard Shaw and Arnold Bennett. That summer, just before the outbreak of war, he dined at the writer Maurice Baring's then walked back with the Chancellor Lloyd George to 11 Downing Street, talking all the way. You could get no higher than this – yet the Kirriemuir boy in him, the Peter Pan figure, was consistently agog at his good fortune.

Hannah Mackenzie was born in 1881 in Inverness, her childhood spent in a succession of streets clustered around the mouth of the city's port: Glebe Street, Waterloo Place, Tanners Lane. Her parents were Jessie and James Mackenzie, a reliably fertile couple who produced twelve children over twenty-four years; Hannah was the fifth-born. Father James was a master shoemaker, an artisan. According to the census returns he had also done stints as a stone dresser, a fruiterer-greengrocer and a 'general labourer'. Jobs were scarce in the Highlands, and with twelve mouths to feed, you did what you could.

The two eldest sons William and James appear in the 1891 census as a compositor (a printer's typesetter), aged 17, and a painter, aged 16. At least three of the Mackenzie girls went into service, working their way to good positions within the English upper classes. In 1901 Hannah, aged 19, had left home and was working for a loom dresser in Lanarkshire as a general domestic servant, the bottom of a hierarchy of four. She moved on, and on again, pushing ever southwards: as many moves as it took to get the top job.

VII

Blood Feud

The story of Wrest Park Hospital – 'Wrest in Beds,' as Barrie liked to call it – has all the right elements for a J. M. Barrie play. As with *Peter Pan* and *The Admirable Crichton* there is an almost Shakespearean removal to somewhere 'other', an Eden-like place apart. For those men who have witnessed the carnage of Liège, Mons and Ypres, Wrest is indeed a kind of Neverland. There is a potentially explosive triangle of the three women in command: Nan Herbert, Sister Martin and Hannah Mackenzie. There will also be a forbidden love affair, intermixing of the social classes, death, and yet more death. Lurking in the background, Prospero-like, is the figure of Barrie – controlling, stage-managing, listening; noting down incidents for future use. (Private Paddy, who slept with a fishing rod so that he might have first chance in the morning, cropped up in the 1917 play *Dear Brutus*.)

If this were a J. M. Barrie play, the first act would now be drawing to a close. Wrest Park Hospital is no longer needed as a convalescent home, the War Office decrees, as there are 'no more convalescents available'. After just one month of 'unbelievable happiness' for all, it closes on 8 October 1914. The curtain rises again on 20 November that same year. On a bitterly cold Friday night a hundred bloody, broken and lice-infested soldiers are being stretchered in, fresh from the Front. There is now an operating theatre at Wrest Park, X-ray rooms and inexhaustible hot water for the line of baths in the stripping room (or 'Louse House'). There are four 'ambulance cars' parked in the stable yard. The hospital has, in this short space of time, moved up a gear. It is now being run on a 'base hospital' footing as a unit with nearby country-house hospital Woburn Abbey. It receives its wounded direct from the Western Front.

The nightmare of the war is being discovered at first hand. With the arrival of the soldiers a direct contact is established between the quiet life of a Bedfordshire village and the grim business of shot, shell and bayonet. Yet the tone of Nan's letters to Bron in London is upbeat, invincible – what one might, in 1914, describe as very *British*.

The work has been terrible, but I begin to see chinks of daylight ahead, and I think in a week it will be going more or less like clockwork. They underestimated the number of nurses needed, and we've had to pour in whatever help we could get; but it's been almost impossible to get even temporary ones . . . The men are *rippers* and are already feeling and looking better, and the wards are beginning to buzz with faint talk and ribaldry.

Where is Hannah in the midst of all this? Mackenzie family legend has it that Hannah once worked as a matron in a war hospital. It's hard to see where she fitted this in (including the training; it took three years just to qualify as a nurse). She was, we must assume, talking about Wrest

Park. She was the housekeeper, but perhaps she *felt* like the matron. The men *saw* her as the matron. She was matronly! Always ready with her sympathetic tone, a rallying quip, a special treat, a cigarette. Whereas that wee slip of a thing, Miss Martin . . . *Matron*? Och, Ward A was in a terrible muddle, that was plain for all to see.

For several weeks there was no time for Nan to write in her diary. She took up her fountain pen again to record the disintegrating relations between staff at Wrest Park Hospital. Miss Martin was the problem. 'Poor Miss Martin now began to show how extraordinarily unfit she was for Matronship, and the inevitable troubles followed,' Nan wrote. 'She tried to please all and in so doing failed to please any; she failed in the handling of the domestic staff, which was natural enough, but also failed to inspire the Doctors with confidence.' There is a photograph of Miss Martin posing timidly in the Italian gardens. All is lush and in full flower; it must date from that 'blissfully happy' month of September, but our Matron looks faun-like and hesitant. The doctors were right: 'poor Miss Martin' does *not* inspire confidence.

'She was always afraid of being short of nurses', Nan continued, and ransacked the country for them. All through those weeks an assortment of nurses came and went – two or three who drank, one who took drugs, stewardesses [kitchen staff] who wanted to do war work, and probationers [trainees] who preferred sharing a chair with a patient to finding an empty one!

Pity Miss Martin – young, anxious, ineffectual – having to assert herself over an attic full of excitable probationers. Nan came to the conclusion, from her vantage point up in her sitting room (perhaps looking down on trysts in the Italian garden), that 'nearly half the nurses were mischievous and at any rate superfluous'.

But this was nothing compared to the terrible relations between Miss Martin and the housekeeper. Nan described it as nothing less than a 'blood feud'. Matron and Hannah Mackenzie were slogging it out for ascendancy, 'neither losing any opportunity to slit each other's throat – Matron clumsily, Hannah with the utmost skill, lashing the men-folk into a state of outraged chivalry on her behalf'. We don't have Hannah's side of the story, so we must imagine the scenario. Their 'outraged chivalry' suggests that Hannah presented herself as victimised, unfairly treated, insulted. Matron was probably presented as sabotaging Hannah's role; denying her authority; even denying her most natural maternal instincts.

Should the soldiers *not* enjoy cut flowers by their beds? Didn't the poor wee laddie from Kirkcaldy get left with not a drop of water one morning? Didn't Mrs Mackenzie have a right to know when Nurse Martin took her luncheon, so that she could keep her eye on those nurses? With Dr Beauchamp now 'tied to her little finger,' Hannah 'steadily fanned his dislike of Miss Martin.' I can hear her voice as she fills a bone-china teacup for the doctor: 'And now Miss Martin is preventing me, *preventing* me Dr Beauchamp – from doing the rounds of Ward A and Ward B with the boys' letters. Aye, aye, I know, I know. Would you credit it?'

Throughout that winter, J. M. Barrie was used by Nan to soothe the staff spats at Wrest Park Hospital. He was a good, sympathetic listener, more interested in the servant classes than those they served (in 1917 he was to write a war play about three charladies, intended to 'make the Society ladies . . . toss their little manes').[10] He gained the reputation of being a 'sensitive arbiter' between the different factions at Wrest. Outwardly, Barrie did not take sides. But he was a man in thrall to powerful women, fixated on his mother, renowned for his dramatisations of the innate superiority of women compared to the weakness, even silliness of men.

The playwright was photographed with the cook Hetty Geyton and her girls in the kitchen, apron on, as if ready to pluck a dozen pheasants. 'What a *ripper*,' as Nan might have said, recording the moment with her Kodak. Did he also regularly cross the flagstone corridor to Hannah Mackenzie's snug seat of power? 'Oh, Mr Barrie!

Well now! What a surprise! And me just finishing my sewing and everything all anyhow . . . Sit thee down, sit thee down, I'll ring for tea.' I can hear her soothing voice with its mournful cadences, barely rising and falling, as she imparts the latest goings-on. And Barrie, hand to drooping Edwardian moustache, nodding sympathetically, one foot on the fender, crumbs of Dundee cake on his tweed jacket.

VIII

A Sedately Married Man

Hannah had a secret. Cecil Argles, Wrest Park's land agent, had fallen in love with her. It might have been wheeled out of her by Barrie's sympathetic manner during one of these imaginary (yet I think plausible) confessional sessions. Perhaps the man in question came to her door once too often in Barrie's presence; perhaps Hannah's embarrassed fluster gave the game away. But really the whole nonsense was an innocent thing at first, and no one could say that she and Mr Argles were not hard at work.

It all started with the accounts books. Hannah Mackenzie was appointed as an efficient, parsimonious, capable housekeeper in the best Scottish tradition – but household accounts were one thing; hospital accounts quite another. Her new role required her to fill out list upon list of minutely graded incomings, outgoings and averages to satisfy not just her mistress but War Office records. Official ledgers from war hospitals of the time are crammed with columns for 'Average Number of Beds available during year', 'Average Number of Inpatients resident daily' and 'Patients' average residence'; moving on to the minutiae of day-to-day expenses such as 'Surgery and Dispensary', 'Salaries and Wages', 'Average cost of Maintenance per Patient per day' – and so on. No wonder Hannah felt faint contemplating these double-page ledgers and the enormous amounts of money involved. No wonder she sought help from Wrest Park's wise and capable land agent.

One accounts sheet survives from this era (May 1915), pasted into the scrapbook: a neat page in fussy, rather feminine writing and signed with a flourish 'Cecil G. Argles'. It is the sort of exemplary accounts page that brings joy to a housekeeper's heart and order to a chaotic regime. This page and others like it were composed in Hannah Mackenzie's basement office at her large leather-topped desk, the two heads close together in collaboration. There was much else to talk over, too, as they discovered. Cecil Argles also came from a large family. He was born the eldest of ten children to Mary Anne and George, later Canon of York Minster. As with Hannah's family, there were three boys to seven girls.

Argles occupied a position of immense power and responsibility. He was employed by Lord Lucas in 1905 and remained in the post throughout the tenure of the American Ambassador, overseeing farms and income not only in Bedfordshire but also at Bron's other estates in Essex, Wiltshire, Leicestershire and Lancashire. He is remembered by his nephew Charles as being 'a somewhat awesome figure' who terrified young nieces with his teasing. In letters he comes across as efficient, sharp-minded and meticulous, yet with that easy manner born of a public-school education.

At the outbreak of war he was aged 42 and married to Muriel, four years his senior. They had one son, Gerry, aged 13. Their daughter Enid had died, aged seven, three years previously. At dusk on midsummer's day, 1914, while driving the heavy estate Daimler back to Wrest Park, Cecil Argles hit a cyclist coming towards him as he overtook a motorcycle. He was driving at 17mph; the cyclist didn't have lights. Harry Chamberlain died that night in hospital – he was a local tax officer, son of an ex-Detective Inspector, a 33-year-old married man with two young children. The inquest entirely absolved Argles, but the trauma and guilt was to scar him for life.

A small, depressed household, then, the numbers made up by four young servants (lady's maid, parlourmaid, cook and housemaid), all living in the substantial Wrest Park Lodge at the gates of the estate. Before its reincarnation as Wrest Park Hospital, Argles ran the show. But since the Honourable Nan Herbert took control, things had changed. Nan was refreshingly straightforward, but she was also highly controlling, didactic and independent. She had a loathing of committees and wanted to manage everything herself, to her own meticulous standards. This led to an exemplary hospital, but it did not always make for easy relations with senior staff.

Argles wanted very much to be involved in Wrest Park Hospital, and not just as land agent. But what could he do? With Nan at the helm – mannish, cigarette smoking, authoritarian – he was effectively emasculated. The two reached a compromise, or understanding, in which Argles would oversee the wounded soldiers' arrival by train and organise their swift transfer to the fleets of ambulances bound either for Woburn Abbey or Wrest Park. Like Nan, he had a flair for organisation.

Midland Railway, Derby, to Cecil G. Argles, Esq., Wrest Park, Ampthill

17 December 1914

Dear Sir,

I find that the ambulance train arrived at Ampthill at 2.22 p.m. and left at 3.35 p.m. The arrangements made were quite satisfactory and I congratulate you upon the smart clearance of the train. We may now look upon the arrangement as permanent.

Yours faithfully – General Superintendent

What drew Cecil Argles and Hannah Mackenzie together? Initially, I suspect, it was a shared antipathy towards their mistress. They would meet for a satisfying little moan, with the coal fire hissing in Hannah's grate, the oil lamp on the table and that dreadfully harsh winter of 1914 blurring the windows with snow. Hannah was a decade younger than Argles. She was irreverent and witty, with a gift for mimicry. Her stories, so her great-nephew remembered, were told with brilliant deadpan timing. She was a warm woman, falling into Argles's upright and respectable life at the right time. Hannah made the estate manager laugh again, perhaps in a way he hadn't for years.

They were obvious allies: two deputies, both being driven slowly mad by the fanatically high standards Nan Herbert set for herself and for the hospital. They weren't the only people to recognise this: J. M. Barrie wrote to Bron in 1916 that Nan 'is so fearfully conscientious about Wrest that her heart gets no rest if everything is not absolutely perfect'.[11]

Nan was bemused by Hannah's popularity with the surgeons and watchful of her. She was also lightly but regularly negative about Argles in her diary. Tellingly, there is not one photograph of Bron's land agent in the Wrest Park scrapbooks where all other staff, domestic and nursing, are meticulously chronicled. The relationship between Nan and her right-hand man was complicated. Argles answered to Lord Lucas; Nan answered to herself. But in the absence of Bron, Cecil Argles was often the only other educated, intelligent man she had reliably to hand. There was friction between them but there was also trust, cooperation and a certain gruff intimacy – for one evening Argles confessed something he might more sensibly have kept secret.

Nan was half tickled, half shocked by what he told her. She'd had no idea, no idea at all. Was she also the smallest bit jealous? How did it feel to learn that stuffy old Argles had a raging crush on her *housekeeper*, of all people, a woman who, at 32, was classed as an old maid (though Nan, at 34, probably thought of herself differently)? Why had Bron's land agent chosen Hannah? In due course it went – discreetly, to save him embarrassment – into her diary. 'A . . . (a sedately married man), in helping Hannah with the hospital accounts, had fallen violently in love, and declared that she was the only thing in life that kept him from going mad!'

IX

Wrest In Beds

I t *was* a time of madness. There was no way of making sense of the abundant horrors of this war from within the gilded environment of Wrest Park – both for the soldiers and for those who helped them recover. Men suffering from shell shock and chlorine-gas poisoning were stretchered to beds facing one of the greatest formal gardens of England. Above them, on the ceilings, they gazed at titillating scenes of embracing, semi-naked girls floating in clouds. Between their beds were French rococo marble fireplaces and pier-glasses with sinuous gilded frames. Doors opened at the turn of an octagonal ivory door handle, a beautiful little object to clasp in one's hand.

The other face of Wrest dealt with scenes such as this:

17 July 1916: '12.15 emergency operation; Dr Kirkwood took off a man's arm. Dr Garner from Ampthill as anaesthetist. Have never seen anything like it', wrote Nan, now fully trained and assisting in the operating theatre as Sister: '– up to the elbow the arm was rotten and blue (gas gangrene). Cleaned up theatre by 2.30.'

There was no time off. Here is surgeon Mr Ewart's timetable for Saturday, 12 August 1916:

1. Walker – Hernia
2. Cleghorn – Paresis of Foot
3. Paul – Ampt. of Toe
4. Leonard – Removal of Plate from Femur
5. Clancey – Shrap. in Knee
6. Hodges – Jaw, wire to remove
7. Pattison – Axilla to stitch
8. Williams – Injury to Perineum

The 'List of Outings' timetable for the same day has fifty men going to Tingrith Manor at 2.30 p.m. 'for tea and games, also cricket match'.

From Wrest the men were sent on to local convalescent homes, where once a month they would be inspected by a captain who would mark out which were fit to return to the trenches. A little leather autograph book survives in the Imperial War Office archives; it belonged to Edith Mary Taylor, a nurse at Wrest Park Hospital in 1916. It is filled with the small, painstaking script of 'the boys': men who had infinite time on their hands to compose their records of the war. Some are gung-ho in tone; many are not.

> Far from the muddy/Dugouts I wont to be,
> Back to Old England/Where bullets wont strick me.
> The man that wants to go/Back shure he is telling a lie.
> *John McKay of the 6th Battalion Oxrs Bucks,*
> *wounded by a bullet in the foot at Ypres, 20 March 1916.*

Private Thomas William Carlton of the 9th Battalion Yorkshire Regiment, a Sunderland boy, cannot even spell his enemy's name:

> We got to Ypres to our sorrow/And it was simply murder
> Because we had to stand both night and day/Up to the knees in water . . .
> Now our Battalion was very lucky/Although we lost a lot of men
> But apart from that we did our best/To keep those fearful jermans back . . .

There is a Private Angus Mackenzie from the 8th Ptt 2nd Infantry Brigade, 1st Canadian Division, called up to help 'the Motherland'. Most of his comrades were now dead:

> Hundreds of that brave band/Have gone from a foreign stand
> Straight to that Happy Land/The Home of the Blest
> But thank the Almighty/There are some now in Blighty
> And this one at Wrest.[12]

They made a big fuss of Christmas at Wrest Park Hospital. It was as if the bottled-up maternal urges of the entire household were uncorked in one ear-splitting pop. Extraordinary to imagine, each of the 130 hospital beds had its own Christmas stocking. Consequently the day began at 3 a.m.,

> when a pandemonium of penny whistles and toy trumpets broke forth, especially from Nurse Mac's little room where she had the three empyemas [fluid on the lungs] – Billows, Rogers and Parker, the latter a very small mild man who was said to have bayoneted fourteen Germans.

There were trick matches and cigarettes, more fancy-dress costumes sent up from London, 'orgies of eating' and a convalescents' band 'braying loudly' on the great staircase. Photographs show the wards crazily festooned with ivy. Costumes are West End quality: J. M. Barrie must have had a hand in securing these. The Herberts' friend Maurice Baring arrived and was hailed as both 'butt and idol' of the boys; Bron was simply their 'hero'. There are pictures of nurses and soldiers, and nurses and surgeons, but none of the domestic staff has made it into the Christmas pages of the scrapbook. Was it Hannah and her girls or Miss Martin and her nurses who wrapped the presents and hung the baubles?

All tried to forget the frightening episode of the week before. Early on 16 December, German warships had shelled Hartlepool, Scarborough and Whitby, killing and injuring hundreds of civilians including children on their way to school. Then, with deliberate timing, a Zeppelin dropped a bomb on Dover on Christmas Eve – the first ever air raid on British soil. 'This is not warfare,' thundered a leader in the weekly *Independent*, 'this is murder.'[13] That year, and for every year after until the war's end, the famous line was cut from productions of *Peter Pan*: 'To die will be an awfully big adventure.'

X

The Supreme Moment

Nan finally got Bron to herself for a long chat in her sitting room on the attic floor. There was so much to be gone through. While she focused on the minute detail ('Statement of problems of carrying on hospital', reads one missive from Nan to her brother) he thought in sweeping, broad-brush strokes ('Don't please worry yourself over it all. This sounds ungrateful, but you know what I mean', he writes back). At times Nan must have felt they were living on different planets, but such was her intense devotion to Bron, she did not complain.

His infectious high spirits were, in any case, a tonic. They restored Nan's pre-war sense of humour – and she had a wonderfully juicy piece of gossip to impart, regarding her housekeeper and his land agent. 'Never shall I forget Bron sinking back helpless with laughter, when I told him this, and gasping between paroxysms, "A of all people, A!"'

Why was Argles's love for Hannah such an object of hilarity for Bron? Was it the preposterousness of the public-school-educated manager falling for a working-class servant from Inverness? Was it that Hannah was way out of Argles's league in looks, youth and charisma? Or was it that pompous, pen-pushing, church-going Argles, with his name vaguely redolent of gargling and gargoyles, had the temerity to enter into a *grande passion* – and claim it to be the real thing?

Cecil Argles was captain of the Wrest Fire Brigade. A photograph shows a small, portly man with protruding ears, slight double chin and a kindly face in shadow beneath the Victorian brass Merryweather helmet. There is something almost feminine about Argles as he stands, small hands hanging passively from what now seems a faintly ridiculous outfit, while the other firemen uncoil the hose and bustle about. The fire engine is a splendid Victorian contraption with gleaming brass work: no doubt he was neurotic about its upkeep.

And then there is Bron, with his inherited wealth, his 'petulant mouth and great wondering eyes . . . like some wild thing tamed and habituated to a garden,'[14] according to a friend. Bron the hero, careering around with his wooden leg (he was hit by shrapnel while reporting on the Boer War for *The Times* in his early twenties), 'just as fine a sportsman as before.' Bron's reaction seems to imply, however obliquely, that adventures of the heart are reserved for the Brons of this world, and not for the likes of Cecil Argles.

Nan's response to Hannah's apparent love affair is also interesting. 'It was, I suppose', she writes in her diary, 'the supreme moment of her life.' I imagine Nan covertly watching her housekeeper queening it; observing with some amusement Hannah Mackenzie supremely in control of this 'sedately married man' who has fallen under her spell. Yet there is also the slightly sneering, patronising assumption that a servant has to take what crumbs of romance might fall her way. The implication is that if this was a 'supreme moment', it was rather a poor one in the eyes of Nan (veteran of the Balkan Crisis, friend of political activist Emilio Bacardi, traveller, heiress, adventurer . . . and spinster). Her housekeeper hadn't caught a man before, and was probably unlikely to in the future. It was her last and best chance.

But it was, of course, ill-fated.

By the new year of 1915, Nan was on the warpath. There was 'general strafing' if the maids were caught serving breakfast late; there were military-style timetables pinned up for the benefit of probationers – 'The men are to form in line at 7.25 and march to breakfast in charge of the NCOs', 'Wards inspected by nurses 8.45 a.m.', and so on. At the same time that the British Navy was bombarding the Gallipoli peninsula, Nan decided it was time to tackle Miss Martin the Matron. 'It was obvious that a change would have to be made', she wrote, yet she quaked at the prospect of having to make it. 'Informing Matron was the first and worst step to take, but no sooner had I commenced to inform her when she stopped me: "I know what you are going to say, Miss Herbert, and I agree that it is best." No words can express the admiration and gratitude I felt.' Nan was to 'step into the post experimentally, and retain it subject to approval of the medical staff'. So she was to be on trial as matron in her own house, *officially* running the hospital she had unofficially been running before. Even she was daunted at the responsibility. 'My dream that night of a huge wave, breaking high over my head, expressed my feelings.'

Was this what Hannah Mackenzie had wanted all along, with her campaign against Miss Martin, or did it come as a surprise? Would Nan now be more involved with the medical side of things, and less obsessed with the housekeeping? Initially, this was so. Nan turned her attention to the 'mischievous' and 'superfluous' nurses, dismissing troublemakers and putting three formidable women – Sister Ife, Sister Rogers and Sister Warner – in charge of Wards A, B and C.

Three more senior women for Hannah to negotiate – but also five more men to wrap around her little finger, now that Dr Beauchamp had returned to his practice in London. The suave, black-haired chief medical officer Dr William Kirkwood and his four surgeons Mr English, Mr Ewart, Mr Hett and Mr Cargill arrived. The hospital became yet more proficient in its patching up and turning around of wounded soldiers, clearing them off to convalescent homes and admitting fresh cases more frequently than ever before. It began to gain a reputation within the War Office for impressive efficiency.

It is often said that housekeepers ran these big houses 'like a sergeant major', orchestrating their smooth management with 'military precision.' The housekeeper's office was like a war office, from which she plotted and manoeuvred with pen, ink and trusted personnel late into the night. Bit by bit, Hannah had found these satisfactions taken off her hands. First, the household treasures had been removed

– the antique furniture, the books, pictures and window drapes – thus denying her the housekeeper's essential *craft* in their upkeep. Next came Nan and Sister Martin, interfering with her staff. Then Mr Argles was doing her accounts, even if this was a boon.

And now a most unwelcome new face – a man – had been introduced into her territory. With the arrival of Sergeant Major Kingsley, life began to get even more circumscribed for Wrest Park's housekeeper. He was brought into the house in May (at Bron's suggestion) to deal with the mounting office work and with convalescing soldiers, prone to misbehave. An old non-commissioned officer, he was an imposing man, tough-featured, mustachioed and brusquely military in manner. It was a source of personal satisfaction that, out of the 1,600 men who passed through the hospital under his watch, there were only eleven cases of 'breaking bounds'.

Sergeant Major Kingsley is photographed writing with intense concentration at a leather-topped desk in the old butler's pantry. There was now no possible excuse for collaboration between Hannah Mackenzie and Cecil Argles. The household they had run between them, however imperfectly, was under scrutiny.

XI

Dangerous And Disorderly

The spring and summer of 1915 brought death upon death to Nan and Bron Herbert's circle. First, and most distressingly, Barrie's adopted son George Llewelyn Davies died at the Front on 15 March, killed by a bullet through the head while listening to instructions from his colonel. He was 21 years old. Barrie received a letter from George two days after his death. As he wrote bleakly to a friend, 'This is now the common lot.'[15] A week after George's death *Rosy Rapture* opened in the West End, but the playwright wasn't present for the first night. Instead Barrie took George's brothers Michael, 14, and Nico, 11, to stay at Wrest Park – it was the best place he could think of in the circumstances. Wrest's domestic servants were stricken by the news. George – exquisitely mannered, handsome, athletic – had been doted on during his visits. Barrie's whole demeanour changed almost overnight. There was a 'deep hoarded sadness in his blue eyes', remembers his personal secretary Cynthia Asquith; 'an impenetrable shell of sadness and preoccupation.'[16] I can see Hannah's mouth tremble as she clasps his hand. 'Oh Mr Barrie. It is a terrible thing.'

More and more headline news was affecting those at Wrest Park Hospital. On 18 May Prime Minister Herbert Asquith, fiercely criticised for failures such as the munitions shortage and the abortive attack on the Dardanelles, asked his Liberal Cabinet to resign and a coalition government was formed. 'As far as I am concerned', wrote Bron to Nan, 'it is a happy release.' Despite his age (39) and his wooden leg, Bron pulled the necessary strings to join the Royal Flying Corps and train as a flight commander.

On 26 May their cousin Ettie lost her 27-year-old son Julian Grenfell, who died at Boulogne Hospital with a splinter of wood in his brain. Two months later his younger brother Billy, 25, was killed at the Battle of Hooge. 'I feel as if all the scaffolding of life was crashing about me daily', wrote Maurice Baring to Nan.[17]

In any war the human response to horror, anxiety and grief is often to act in extremis. Norms of behaviour get forgotten. Opportunities are clutched at wildly. Confessions are made; risks are taken. Falling in love, however inappropriately, might have seemed to Hannah Mackenzie and Cecil Argles the only way of forgetting the nerve-jangling uncertainties of the time.

Photographs taken by Nan in the grounds of Wrest Park during the summer of 1915 depict a slightly crazy fairground atmosphere. While Zeppelins began their raids on London, uniformed soldiers were photographed astride 'Major Wingfield's camel' – a pale, proud beast with one hump and fuzzy pelt; or sitting six abreast on small donkeys and Shetland ponies (all hunters having been requisitioned for the war). Others are dressed as women (a very beautiful, slim 'nurse' coyly holds the hand of laughing young Nurse Cockburn), or posing in medieval tights and tabards. As the weather grew warmer, hospital beds were dragged out to line the wide terrace outside Ward A. Here, handsome soldiers lounged under improvised shades like subalterns in some colonial outpost. It was a summer of camel rides and amputations; of poisoned lungs and bowling parties. Nothing was remotely normal any more – although the *Bedfordshire Times* tried hard to keep a rousing, patriotic tone as it reported each and every event at Wrest Hospital, Silsoe.

'On Saturday a cricket match took place in the splendid grounds of the hospital between teams representing the Mother Country and Colonials. It was a splendid game, played in the sporting spirit that soldiers love, and was greatly enjoyed. The Mother Country won by 74 runs.' The Greenfield troop of Boy Scouts 'were allowed to distribute the cigarettes among the soldiers.'

Away from the cricket and croquet matches, the oompah tunes of the Ampthill Camp brass band and the gimlet eye of Sergeant Major Kingsley, Wrest was a paradise for lovers. It was here that Nan's cousin Ettie learnt to flirt so adroitly at house parties in the 1880s and 1890s. 'You never came to an end of the lovely surprises in those huge pleasure-grounds,' she wrote; 'the little hidden pavilions, secret Lovers' Walks, Chinese hedges, the long canal encircling all.'[18] Arthur Balfour, writing to a female friend in 1891, depicts Wrest as the perfect setting for clandestine assignations: 'Shady alleys, delicious yew thickets, ponds, summer houses and gardens make it perfect for all conversational purposes. Every taste, and every "*systeme*" is suited.'[19]

How far did Cecil Argles dare pursue his passion for Hannah Mackenzie? Or was it, rather, the other way round – was Hannah the corrupting influence on this married man? She was, according to her great-nephew, a woman who 'did things to excess'. She drank, she smoked, she pushed a joke to its extremes. She lived life boldly. Hannah was now 33 years old, but she did not fit the contemporary image of spinster. She was a dab hand at making scones and Scotch pancakes, but she was not one to knit or read mind-improving books in her spare time. 'An old maid is only an old maid when she makes up her mind that she is one and gets upon her shelf unaided', ran an article in *Woman's Life*, 1920, in response to the acute shortage of marriageable men after the war. 'Girls get married so late in life sometimes that no one can really be called an "old maid".' Cupid's bow and arrow are waiting for everyone.'[20]

The stereotypical spinster housekeeper was required to keep an eye on her girls: to safeguard their virtue vigilantly. Yet that summer of 1915, Hannah Mackenzie's focus was not on her housemaids, and her mistress spent most of her time in the operating theatre. With no one to peel those young maids away from girl-starved Tommies and push them back to their duties, the domestic harmony of Wrest Park Hospital began to unravel.

I would love, at this point, to produce a snapshot of a forbidden moment under the weeping willows. Dusk is falling: Argles turns, trembling, to Hannah, pulls her slim waist towards him, speaks of his passion. And there is Nan, slowly stalking them with her Kodak, her matron's apron stained at the hem with cut grass – Nan the hunter, who later writes of 'a most marvellous rabbit stalk' in her diary.

But I can't. We do not know what led to Hannah's downfall – whether there was a specific unforgivable incident. It's possible, of course, that our housekeeper did not reciprocate the land agent's feelings; that she was embarrassed by his attentions; that his spaniel eyes were the talk of the basement corridors and it was undermining her authority. It appears that the violence of Argles's crush had, in the end, made Hannah's position untenable, just one year into the job. Nan's daughter paraphrases this part of her mother's diary in the scrapbooks. She (or Nan) is tight-lipped, and the language she uses is extreme. But what exactly did she mean? 'In 1915 the domestic situation had become dangerous and disorderly and it was obvious that Hannah Mackenzie would have to be replaced.'

It is unclear whether Hannah herself is the cause, or whether she is unable to handle the insurrection. Probably it was a combination of the two. On 1 July the housekeeper was forced to place two advertisements in *The Times* to replace the scullery maid and third parlourmaid, teenage girls who had fallen foul of the regime. Did the word 'dangerous' hint at sexual impropriety?

It was the *disorder* that Nan, in the final analysis, could not bear. She was fanatically systematic and she would not have her 'A1' hospital compromised from the basement up. Yet she was not a natural manager of people, and as with the sacking of Miss Martin she could not bring herself to have an honest chat with Hannah. First Nan waited until Hannah's ally J. M. Barrie left for Scotland on holiday (where he found it 'as bare of population owing to this war as if this were the month before Creation').[21] Then, seeing that there were very few wounded soldiers coming in, she decided to close the hospital for a month for general repairs. This gave her the plausible excuse she needed to talk to Hannah Mackenzie.

If this were a J. M. Barrie play, our second act ends abruptly with the denouement between Nan and her housekeeper. 'August 30 1915: Settled Hannah's "holiday" and installed King in catering department. All day job.'

XII

Up In Smoke

Hannah was replaced, elbowed out, by a man. Nan had been plotting it all along. Mr King was her excuse, her trump card. This was a hospital now, not a country house, and it had to be run along War Office lines. Nan needed to be surrounded by professionals who understood such things, and an old-fashioned housekeeper was no longer appropriate. Hannah was duly paid off, her staff fed the unlikely excuse of an extended holiday. Argles returned from his own short summer holiday to find King – a portly, white-haired ex-head steward from the Orient Line – at Hannah's desk in the housekeeper's sitting room. His effects were on the mantelpiece. A masculine smell of Macassar oil and tailoring filled the room.

This was a fait accompli of Nan's. Housekeeping, and Mrs Geyton's kitchen, now fell under something called 'the Commissariat Department', and it was to be run, with bureaucratic efficiency, by a man. Nan, who was at heart one of the boys, had surrounded herself with men. She dined with five surgeons and a Sergeant Major. She gave orders to an ex-ship's steward. But land agent Cecil Argles, who had become increasingly contrary and opinionated, was not a welcome part of the new regime. I suspect he never forgave her, as their relationship soured from that moment on.

King ran Hannah's domain for one year, then died of a heart attack. He is eulogised in Nan's diary for running 'one of the happiest and most successful departments in the hospital', his death causing 'the deepest regret at Wrest, as all realised how wonderfully and capably he had assisted the Hospital. So successfully had King systematised the catering,' she continues, 'that it was by now almost a matter of routine.' She decided to hand the job over to her secretary, Mrs Barrett – 'a really capable responsible woman' – who found the hours 'long and exacting' but the work 'less difficult than anticipated'. From this we might deduce that Hannah made the place unhappy and ran it sloppily and badly; that she was incapable, irresponsible and, intellectually, wasn't up to the job.

The swift, final act of 'Wrest in Beds' begins one year later. Our house-keeper long departed, Nan is on the prowl early one evening. She thinks she smells smoke but cannot find its source. Finally she sees, with a kind of calm detachment, 'a most exquisite pattern of blue smoke frills outlining the slates. So it had come!' On 14 September 1916 a chimney fire broke out in the eastern end of the roof of Wrest Park. There were 150 patients resident at the time. As Nan sounded the alarm, domestic staff appeared 'with puzzled, resentful faces at what they evidently thought was "one of Miss 'Erbert's antics 'aving drill like this"'. She put them to work dragging out the precious contents of the cellars through the great window of the stewards' hall.

While the nurses evacuated the patients, Nan and forty men ran up to clear the attic floor of all valuables, even as smoke clouded the eastern end. Everywhere, water from the hoses of Hitchin Fire Brigade (drawn by three horses abreast) and London Fire Brigade (motorised, with a 'great show of headlights') was 'dripping down the inside walls and streaming down the stairway into the Hall, several inches deep, and gushing along the passages and spluttering down the stairs into the basement'.

Nan paints in her diary an intensely vivid scene – no doubt because she knew that this was the end, and she wanted to remember every detail: the men grouped haphazardly outside in their red-blanketed beds like 'a garden of scarlet geraniums' in the dusk; the 'shouts of delight and excitement' when the firemen managed to pump water from the fountain basin. The only mention of Captain Argles and Wrest's own fire brigade are his 'bitter remonstrations' when she nabs some of his men to help her move furniture. By 10 p.m., with half the roof collapsed and two-thirds of the upper storey burnt, the fire was brought under control. The house was salvageable, but this was the demise of Wrest Park Hospital.

The next day, head housemaid Maggie and her squad 'toiled at cleaning' those parts of the house which were reasonably dry. There was no keen-eyed housekeeper to direct them. The Staircase Hall, scene of all those evenings of entertainment, was twelve inches deep in water. The fire was reported in detail in the national press, and letters began to trickle in from soldiers all over the country who had stayed at Wrest Park Hospital. Hannah, too, would have read the reports and been shaken: all that teamwork, all those memories, good and bad – gone up in smoke.

'My dear, what a bloody time you must have had', Bron wrote to Nan from the Royal Flying Corps in Cirencester. 'It's rather disappointing that it's not more burnt. We could have collared the insurance money and sold the land as farmland. Perhaps we could do that still. Is it worth repairing it?'

Two weeks later, Nan saw her brother off for the Front at Charing Cross station. 'I went back to the cab to get something which had been left, and when I came back saw Bron standing by the barrier, looking utterly radiant and as if bathed in glowing light. I felt stabbed through the heart by the premonition that I should never see him again.' She was right. Within a month Bron was reported missing, having flown his two-seater biplane over German lines. J. M. Barrie wrote the obituary for Lord Lucas – 'Bron the Gallant' – in *The Times*: 'No ill will, I am sure, to whoever brought him down, but rather a wave of the hand from one airman to another. There is still that sort of chivalry on both sides in the sky.'[22]

Nan's diary stops abruptly at her beloved brother's death. Subsequent letters show that relations between Cecil Argles and his new mistress – now The Right Honourable Baroness Lucas of Crudwell and Dingwall – deteriorated rapidly. The sale of Wrest Park – decided on by Bron straight after the fire – was fixed for the summer of 1917. 'Argles was to start looking at once for another post', Nan had noted back then. Letters to her lawyer Mr Surtees refer to the 'private spite' of Argles against Land, the gamekeeper, as well as 'the trouble between A and myself'.[23]

In September 1917 Wrest Park was bought by John George Murray, a brewing and mining magnate from the North-East: a war profiteer. Unpopular with the villagers, and knowing nothing about the running of a great estate, he kept Argles on as his land agent. Nan successfully fought for their old gamekeeper Land to keep his cottage, fearing some kind of retribution since 'Argles is remaining in the neighbourhood (and apparently in authority)', as she wrote to Surtees. She was controlling – and conscientious – to the last.

Six months later Nan surprised everyone by marrying Lt. Col. Howard Lister Cooper, a friend of her brother's, owner of a 'darling' Stellite car and one of the few men in her circle to survive the war. She was 36 and lucky to find a man; two million women remained single after the Great War. The couple moved to Wiltshire, brought up Anne Rosemary and Rachel and lived the 'sedately married' life she had once disparaged.

Cecil Argles remained land agent at Wrest Park for some years, increasingly disturbed and aggrieved by what was happening. The Essex Timber Company felled many of the great trees, and the estate was finally sold in 1939, in disrepair, to the Sun Insurance Company for use as their wartime headquarters. His son Gerry produced no children – but Argles, being Argles, kept busy. To atone for the death of that young cyclist, still heavy on his conscience, he sat on the committee for the first Highway Code in 1931. He lived not far from Hannah, in the end: she in Northampton, he and Muriel in Wansford, Huntingdonshire. It is just possible that they met again, many years after that strange time at the start of the First World War when life was lived at a heightened pitch.

XIII

Hannah Triumphant

It is not remembered where Hannah Mackenzie spent the remainder of the war. It is thought that she stayed on in Bedfordshire in domestic service. Whatever she did, she found the time and confidence to start another relationship with a man roughly her age – a man who was then picked off by the Military Service Conscription Bill of 1916 which demanded that men aged 18 to 41 sign up. Hannah's unnamed sweetheart did not survive the war.

The Mackenzies, like all families, bore their losses. Younger sister Nellie was widowed on the first day of the Battle of Loos in Flanders, September 1915, a month after Hannah's departure from Wrest. Nellie was pregnant. Baby 'Vermelles Hughina Munro' was named after the cemetery where her father lay, near the battle that took his and 50,000 other British lives. Two years later Hannah's older sister Jessie lost her second son William at the Battle of the Somme, 26 November 1917. He was 19 years old.

Hannah's response to the bleak post-war years of poverty, strikes and unemployment was typical of her chutzpah. On 25 November 1922, aged 41, she left her brother Alick's house in Bedford and set off by train for the Liverpool docks with two friends, Ethel Nobbs, 23, and Jessie Quarry, 35, both domestic servants. Here they boarded the *Titanic*'s sister ship the *Adriatic*, White Star Line, for the thirteen-day crossing to New York. Two years later she was photographed at a studio in downtown Greenwich Village, close to the First Presbyterian Church where the Scots in New York congregate. Her great-nephew Ross still has the portrait.

This 43-year-old Hannah is stouter, with a daring shingled hairdo and fashionable 'barrel line' dress falling in soft ruched waves from her hips. She still has that poise; that quiet air of self-possession. And something else: a hard-won satisfaction. The look in her eye in this portrait of 1924 might say to her old employer Nan Herbert, that no, Wrest Park was not the 'supreme moment' of her life. There was far, far better to come. Clearly Hannah was none of those things – sloppy, stupid, chaotic – that were levelled against her at Wrest. Or perhaps she was: but only momentarily, in the madness of love and war. Hannah must have been a class act among housekeepers, for she ended up working for the most famous party-giver on Fifth Avenue.

There was a certain snobbery attached to having a Scottish house-keeper (thought by many to be the best), which might have proved irresistible to Mrs Cornelius Vanderbilt III. The 'top-flight hostess of her era' was addicted to a lifestyle that had all but fizzled out in the post-war world. "They just went on the same."[24] She would routinely spend $300,000 a year on entertaining; guests included the Queen of Spain, the King of Siam, Lord and Lady Mountbatten, the Duke of Kent, Herbert Hoover and Winston Churchill. She moved between the vast, Italianate mansion at 640 Fifth Avenue with its thirty liveried servants in Vanderbilt maroon (now the site of the department store Bergdorf Goodman), the family's Rhode Island summer house, The Breakers, and a three-month stint in London followed by Kelso Castle in the Scottish Borders every summer, with full retinue of staff in tow.

Grace Vanderbilt was in thrall to all things English – from her monogrammed linen, to her marriage hopes for her children, to her servants. Each summer she set about poaching the staff of her upper-crust English hosts. In 1927 she persuaded Prince Arthur of Connaught's steward to become her butler; Stanley Hudson was to stay with her for twenty-five years, remembered by fellow servants as 'a stalwart, heavy British, very true to his calling.'[25] I like to imagine Hannah Mackenzie falling under the scrutiny of this 52-year-old Queen of Fifth Avenue, perhaps at an efficiently run 'Saturday to Monday' country-house party in Bedfordshire in the summer of 1922. Or perhaps she came recommended by her old friend J. M. Barrie, a regular at Mrs Vanderbilt's famous soirées when in New York.

Working for the Vanderbilts – the American equivalent of royalty – was exacting. Grace did not pay high wages, and her servants were 'expected to do their work to perfection'.[26] There was little time off, but few left her service. She knew, said her son, 'exactly what she wanted and how to give directions'. She expected the same firm hand from her housekeeper. It seems that Hannah – 'Mrs McKinsey' as the Americans called her – delivered the goods. For chauffeur Howard 'Happy' Grant, one incident stood out. On a Saturday night in the summer of 1926, four years into Hannah's sojourn in America, Grace Vanderbilt gave a big dinner party at The Breakers, her in-laws' sumptuous mansion at Newport ('The Breakers was the ultimate', said Happy). The two young footmen in maroon livery flanking the door suddenly started fighting. 'In the meanwhile the guests are arriving. And there was a Mrs McKinsey', remembered Happy, 'who was then the housekeeper for Vanderbilt. And she came to the front door and she said to the head chauffeur, she says, "Well, Mr Sanguine, will you break this up?" And he said, "No, I got nothing to do with this".' So Hannah herself waded in. The men, a footman and Mr Vanderbilt's valet, were fired the following Monday.

The Vanderbilts lived and entertained on a scale unimaginable in post-war Britain. Mrs Vanderbilt threw a ball once a month. Twice weekly she hosted dinner parties for a hundred people. On a daily basis she gave 'smaller' dinners and brunches for up to fifty. One hundred people would 'drop in' for tea on Sundays, making the house feel 'like Grand Central' (according to her antisocial husband Neily, 'the General'). There were six footmen in maroon breeches and jackets with white stockings and buckled shoes. There was the obligatory highly strung French chef, Charles Massé, who would spoil the staff with 'individual shepherd's pies in little dishes, lemon meringue pies and little tartlets'. (The servants, it is remembered, loved their desserts.) The bed sheets were changed *twice a day*; a bath towel would be used once and once only. It was like running a five-star hotel.

When the family moved to Rhode Island after the New York opera season, a fleet of hired vans moved the Steinway, the Gobelin tapestries, the gold service and the trunks of Vanderbilt silver with them. The house at 640 Fifth Avenue was shut up for the summer; 'everything had to be draped and everybody pitched in,'[27] according to chambermaid Norah Kavanagh Sarsfield. Norah had made the journey over from Ireland in 1926, steerage class. She described the house rules for a lowly chambermaid thus: 'You don't cross the housekeeper ever. That is a mortal sin. You stay out of the way of the family. But you're right there at a moment's notice when the family wants you.' 'Mrs McKinsey' by all accounts, ran a tight ship below stairs. Norah learnt 'very early' not to cross her; 'that was a rule. You followed to the T what the housekeeper wanted you to do. You did it, and you kept your mouth shut.' If you didn't, you were out. But there was also 'great camaraderie' among the staff. Servants ate the same food as the Vanderbilts, drank the leftover champagne and when the family was away, the kitchen maids and footmen would roller-skate around the 'humungous' kitchen. Young Irish maids Norah and Mary remembered once being 'intoxicated' while on duty. And their housekeeper, for all her formidable manner, kept her sense of mischief – the way she put those champagne corks in the fountains, giving Hudson the butler the fright of his life when he turned on the water jets each morning! *Bang, bang, bang!*

Hannah returned to England in the mid-1930s with an American accent and an extraordinary stock of first-hand anecdotes about the likes of Lillie Langtry and Lady Docker. More importantly, she brought back from New York a tremendous confidence, which signalled the end of her career in domestic service. She took on a boarding house on Fellowes Road in Hampstead, her tenants eventually to include two brigadiers and an alleged German spy. When the Blitz made her living too dangerous she moved to Northampton to look after brother Alick, who'd lost his leg falling down a lift shaft during a blackout. Having installed a large American-style fridge, there she stayed, the classic spinster-sister housekeeper figure – and yet nothing like that in spirit.

Even in old age, as great-nephew Ross remembers, Hannah was formidable trotting around London in feathered hat, fox fur and pearls, taking tea at Jackson's of Piccadilly where she was treated like family. In a large deed box initialled 'H.M.,' she kept her stocks and shares certificates for gold mines, Scottish & Newcastle breweries and British American Tobacco (given to her by the Vanderbilts). Ross has the box still: dark brown crinkled Moroccan leather made by J. C. Vickery of

Regent Street – a shop with so many royal warrants that this was surely another gift from Mrs Vanderbilt.

By 1981 Hannah was resident at St Crispin's Hospital, Northampton – one of Britain's last long-stay hospitals for dementia sufferers. Here the *Northampton Chronicle & Echo* caught up with her and took her photograph: 'A glass of champagne for Miss Hannah Mackenzie, who reached her hundredth birthday at St Crispin's Hospital on Monday', reads the caption. 'She enjoys a glass of whisky and a cigarette, too.' By then she wasn't able to tell them her story – but, almost inadvertently, the local reporter got it right. Even with dementia, Hannah still liked the good things in life. She died two years later, aged 102.

Part 5

Grace Higgens

Charleston, East Sussex 1920–1971

I cannot regard Grace as anything but a family appendage.

DUNCAN GRANT

Timeline

1931 – Five per cent of England and Wales employs a resident domestic.

1933 – Dettol, antiseptic liquid, goes on sale.

1935 – Penguin brings out paperback books at 6 pence each.

1936 – George V dies. Edward VIII succeeds and abdicates.
George VI becomes King.

1938 – First electric steam iron.

1939- – The Second World War. Half a million women employed by
1945 the armed forces.

1939 – Instant coffee first available.

1940 – Ration books introduced.

1943 – Conscription of all single women aged 19 to 24.

1946 – The biro invented.
Family Allowances introduced for the second child onwards.

1947 – Education Act: school leaving age rises to 15.

1948 – National Health Service founded.

1949 – Family Planning Association clinics open at the rate of
five weekly.

1951 – 0.72 million servants in England and Wales, a fall of 46 per cent.
Britain's first automatic washing machines.

1953 – Over 20 million people watch Elizabeth II's Coronation on
television.

1959 – The Morris Mini-Minor goes on sale for £500.
First Spanish package holiday: 15 days in Majorca for 55 guineas

1960 – Contraceptive pill available to women.

1963 – 'She Loves You' by the Beatles.
Assassination of President John F. Kennedy.

1966 – England wins the football World Cup.

1971 – Upstairs, Downstairs airs on ITV.

Forty-Four Little Books

I

Here is a different story. Our housekeeper occupies not a grand country house but a ten-bedroomed, isolated farmhouse at the foot of the South Downs. She has none of the obvious trappings of power: no black dress, no keys around her waist, no wood-panelled sitting room with fireplace stoked by a cowed young maid. There is, in fact, no retinue of underlings to keep in line: she has just the house (damp, decaying) as her gruelling charge. She lives in close proximity to her mistress, eventually to share a familiarity unimaginable to previous generations on both sides of the class divide.

The tale of Grace Higgens is a story of loyalty – excessive loyalty, perhaps – and it unfolds over fifty years of the greatest period of social change Britain has yet seen, defined by the central event of the Second World War. Grace entered service as a housemaid for the Bell family in 1920, when deferential teenage maids still curtsied and averted their eyes and cooks were hidden away in dark basement kitchens. By the time of her retirement in 1971 she was the last of her line: an anachronism serving a household of one in the same year that a drama called *Upstairs, Downstairs* made its debut on ITV. No one in 1971 had live-in servants. No one could *find* live-in servants. Or if you could, you kept quiet about it.

Even though Grace married and became a mother, she chose to remain living in the freezing attic at Charleston working for Vanessa Bell (on £5 a week, bath night Fridays) right up until her sixty-seventh year, though her husband Walter clearly wished it otherwise. Having finally made the break, she was found a decade later by a *Sunday Times* reporter sitting in her Ringmer 'chalet', fulminating about a disrespectful TV documentary on the Bloomsbury Group ('What rubbish!'). Through retirement and right up to her death, Grace kept scrapbooks of every press cutting she could find on the circle – *her* circle.

The individuals she worked for had – and still have – a reputation for being wildly unconventional, so much so that it is odd to think of servants being a part of their *ménage* at all. The household of artist Vanessa Bell waxed and waned over Grace's half-century to include her separated husband Clive Bell, their children Julian and Quentin and her one-time lover and lifelong companion, the homosexual artist Duncan Grant. There was also her younger daughter Angelica, secretly fathered by Duncan, whom Clive Bell had agreed to pass off as his own. Vanessa's sister, the author Virginia Woolf, was central to this family, as was her husband Leonard Woolf. So intriguing and well documented is the group that its clamorous voice threatens to overwhelm this housekeeper's tale. My aim is to turn down the volume on the 'Bloomsbury Set', on its clever irony and self-conscious wit, and to coax into life the unheard voice of domestic servant Grace Higgens.

After her death in 1983, a hoard of forty-four little books was discovered among Grace's possessions. She had been an inveterate diarist. From the first ruled exercise book kept beneath her mattress, aged 16, to the hardbacked, illustrated recipe diary written in her seventy-ninth year, Grace recorded her day-to-day life with an eye for pithy detail. There are the Provençal peasants on her first trip abroad with the Bell family in 1921, 'who came & stared & jabbered in French'; the dinner guest resembling film star 'Fatty' Arbuckle; the Woolfs on their bicycles in Sussex looking 'absolute freaks, Mr Woolf with a corduroy coat which had split up the back like a swallow tail, & Mrs Woolf in a costume she had had for years'. Later – thirty or forty years later – Grace was still trenchant. 'Sat for my portrait after lunch . . . I had a peep & think I look a peevish woman'; 'The house looks as if a tornado had hit it';

'Heard our voices on Tape machine. Sounded ghastly'; and, returning to France for the last time in 1960, 'I spilt so much Chanel 5 on myself I smelt like a whore, but better I hope.'

The cache of diaries, along with letters, photographs and scrapbooks, was acquired by the British Library in 2007 as background material for scholars of Bloomsbury, every famous name carefully annotated. But the mundane nature of much of her diary entries ('Whist drive'; 'hen on goose egg'; 'cricket match Firle') give us perhaps a truer picture of Charleston than Bloomsbury's own descriptions of the notorious house parties where T. S. Eliot was served two whole grouse, or when Quentin Bell dressed up as a stout lady and spoke in a falsetto. The arc of Grace's story has its own validity: this was her house, after all, for thirty-seven years. In some senses it was more hers than Vanessa Bell and Duncan Grant's, who shuttled between London and Sussex. And for Grace's son John, it was the only childhood home he knew.

Grace was practically a child when she started working for Vanessa Bell; she was 16 years old. She did her growing up with this family. But at 30 she became a wife and soon afterwards a mother – and this is when she decided to make her married home in the attics of Charleston. She wouldn't leave the farmhouse until she was 67. The intimate moments of family life were played out in small, squeezed spaces, under the noses of those she served. The Higgens family and the Bell family lived on top of each other, quite literally, in a claustrophobic unit that would have been unthinkable to previous housekeepers and their mistresses. There was no question as to which family had the worse deal – but what did it feel like to be on Grace's side of the master–servant divide? Was this simply a tale of sacrifice, or was it perhaps one of an identity gained?

II

Very Peculiar People

There is, for this housekeeper, a wealth of material – almost too much material. After excavating the ghosts of Mrs Doar, Mrs Wells, Mrs Penketh and Mrs Mackenzie through census returns, prison records and shipping lists, delving into the life of Mrs Higgens was a very different process. There are the prolific writings of the incestuous Bloomsbury group: letters, memoirs, novels, biographies. But, as a counterweight, there are now the Higgens Papers. Grace's early diaries allow us to see right into her young mind. She is obsessed with her hair, fashionably bobbed, and with her clothes ('Bought a hat, it is quite charming all Black, with a black georgette streamer'). We witness her 'getting off' with the violinist in the 'Lyons Popular' orchestra in a London tea room, working her way through *Moll Flanders* and *Gulliver's Travels* and battling her black moods ('I have a restless longing which I do not know how to satisfy'). We are with her on her eighteenth birthday in St Tropez, feeling 'very old & important' until Mrs Bell ruins it all with an accusing look – it seems that Grace has eaten all the figs from the garden. 'Oh, I hate, hate it all, I wish I never had come, something all ways come to damp my happiness.' Mostly, though, she is upbeat, 'full of fizz', delighting in her new and extraordinary circumstances as housemaid and then nanny for the bohemian Bells.

Clive Bell was captivated by this fresh, freckled girl with her slim 1920s figure, bobbed hair and soft Norfolk accent. 'Mr Bell came to lunch, & as usual said some very idiotic remarks, making me feel very uncomfortable', Grace wrote in her diary. He gave her for Easter a 'lovely' egg containing a pair of silk stockings. 'I must not let Alice Mary know.' (Alice Mary was another maid, attractive but prone to violent moods.) Grace paid to have a photographic studio portrait done every year, postcard-sized, which she signed in ink on the back. By the age of 18 she was already beautiful: serious mouth, full lips, intelligent eyes. Her looks were such a magnet that she often found it easier not to go out – 'Both Ruby & Mrs Harland think I will go mad, as I am turning Hermit, but every time I go out I have so many lies told about me that I dread to go out at all, besides, I am very happy with my books.' Grace was to be an early sexual fantasy for the teenage Bell boys Julian and Quentin, who would return after long stints at boarding school to hang around in the kitchen.

Today when visitor guides at Charleston evoke the memory of Grace Higgens, they conjure up the 'Angel of Charleston' – a rheumatic woman in flowered overalls with grey permed hair; a 'treasure', rather like housekeeper Mrs Bird in *A Bear Called Paddington* (1958). They neglect to tell you that Grace was *sexy*. The Bells and Mr Grant saw her bloom and then fade over the decades, but the impression she made on random visitors, well into her thirties, was vivid. Friends of Julian, young graduates from Cambridge, remembered the frisson of this astonishingly good-looking woman bringing them cans of hot water in the morning and serving them dinner. She was not your average cook-housekeeper.

Grace's early diaries show us a girl young in manner, but she was no ingénue. She had left school at 13, a year before the Education Act of 1918 raised the leaving age to 14. There were seven small children at home in Banham, a village in the flat fenlands of Norfolk. Grace was the eldest, and she needed to earn a living. Her father George Germany was a warrener: a rabbit catcher and gamekeeper who worked the flat acres surrounding their cottage at Coppins Fen. Her brothers would eventually take over the family smallholding; Grace and her sister Alice would have to go out to work.

And so she had travelled with her small leather trunk to a childless aunt's house in Hayes, Middlesex, sent by her parents in the last year of the First World War. Here, in this industrial town ten miles from London, she tried them all: the Scotts jam factory, a stamp factory, a gramophone factory, a chocolate factory. She earned between 4s 7d and £1 a week, less than half of what a female factory worker might expect to earn in 1920. Grace, who had a brain, was crushed by the mind-numbing monotony of these sweatshops, and decided that domestic service had to be an improvement. She was wrong. She began working for a Dr Spowart in Norwich, a man with a temper so 'awful' (as she told her diary) that she gave this up too, returning home that May. Bessie and George Germany had not wanted Grace to go into service, but their eldest girl had no future in the Fens other than agricultural work. Within days she took herself off to the Collins employment agency on the Prince of Wales Road in Norwich. Here she was given Mrs Bell's address: 46 Gordon Square, London.

The woman who interviewed Grace Germany on that early summer's day in 1920 was a curious mixture of the permissive and the repressed. With the children her word was law, yet 'Nessa' also hated them to feel restricted (clothes, school, manners, sexual relations). Her handmade outfits were loose and flowing, her shoes unfashionably flat and her handsome face bore an 'awesomely noble resemblance to a Greek statue of the archaic period.'[1] Vanessa Bell's take on life was habitually ironic: when she spoke it was usually to give some dry utterance. She lacked an easy manner, and was painfully aware of this when interviewing nervous young housemaids. Her instinct was to summon all her mother's Victorian reserve.

Vanessa had grown up in a tall Kensington house where ranks of servants toiled in the basement and sweltered in tiny attic bedrooms. When their mother Julia Stephen died prematurely, the 15-year-old Vanessa had taken on the mantle of housekeeper for a controlling and parsimonious father. On his death in 1904, Vanessa, Virginia and brothers Thoby and Adrian moved boldly north to raffish Bloomsbury. Life at 46 Gordon Square was nothing short of a domestic revolution, and much has been made of this. But their new, apparently carefree and sensual existence could not work without servants.

For all that she was the 'Queen of Bloomsbury', famed for her ribald wit, soulful looks and open sexuality, Vanessa Bell had an almost obsessive need for tidiness and cleanliness. She couldn't paint surrounded by chaos. Although she professed to dislike the old 'them and us' stance with the servants, others found her so fierce with her maids – 'splendid, devouring, unscrupulous' thought her sister Virginia[2] – that Maynard Keynes nicknamed her 'Ludendorff Bell', after the German Quartermaster General.

Grace dipped her head meekly as Mrs Bell outlined her duties as house-parlourmaid. No white cap or uniform; no waiting at table; four bedrooms to do each morning, two sitting rooms in winter and three in summer; no church attendance compulsory. There would be regular travel to Firle in East Sussex for spells at Charleston, their country residence – a little dilapidated; no hot water or electricity; she was to understand, but it was a work in progress. Long periods would also be spent in the South of France each winter helping with housework, cooking and the children (Julian was 12, Quentin nine and Angelica just 18 months), while her mistress painted. She was to be known as 'Mrs Bell', not the conventional 'ma'am'.

Vanessa had seen so many unsuitable, flighty girls come and go that she rattled through these duties in a monotone. Was Grace Germany from Banham straightforward and trustworthy? It was the most she could hope for. The fact that it was Vanessa's forty-first birthday might have seemed like a good omen. She decided to engage the tall, gangly girl with bobbed hair, slim face and direct, appraising gaze. If nothing else, she would do as an artist's model. For a working-class girl, Vanessa thought her looks unusually 'aristocratic'.

Grace started work on 30 June 1920, sharing an attic bedroom with nursemaid Nellie Brittain. It took a special sort of servant to work for the Bells. The ménage was spread over two houses in Gordon Square:

Clive (art critic and womaniser) at number 50 and artist Vanessa at number 46 with the three children. Also living at number 46 was the celebrated economist John Maynard Keynes, joined in 1925 by his new wife, the Russian prima ballerina Lydia Lopokova. Duncan Grant was a constant visitor – dark and tousle-haired, magnetically attractive to both sexes – though from Angelica's birth in 1918 he no longer slept with Vanessa, preferring the male models that turned up at his Fitzroy Street studio. In 1920 Duncan was held to be the 'best painter in England' (according to Clive Bell); Vanessa, meanwhile, was working determinedly towards her first major solo exhibition.

Was Grace shocked by the permissive, bohemian world of her employers and their unconventional arrangements? She must have drawn conclusions: as a housemaid she changed the bed linen, sorted the dirty laundry and emptied the wastepaper baskets. Mrs Bell and Mr Bell *lived apart*. This was curious, but it seemed to be common in Bloomsbury. (Both addresses are entered in the flyleaf of Grace's diary.) As with any big house, there was gossip in the basement. She writes in February 1924 of spotting Vanessa's youngest brother Adrian and his wife Karin walking along arm in arm in Gordon Square: 'Who would think they were living apart, & that Mr Stephen was broken hearted, & has considered taking his life, perhaps it is only talk, (I mean the broken hearted part) but I think they are very peculiar people.'

For the servants, too, there was plenty of opportunity for intrigue. Vanessa's parties were renowned in Bloomsbury, not just among her guests but among the domestics, who saw them as an exciting opportunity to dress up and put themselves forward. At Gordon Square you rarely got ticked off by the mistress for presumptuous behaviour – just by the cook, Mrs Harland. 'We had a big dinner party tonight,' Grace wrote in March 1924, '& I had my hair waved, & it looked lovely, every body kept telling me so, & Mrs Harland was mad, especially when Mr Harland [the butler] said so, she was very jealous, was not that a catty thing to say, but it is true, everything went off lovely.' There was a concert after dinner to which the maids were invited, sitting at the back until they could keep their eyes open no longer. In such a liberal environment Grace began to blossom.

III

The Kitcheners

Grace went down to Charleston one month after she started working for the Bells, in August 1920. This was to be her home, on and off, for the next fifty years. The farmhouse lies at the end of a deeply rutted pale chalk track, half a mile long. It has a faintly Sleeping Beauty air, softened at the edges by feathery elms and weeping willows, half buried beneath a tangle of pink roses climbing up its cream facade, topped by a steeply pitched red-tiled roof. Cows chew the cud in a large flint barn to one side, filling the air with the fermented, sharp tang of fresh manure. Behind is a cornfield, then the gently rising heft of the South Downs. In front are a pond prone to duckweed, a lichened apple orchard where children love to hide and a tousled, north-facing walled garden perfumed in summer with syringa, sweet peas, tobacco flowers and stocks.

Visitors come to Charleston today primarily for the farmhouse interior: all those walls, tables and chairs covered in exuberantly painted nudes, vases and swirling patterns in blues and yellows, midnight greys and earthy reds: the fruit of Vanessa and Duncan's excessive creative energy. But Grace would have seen none of this as she entered the side door into the servants' quarters. A dark little hall, more of a vestibule really, opened to the right on to the dining room and to the left on to the kitchen. Here was the heart of operations, the only place in the house one could ever get properly warm. The kitchen at Charleston stood in stark contrast to the rest of the house. It was grubbily whitewashed, low-ceilinged and small-windowed, with a temperamental coke-fuelled stove and a gritty, sloping concrete floor. Lead pipes snaked along the wall over a small sink. A large scrubbed table, a place of work, stood in the middle, around which people would congregate.

Grace was shown up a steep and creaking double flight of stairs to the attic bedrooms, where camp beds were lined up in a makeshift dormitory under the dusty rafters. They had one day to get the house right before Mrs Bell arrived with the children: one day to air the many mattresses by heaving them out of the windows, to sweep up the mouse droppings and scrub the brick passageways down on their knees. In Angelica's imagination it was a swift and cheerful process:

At the beginning of the holidays it took the house one short night to wake from its torpor: by morning, the servants, whose names – Grace, Louie, Lottie, Nelly – were so typical of their generation, had it singing like the kettle on the hob; without them, Vanessa's creation would have been impossible.

But hours before one could even make a pot of tea, the stove had to be cleaned out and stoked with coal from the cellar, which might – or might not – have been ordered by Mrs Bell in time for their arrival.

What did Grace think, on entering the family's exuberantly decorated rooms for the first time? She doesn't say. After one month at Gordon Square strange things had, no doubt, quickly become ordinary. But really, it was as if a child had been let loose with several fat brushes and half a dozen cans of paint. The furniture was *covered* in experimental swirls, dots, chequered squares and overlapping hoops. The walls were similarly painted, roughly so, with damp spots now breaking through from beneath, crumbling the plasterwork to dust. Portly women splayed their legs on door panels; acrobats tumbled brightly down cupboards. A slightly shocking sense of fearlessness danced across the surface of every room. The effect on all entering, it is said, was one of intense liberation.

*

This was the reputation of Charleston. It was a 'paradise on earth' of sensual pleasures and freewheeling conversation into the small hours, of music on the wind-up gramophone and a relaxed attitude in the bedrooms. The 1920s are remembered by those who were there as the heyday of Charleston, with its 'holiday camp' house parties. But was it really like that? By the 1920s Vanessa Bell led a celibate life while Duncan pursued his adventures elsewhere, ever nervous of censure. Angelica, a child at the time, distinctly remembered an atmosphere of constraint, even gloom in the house. She wrote of the adults' 'lack of physical warmth and animal spirits', recalling her mother in particular as unable to show 'human warmth'. This was compared to the 'warm, earthy humour' of the 'harum-scarum' girls in the kitchen. Grace's summer diary for 1924 similarly suggests a more inhibited atmosphere. 'Rained like the devil, & I laid on the bed, & read *Hajji Baba*. Mrs Virginia Woolf arrived after tea to the great joy of the household, as she is very amusing, & helps to cheer them up.' (Her abiding memory of Mrs Woolf was of a 'very frivolous' lady – not the melancholy neurotic of popular imagination.)

By contrast, Grace's diary conjures servants' quarters echoing with shrieks of laughter, practical jokes and flirtatious, physical horseplay. The kitchen was where the *real* sexual anarchy dwelt at Charleston, among what Vanessa called the 'crop-haired generation' of maids. 'Arthur West, Will White, E. Kemp, Spenser Wooller called in & started chasing me, they were a terrible nuisance', Grace writes in September 1924. 'Tom West told Mrs Upp he was my young man & tried to kiss me, thereupon I called upon God to let me die, & he could not kiss me & gave it up as a bad hope. Arthur West did, the rotter. Mrs Upp so amused she made water, & had to go upstairs. Alice very mad.' Teenagers Julian and Quentin lurked in the kitchen, watching the goings-on between the 'kitcheners' and local lads, waiting for a chance to insert themselves.

At the end of that long, playful summer, the boys persuaded the 21-year-old Grace to come on a slightly risqué adventure. 'Julian & Quentin very set on my climbing the beacon to see the sunrise tomorrow', she wrote on 5 September 1924. Charleston stands isolated at the foot of Firle Beacon, the highest point in the range of Downs that extends, 'like a row of half-submerged ancient elephants', as Angelica put it, from the River Cuck in the east to the Ouse in the west. Julian and Quentin – heavy-breathing, fantasising adolescents of 16 and 14 – hatched a plan to scale its summit.

And so it happened: Grace and a blushing Louie Dunnett, Angelica's nursemaid, met the two boys in the still small hours outside the back door and set off together through the dewy cornfield. One hour later and warm with the effort, the four sat close together on top of the Beacon and watched the clouds turn 'a gorgeous Salmon Pink', wrote Grace. 'We came back by the Winding Path, and arrived back at Charleston, after Julian, Quentin & I had paid each other extravagant compliments, about 7.30. Alice looked mad.' The expedition was recorded in their home-made newspaper, the *Charleston Bulletin*, but as the boys told it just the two 'intrepid explorers' went up to the top. That two young maids came with them was too complicated, too unsettling to laugh off to the adults. Friendship with the servants was encouraged by Vanessa, but not intimacy.

IV

Practically No Ground In Common

The joyful climate in the kitchen, and the flirtation between Grace and the boys, seems to suggest that old-fashioned rules for servants no longer applied and that a modern chumminess was the order of the day. But this was not the case. Vanessa Bell began the morning like a

Victorian mistress. After breakfast she would appear in the kitchen to give her orders, just as her mother had done in Kensington in the late nineteenth century. For the fifty years that Grace worked for Mrs Bell the ritual never altered: Vanessa sat at a chair at the table and, notebook in hand, the cook (Mrs Harland, or Lottie Hope, then finally Grace) would stand by her side.

Vanessa was 'faced with half an hour in the kitchen', wrote Angelica, 'deciding whether to have spotted dog or treacle tart for lunch, and listening to Lottie's suggestions, jokes and complaints'. *Faced with*: it was a chore, an effort, and somehow beneath Vanessa to engage on such corporeal matters as food and clean linen. Spotted dog or treacle tart – the hilarious banality of such a choice! Time spent with the 'kitcheners' was felt to be time wasted. Although Vanessa saw herself as an enlightened and egalitarian employer, she passed her class prejudices on very thoroughly to her daughter. The subject of servants formed a bond between her and Angelica (just as it did between her and her sister Virginia); an opportunity for eye-rolling, exasperation and cattiness, for jokes told at their expense.

Both Vanessa and Virginia fought against their ingrained social reflexes – they were part of a group, after all, that celebrated the flowering of working-class culture. Doesn't the charlady's life have as much validity as the barrister's? Virginia Woolf asked in *A Room of One's Own* – yet at the same time she hated living in such close quarters with working-class women and found it 'detestable, hearing servants moving about'. Vanessa wrote to Virginia from one early holiday home, Studland, that 'My brains are becoming as soft as – yours? – by constant contact with the lower classes . . . I shall be glad to have one floor beneath & one above between me & them again.'

Angelica absorbed her mother's snobbish attitudes, reproducing them in her autobiography many years later. Nellie Brittain, her strikingly beautiful first nursemaid (Grace kept a photo of her, playing affectionately with a naked Angelica), was connected 'with the peculiar smell of linoleum, of a back lavatory and a dark little bedroom on the ground floor'. She was shortly after replaced by Louie Dunnett, with 'a face like a squashed red apple with pips for eyes'. Louie cowered from her master and mistress, blushing all over her neck when she passed Mr Grant or Mr Bell on the stairs – unlike Grace, 'who was always ready to pass the time of day, and perhaps say something foolish which was repeated with laughter at the lunch-table'. Louie would do, wrote Vanessa to Duncan, but 'she isn't half as aristocratic as Grace'.

Grace replaced Louie as Angelica's nursemaid, and Vanessa seemed to find the guilt-ridden relationship easier to navigate by treating her almost like another daughter – *almost*. In January 1927, Vanessa took the two to Cassis in the South of France. 'Angelica and Grace are in a wild state of excitement', she wrote to her ex-lover, the art critic Roger Fry, 'and enjoy everything, food and travelling and all they see and do.' The two are lumped together both in letters and in photographs; one picture, kept by Grace, shows them rolling around in the long grass, arms around each other. They were packed off for French lessons together, one hour a day, like a couple of schoolgirls. And yet, as soon as Angelica went to bed, Grace's company began to grate. Vanessa let off steam to the only woman who would understand and forgive her uncharitable sentiments: her sister. It is Vanessa Bell's most detailed assessment of Grace.

22 February 1927: 'I shall be very glad to have some grown up educated companions again, which I haven't had since Charleston early in January, not to live with, that is to say', she wrote.

Angelica is so intelligent and vivacious that she's much better than most grown ups in many ways, but of course no child, however charming, can be talked to equally.

Since we have been here I have had practically to live with Grace – she has had all her meals with us, generally alone with me in the evenings, as it seemed too absurd for her to bring in my food and then have her own rather later in the next room. But it is curious. Though extraodinarily nice and free from any of the tiresome qualities of many of our friends she is, like all the uneducated, completely empty-headed really, and after a bit it gets terribly on one's nerves. She either asks me questions, which it is obvious she could answer as well as I can, or she tells me things she has already told me dozens of times about the Harlands. One has practically no ground in common.

I am rather interested to see what does happen with the lower classes, as she is a very good specimen, not only unusually nice, but much more ready than most to try to understand other things, reading all she can get hold of and making desperate efforts towards culture. But there's something I suppose in having educated grandparents, for already Angelica is capable of understanding things in a way one can see Grace never will. However my enquiries into the lower class mind will come to an end in a few days now I'm glad to say, for I shall relegate her to the kitchen again when Duncan comes here.

Pity Grace with her doomed gestures at culture, struggling to make awkward conversation with her taciturn mistress when she'd much rather be laughing with Louie or reading *Gulliver's Travels* on her bed. But also pity Vanessa Bell, longing to be alone with her intelligent thoughts and the background cicadas, but feeling duty bound to make an effort with dear Grace, now almost seven years with her family.

V

The Dolt

Between 1924 and 1944 there is a gap in the Grace Higgens diaries. Did life get too busy, or just too humdrum to record? The missing years covered a period of many boyfriends, including two proposals in the South of France. Right in the middle of this twenty-year period came Grace's decision to get married, to have a life outside her work.

For most women this would spell the end of service. In 1934 it was unconventional to continue working once married; husbands liked to be seen to provide for a wife kept at home. Given Grace's commitment to Vanessa Bell and the family, choosing Walter was a brave assertion of *self*. But she was torn. The Bells had become like family to her – now 30, she'd spent half her young life with them, and was anxious at the thought of leaving their protection.

Why did she settle for the deeply ordinary Walter Higgens, ten years her senior? Here was this avowedly 'exquisite' girl, chased around the South of France by would-be suitors (two who presented themselves to Mrs Bell to ask for her hand in marriage – one the owner of a patisserie, the other allegedly an Eastern European count). Grace was a favourite artist's model; her bone structure was so good that Duncan Grant once mistook her for society beauty Lady Diana Manners when he spotted her on the Lewes bus. She was an avid reader, a feminist, a pacifist and socialist in her instincts. She had her views. Bloomsbury could have been her jumping-off point, her springboard out of domestic service and into a marriage or career that might have seen her continue to bloom. Vanessa's great-aunt, the photographer Julia Margaret Cameron, saw her own maid (and favourite model) Mary Ryan marry a gentleman and become Lady Cotton. Another maid of Vanessa's, pretty Trissie Selwood, had married a local well-to-do farmer's son near Charleston. Grace's employers thought she could have done so much better. Instead, this 'very good specimen' of the working classes reverted to type.

But by the standards of Grace's Norfolk family, Walter Alfred Higgens was a catch. He came from solid farming stock; his father had been a substantial Hampshire dairy farmer who employed extra men (and a housemaid). Like Grace he was the eldest of a large family – there were eight Higgens children. Walter had had an extraordinary Great War by any standards. With the Eighth Hampshire Cyclists (later Infantry) Regiment he had circumnavigated the globe, ever hopeful for active service but 'never a shot fired in anger'. He went by boat to India and trained for mountain warfare in sweltering conditions with

Nepalese battalions; he went to Vladivostok in Siberia and thence to Omsk: 4,000 miles on the Trans-Siberian Railway, 23 days in closed cattle trucks through temperatures of minus 40 degrees, arriving as the armistice was signed. Here Walter's battalion joined the new Anglo-Russian Brigade, a mob of Russian peasants commanded by English officers to help the doomed Russian royal family. When cornered by the advancing Bolshevik army, they embarked hastily for Vancouver. Crossing Canada by train, Walter saw brown bears in the forests, a sight that would stay with him all his life. Four years after leaving home, he and his comrades returned to Southampton, soldiers with a mine of memories utterly unlike any other battalion's. Walter had three medals and a glamorous past. He had lived a bit.

As for Grace, perhaps she looked at her essentially solitary mistress's world, with its fractured, complicated relationships and that slight unhappiness that afflicted them all, and made her choice. She had enjoyed her time in the Lyons tea shops and Tivoli Picture Palaces of London, but marrying countryman Walter was a return to her rural roots – and a chance, at her advanced age (for the times), to have a family. Grace had been so keen to preserve her job and her independence, shunning the approaches of so many young men, that she had perhaps found herself on the shelf. Her great friend Ruby, housekeeper to Lady Keynes at neighbouring Tilton, had married Grace's old flame Edgar Weller. Men were in short supply after the First World War. Walter was available, and Walter was willing.

He was not a man of great physical presence. He had a habit, when being photographed, of ducking his face down away from the camera and squinting upwards, compared to Grace's direct gaze. As the years went by Walter grew a comb-over hairstyle to cover his bald patch – but then so did Clive Bell. He is remembered by Anne Olivier Bell, Quentin's wife, as 'a very boring little man, not at all attractive, insignificant'. Walter would have been in his mid-fifties when Olivier, as she was known, first visited Charleston. The younger generation was more forgiving: Angelica's daughter, Henrietta Garnett, remembers being bounced on his knee and giggling at his jokes: he was 'a honeypot' – very kind, very funny. Not once in her diaries does Grace complain about her husband; he is unfailingly recorded as supportive, protective, a bringer of fancy chocolates, 'a great comfort' all round.

Walter was immediately nicknamed 'the Dolt', or 'the D' by Vanessa and the family. When Vanessa Bell's letters were published in 1993 and her contempt for Walter laid bare, it incensed son John Higgens and daughter-in-law Diana. But apparently Grace had always been relaxed about it. She knew the nature of the beast; she knew that nicknames at Charleston were an occupational hazard. Lettice, a girlfriend of Julian's, was known as 'Cabbage'; Duncan's close friend Paul Roche was 'the Cockroach'.

Vanessa liked to think that Grace also found Walter a bore, but Grace's diaries (and the memories of her son John) suggest this was her mistress's invention. Vanessa writes to Angelica, for example, of 'the D' singing at a Victory in Europe party 'to ill-suppressed giggles', while 'Poor Grace hid her head in the background.' When Walter tried to whirl Grace round in a waltz, she 'simply sent him packing'. Walter was a fine singer, according to John: 'Loved singing. Loved it. [He was] in various choirs, even on the radio from Lewes town hall at one time. Piano in the pub, he'd sing to it.' Again writing to Angelica in 1952, Vanessa told the story of Grace 'jumping up in a rage' at three in the morning to get 'the D' some dyspepsia tablets, slipping on the stairs and falling all the way down on her behind (and cracking her spine). 'The Dolt I imagine lying comfortably in bed all the time,' she adds drily.

Probably Vanessa Bell had not wanted Grace to marry at all, and her aversion to Walter was in part simple jealousy. She felt proprietorial; felt she owned Grace. Marriage was a distraction from her service to the Bells. In this, Vanessa's attitude was the same as the Duchess of Sutherland complaining about Mrs Doar a century earlier. 'Her Ladyship will never again have a married House Keeper', as one Sutherland agent wrote to another, 'it is attended with many bad consequences.'

Vanessa's treatment of Grace was necessarily more enlightened. She could not afford to lose her prop and mainstay at a time when servants everywhere were handing in their notice.

VI

So Glad I Need Not Say Goodbye

Few women wanted to work as a live-in servant by the mid-1930s. It had become an embarrassing profession to admit to, particularly if you were in search of a husband. 'If you said you were in domestic service it was still the same old story', wrote former housemaid Margaret Powell of her attempts to snare a man in the thirties; 'you could see their faces change. The less polite ones used to say "Oh, skivvies!" and clear off, and leave you cold.'[3] Working women had a new sense of self-worth, fired by increased literacy and the rise of Labour politics. The hard-pressed middle classes began instead to rely on ageing 'dailies' and charladies. There were concerned debates in the national press and on BBC radio about 'missing maids', the decline of deference and the 'class war in the home'. An advertisement for Fry's Cocoa at this time shows a mob-capped maid cheerfully savouring her mid-morning cup, while her mistress's bell jangles unheeded behind her. 'Let 'em ring!' is the disconcerting slogan.

The upper classes fared better, since there was still a certain prestige attached to working in a large country house. Many estates remained generously staffed, still functioning on Edwardian lines both in opulence and attitude. Lady Astor's personal maid Rosina Harrison routinely worked an eighteen-hour day, seven days a week, seeing to the needs of a woman who got through five sets of clothes in a day.[4] At Shugborough in Staffordshire, the Countess of Lichfield told laundry maid Nesta MacDonald that her fashionably bobbed hair was out of the question, since the young ladies of the house had just had *their* hair bobbed.[5] In June 1936 the MP Harold Nicolson, house guest at the Astors' immense country seat in Buckinghamshire, wrote the unthinkable in his diary: what was all this show *for?*

Cliveden, I admit is looking lovely. The party also is lavish and enormous. How glad I am that we are not so rich. I simply do not want a house like this where nothing is really yours, but belongs to servants and gardeners. There is a ghastly unreality about it all. Its beauty is purely scenic. I enjoy seeing it. But to own it, to live here, would be like living on the stage of the Scala theatre in Milan.[6]

Vanessa Bell was made uncomfortable by her annual visits to Clive Bell's large parental pile, Cleeve House in Seend, Wiltshire. Playing the role of conventional wife (though long amicably separated from Clive), she would retreat to her bedroom to write tartly comic letters to sister Virginia describing the ranks of humble servants and the household's footing, pointless existence. 'I don't think this establishment can last very much longer', she wrote at Christmas in 1929. 'I suspect one's trial at Seend will soon be over. Already it seems quite unreal and only hanging by a thread to the year 1929. It all belongs properly to 1870 and the wonder is that still servants can be found to keep up the illusion.'

Yet for all her poking fun at Seend, Vanessa Bell and her sister could not seriously imagine life without servants. When Virginia Woolf took to doing the housework as a way to manage her nerves during the Second World War, 'I'd no notion', she wrote to a friend in 1941, 'having always a servant, of the horror of dirt.' On a rare occasion when she found herself doing the dishes, she was amazed at the effort: 'I've been washing up lunch – how servants preserve either sanity or sobriety if that is nine 10ths of their lives – greasy ham – God knows.'

With Grace about to marry Walter, Vanessa thought hard about how they could keep her and whether this would work, weighing convenience (a live-in housekeeper for Charleston) against imposition (the Dolt in their attic). Grace must have worried too. Would she be allowed to stay? Should she leave service after fourteen years with the Bells? Walter would have preferred this, but he did not have a reliable income. After the army he worked in farming, for the council, then at the local brickworks, earning a slender living.

When he and Grace got engaged he looked hard for a cottage to rent, but nothing comfortable could be found. Grace's wages were low for a domestic servant (it is not remembered precisely what she earned at this stage; her son claimed she never once asked for a pay rise) – but at least board was included. From 1933 there was electricity at the farmhouse, too. With Vanessa Bell's blessing, the newly-wed couple moved into the attics at Charleston.

On 23 May 1934 Vanessa wrote to her servant from London.

My dear Grace,

I am sending you two cheques, one for your wages the other a wedding present from Mr Bell, Mr Grant & myself. I am so glad that I need not write to say goodbye, but only to send you every affectionate good wish from us all & hopes that you will be very very happy & make yourselves a lovely home.

Yours affectionately

Vanessa Bell

Duncan Grant gave the married couple a painting of the Coliseum in Rome: his touch was always more personal.

Grace wrote to Clive (who, earlier that year, had sent her a provocative postcard of a naked African woman with pendulous breasts posted 'between Daka and Port-of-Spain'):

Dear Mr Bell,

I am writing rather late I'm afraid to thank you for the lovely and generous present which you sent me. It was very kind of you, I feel I have done nothing to deserve so much; I have never been so wealthy before, & although I had a great temptation to spend some of it, I put it all in the Bank. I am so glad that although I am married, I am still living at Charleston, it is very kind of Mrs Bell & yourself to allow me to stay on, I hope some day to be able to repay the many kindnesses to which I am indebted to you both.

Yours sincerely,

Grace Higgens'

Both mistress and servant professed to be 'so glad' that nothing would change: it was a source of relief all round.

Three months later, Grace was pregnant. Wearily Vanessa took this new yet inevitable development on board. As a rule, Bloomsbury did not like babies. 'Sticky fingers, sticky fingers,' Clive Bell would say with jocular distaste when young children clattered through the house. But he meant it. Children were anathema to clever conversation, to civilised mealtimes and silent hours in the studio or library. Although Charleston had been a haven for the wild antics of young Quentin, Julian and Angelica, those years were over. Now, when Julian and his Cambridge friends came to stay, they debated politics late into the night.

In the spring of 1935 – just before Grace reached full term – Vanessa and the household went to Rome for five months, promoting her servant to cook-housekeeper of Charleston. This was the top job; Grace could do no better with the Bells. And yet the role was nothing like the impressive equivalent of the previous century. Cook-housekeeper in the 1930s meant doing it all: the pastry making, the hallway scrubbing, the sheet changing, the household accounts, the chamber-pot emptying. Charleston always employed a series of ageing charladies who came weekly to 'do the rough', but Grace's daily round was a relentless one.

'Have you heard whether Grace has had her baby yet?' Vanessa wrote to Virginia on 27 April. 'I hope I shall hear somehow when it does arrive, but I doubt her husband's capacity to write.' On the same day she wrote to Grace, a letter quite delicate in tone:

I am beginning to wonder whether you are through your troubles yet . . . You seemed to think it might be very soon when we left you . . . . It is a pity that I who really adore tiny babies should miss seeing yours. Never mind, it will be fairly small still I daresay by the time I do see it.

She then gave instructions about a wardrobe being removed, chair covers and china delivered and a request for Grace to write to Foley China at Stoke-on-Trent to chase an order. As if that might be too much of an imposition for a woman about to give birth, she added:

Walter will be able to see to all these things if you can't I suppose. Or else I wouldn't bother you. You will have enough to do for the first fortnight at least I'm sure with Peter John. Or Elizabeth. Or both! Take care of yourself.

Heaven forfend there should be twins in the attic. Peter John was delivered on 10 May 1935 in his parents' bed in the eaves of Charleston. The farmhouse had been rented out to friends by Vanessa, ever frugal, leaving Grace and Walter in their new home on ambiguous terms. Clearly Grace could not be expected to work, but the tenants needed their maid to use the kitchen, which was also the Higgenses' kitchen. The one bathroom could be used only by the tenants, so Grace and Walter would have to forgo their weekly bath (as negotiated with the Bells, between 8 and 10 p.m. on Friday while the family ate their dinner), and rely instead on cans of hot water which Walter would have to carry up the vertiginous twenty-six stairs to the very top. The attics at Charleston are surprisingly roomy – at one end is Vanessa Bell's studio, at the other a small sitting room and bedroom, plus space for visiting children on camp beds and maids needing a berth. But for a family of three, the steeply pitched walls seem to contract. You can never forget where you are (so says Mark Divall, the gardener who lives there today): car tyres on the gravel outside, voices in the rooms below, the creak of those wide oak floorboards as anyone moves across them. Every window overlooked the Bells' realm below – hence Grace's nickname for the attic, 'High Holborn', since it 'looked down on Bloomsbury'. By the same token, those in the bedrooms below would hear every squeak of the Higgenses' bedsprings, every footfall across their sitting-room floor, every murmur of conversation. The cry of a newborn baby would have carried throughout the house.

'How I wish I could see him,' wrote Vanessa Bell with touching warmth from Rome that May.

You must write when you can & tell me exactly what he's like. The colour of his eyes & hair & whether he's good or naughty. Boys are generally said to be naughtier than girls. I hope he's gaining weight properly, perhaps my old baby scales will come in useful . . . I'm afraid you've had horrid cold weather for the first few weeks of your baby's arrival but I daresay he takes after you & enjoys the cold . . . When you're quite well enough & have a minute to spare do send me a short letter & tell me about yourself & the baby, as you know men aren't much good at describing babies.

We assume that Grace wrote back to her mistress, though no letter survives; a proud little paragraph about her baby; nothing flowery. Now she was a mother just like Mrs Bell. Who knew how the relationship between housekeeper and mistress might change? Vanessa was asking herself the same question, but in an altogether different way. On 18 July she wrote again to her housekeeper from Rome: could Grace get the electricity company to come and read the meter in London – 'see about it as soon as possible'. She was, as usual, vague about her plans – 'We will be back I think at the end of August or beginning of September' – and would come straight to Charleston, but was thinking of asking Lottie and Louie to come to help. In the course of the long letter (mostly filled with instructions) Vanessa circled, warily, ever closer to the nub of the issue: what use was Grace going to be with a small baby, and when could she properly get back to work? 'Perhaps it will be best', she suggested, if you don't try to do anything for us, but lead a separate life. What do you think? I expect John Peter gives you plenty to do . . . We could get Mrs Stevens I suppose if we wanted her. Mr Bell won't be there & I don't know about Julian. But it shouldn't be a very large household most of the time.

This pragmatic letter might well have panicked Grace. What did Mrs Bell mean, 'lead a separate life'? Would she still get her wages? Would she and Walter have to pay for board? She was on maternity leave, of a kind – yet she was being asked to scurry around getting the London house ready, having windows cleaned and meters read. How was she to manage this with a new baby? Perhaps, in her sleep-deprived state, she could focus on just one thing in Vanessa's letter. 'I expect *John Peter* gives you plenty to do.' Hadn't Grace written to Mrs Bell about her baby *Peter John*? Hadn't she even sent a precious portrait of him, taken in Eastbourne at great expense by a studio photographer? It was just a careless mistake, of course; but somehow a telling one.

VII

Peter John

As it turned out, the Higgens family did get to live a separate life of sorts. When Vanessa and Duncan were in London, which was much of the time in that decade before the Second World War, the Higgenses had Charleston to themselves. It was as much Peter John's home as it was Vanessa Bell's. Photographs from Grace's albums show a beautifully dressed toddler with buttoned Mary Jane shoes and a cream double-breasted swing coat, sartorially every inch his mother's son. Walter lounges on the lawn next to him with a magazine. There he is again, Peter John, a little older now and stark naked, dangling his legs in the Charleston fish pond, a wooden toy truck by his side.

Half the time they could lounge by the fish pond in deckchairs. The other half, they had to make themselves scarce. When Grace had lived in London, Vanessa would often refer to 'the Grace problem' in letters to Duncan, a problem that by 1930 was beginning to make her lose her 'reason'. Her servant would suddenly intrude just when she was in the middle of painting and start chatting about some household business, oblivious to Vanessa's silent concentration. Or else Grace would come in to tidy up and find a nude model posing on the divan. The solution was a large pair of curtains, erected across the entrance to the studio at 8 Fitzroy Street. 'I don't mind hearing her as long as I know I'm inviolate.' Vanessa wanted a servant, but at the same time didn't want to be constantly reminded that she had one. The ideal was a sort of absent presence.

Peter John grew up to be a gangly little boy, 'shy and self-conscious, like a spider, all arms and legs', as he said of himself. He was good at making himself invisible, shrinking back into the shadows and keeping quiet when the mistress of the house approached. This was a potent memory that stayed with him all his life. He remembered playing football in the kitchen, kicking his ball hard against the painted cupboards (now encased in Perspex to conserve the artwork). 'I used to be kicking or pinging a ball about in there, and would hear Mrs Bell coming through from the other side, and would have to stop, or think about stopping.' He would also play in Vanessa and Duncan's old car, left in the apple room throughout wartime due to petrol rationing. 'I didn't do it if Mrs Bell was going to possibly come round the corner. No, I'd leap out again! I had good ears in those days.'

Vanessa used to gaze out from her attic studio, deep in thought – only to snap to when she spotted a small boy climbing the wall by the chicken run, hand outstretched towards a juicy pear. A Bell pear. 'Would you stop Peter John helping himself to our fruit?' she would say to Grace, who would have to nod her head and bite her lip. When visitors were sitting round the dinner table, Vanessa objected if the Higgenses cut across the garden in front of the house, past the small dining-room window. They were supposed to go the long way round, by the chicken run.

She was a dominant, rather terrifying figure to young Peter John. Mrs Bell had, as he put it, a 'foreboding appearance'. She was 'strange with her attire. She struck me as one of the original hippies, long before the hippy people came about, with her large hats and shawls and scarves.' When he became a father, his young daughter Jacqueline refused to visit the farmhouse because she was convinced there was a witch, even though Mrs Bell was no longer alive.

For all his skulking in the shadows, Peter John enjoyed a childhood of tremendous freedom, playing in the outlying fields and barns with his friends, servants' sons from the local big houses Tilton and Firle Place. He was allowed to use Vanessa's piano, although he hated the lessons Grace forced upon him at great expense. She tried him at the piano and she tried him at the violin, but Peter John did not excel in music. He didn't have an ear. He would nervously knock on Clive Bell's study door, where the master of the house sat at his desk surrounded by piles of books, to ask for help with some esoteric piece of schoolwork. 'He was a charming person, but he would be very aloof if he had any of his friends . . . then I'm afraid you were just a little boy and you were not to be seen.'

His first birthday in May 1936 marked the last blithely hedonistic summer at Charleston. While Grace laboured in the kitchen and the stuffy attic, cooking the food, changing the bed linen, keeping herself, Walter and the baby out of the way, Vanessa wrote letters describing gay house parties and bright young things. Angelica was now a strikingly beautiful 18-year-old who had made her 'debut' in Bloomsbury in a hat 'which she said (and I believe it!) had caused a sensation in Paris', as Vanessa wrote to her eldest son Julian, who was teaching in China. Charleston, she told him, was in a state of pandemonium . . . full of young people in very high spirits, laughing a great deal at their own jokes, singing and playing all the time and lying about in the garden, which is simply a dithering blaze of flowers and butterflies and apples . . . Everyone has been going about half naked and getting brown, Angelica looks very well and wears hardly any clothes.

By the summer of 1937, everything had changed. When Peter John was two, Julian Bell set off hot-headedly for the Spanish Civil War, despite the anguished warnings of his mother. 'It can happen so easily,' she had prophesied that February, 'but it mustn't happen to the really valuable people if one can possibly help it.' Six weeks later, aged 29, he died of a shrapnel wound to the chest while driving an ambulance. Vanessa broke down and took to her bed at Fitzroy Street. Grace wrote to her mistress about her loss – this same teenage boy she had once sat close to at the top of Firle Beacon, seeing the sun rise gloriously. She still had two schoolboy portraits of a brooding, bespectacled Julian, probably pressed upon her that flirtatious summer of 1924. She kept these to her death. It is the only letter from Grace to Vanessa to survive, kept as it was with her mistress's letters of condolence.

Dear Mrs Bell,

Please forgive me writing to you now, but I wish to tell you, how terribly sorry I am to hear of Julian's death, & how deeply I sympathise with you. I'm afraid this is not a time, when I can do anything to help you, although I wish I could.

Yours sincerely,
Grace[8]

When Vanessa was well enough to return to Charleston, Grace found her weeping uncontrollably in the garden. No one understood her need to talk about Julian.

VIII

Wartime

In 1939 the Bells purchased a wireless: heavy, chunky, in a Bakelite frame. It benefited the servants more than their masters, for while Vanessa and Duncan lived their lives in London, Grace and Walter took to sitting around this new and extraordinary device that brought them a sense of connection with the wider world. Short plays, organ music, seaside songs and Children's Hour at 5.15 p.m. were wonderfully entertaining, but the six o'clock news brought with it an increasing unease. Grace, working on a succession of rag rugs, listened anxiously to the escalating fears of another war with Germany. 'We are naturally all rather agitated about the news here & you must be too', wrote Vanessa to her housekeeper on 13 March that year. 'I do hope things will calm down soon but one simply doesn't know what to think or expect. The world is certainly mad.' She signed it with her customary formality, 'Yours sincerely, Vanessa Bell.'

The Second World War was the most turbulent episode of Grace's life – as it was for every working woman in Britain. It blew all the old certainties about class distinctions out of the water. As the Blitz bombs rained down, ladies sheltered with their maids for hours on end in Anderson shelters and mansion basements, making small talk to ward off hysteria. Servants in their thousands, men and women, gladly left to join the war effort. Who could say who Vanessa Bell's 'really valuable people' were, now that half a million ordinary women were employed by the services and countless more in essential war work on farms and factories throughout the country?

As a married mother of a small child, Grace was exempt from

war work. But as housekeeper of a farmhouse lying directly on the predicted route of invasion, just three miles from Newhaven, the war insinuated itself into her every living moment. Britain had long held dear the idea of the home as a fortress, a place of sanctity and safety. The housekeeper's role was to safeguard this fantasy; to keep the wheels running smoothly and the rituals unchanged. But if a single bomb could destroy a house in seconds, what fundamental value did her job hold? Was this a time to give up on slavish attention to floor waxing, mattress turning and silver polishing and put other, more vital priorities at the centre of one's life?

And yet perhaps this was precisely the time that the sanctity of home mattered more than ever; a time in which satisfying domestic routines were the only balm to the madness outside. Picking and bottling blackberries; transforming an army blanket into a winter coat; turning a worn collar on an old shirt: many women wrote of the fulfilment, even joy, that finite domestic tasks gave them during wartime. Both Vanessa Bell and Grace Higgens turned to their knitting needles, to bread making, to vegetable growing and pig rearing in an unforeseen merging – not always harmonious – of two previously opposite lives. At Charleston, mistress and housekeeper both rolled up their sleeves and made the best of it.

There are no diaries from Grace for the outbreak of war; they resume in 1944. But there are letters from Vanessa Bell that fill in the blanks, describing how Charleston was transformed into the family's retreat. For several months, as the country prepared for war, the Higgenses found their home turned upside down with building dust and chaos through every doorway. 'Piles of brick and rubble arise and then disappear and there are holes in the floor everywhere,' wrote Vanessa to Virginia in June 1939. 'Baths and WCs sit about in odd places . . . I dash into cupboards thinking they are passages . . . Clive is arriving presently and I rather dread thinking his horror when he finds what a state it's all in, though he has been warned.'

Clive Bell was moving in – an unusual decision for a former husband, yet one that probably seemed perfectly logical to Grace, since she had always regarded him as her master. Vanessa's close companion Duncan Grant was just a dear addition to the family, relaxed and informal in his relationship with the servants. Clive, used to far more luxurious surroundings, was to have the best: the whole north end of the first floor, including a bathroom, which pushed Vanessa downstairs into the old kitchen pantry, now with new French windows opening on to the garden.

The Higgenses, too, were to benefit. For the first time in twenty years of service, Grace was to get her own sitting room on the ground floor. She would have somewhere to put her feet up while she waited all evening to clear the dining table. The family wouldn't have to climb up and down twenty-six stairs every time they needed a magazine or a pair of knitting needles or a toy. This space – 11ft by 8ft – was 'so as to give you a place to put things in,' wrote Vanessa. But really it was somewhere they could stake out as their own, and it became the new hub of Higgens family life.

They needed it, because their personal space was under threat. On Sunday, 3 September 1939, Vanessa, Duncan, Clive, Quentin and Angelica gathered round the wireless at 11.15 a.m. to listen to Chamberlain's speech. '. . . I have to tell you now that no such undertaking has been received, and that consequently this country is at war with Germany.' How unreal it seemed, with the garden outside 'glowing with the reds and oranges of the dying summer', Angelica remembered. She did not mention the Higgenses, but they would have been there too. Servants all over the country were at that moment taking their places next to employers to listen, tensely, to this historic broadcast.[9] Standing next to Grace and Walter was Lottie Hope, turbulent cook-housekeeper of 50 Gordon Square. Lottie had arrived along with Clive's vast collection of books, his exquisitely tailored tweed suits and his eau de cologne bottles cluttering up the bathroom. She was to work alongside Grace in the kitchen.

IX

Too Many Cooks

In a buff-coloured folder in the British Library is a collection of old recipes snipped from papers by Grace throughout her fifty years in service – from *The Times*, the *Express* and *Woman's Weekly* magazine. There are dog-eared favourites, part of her reliable repertoire, for roast pork roll, beef in mustard sauce, cold veal and tomato soup and walnut and coffee slices. By the time of Lottie's arrival, Grace knew what worked, what was popular and what was economical. But still she snipped out wartime suggestions, responding to the national mood of mounting anxiety. In January 1940 bacon, butter and sugar were rationed, followed shortly by meat, tea, jam, biscuits, breakfast cereals, cheese, eggs, lard, milk and canned and dried fruit. By August 1942 almost all foods, apart from vegetables and bread, were rationed.

The Ministry of Food issued daily recipes via the press for housewives trying to rustle up a treat with poor substitutes, such as chocolate cake made with dried eggs and two ounces of margarine, or 'mock cream' made with milk, margarine and cornflour. Newspapers quickly brought out their own wartime cookery books full of ideas to stretch non-rationed food further, such as 'savoury sheep's tongue', or 'cod's roe pie' (livened up with an ounce of margarine and a teaspoon of dry mustard). Dried egg, pronounced the *Telegraph*, could be viewed as 'a fascinating and progressive branch of present-day catering'.

But Grace never had to reconstitute the dreaded dried egg: whisking hard to get rid of the lumps. She had no need of dried milk, and probably did without sheep's tongue too. She was lucky to have at her disposal fresh and bountiful ingredients, thanks to the neighbouring dairy farm and the forward planning of the household. 'I suppose the sensible thing to do would be to grow as much food as possible at a place like Charleston,' Vanessa had written to Grace in October 1939 (the 'phony war' having lured her and Duncan back to London); 'vegetables, pigs, ducks & all we can – anyhow it could do no harm – we might be very glad of such things as we would have been in the last war.'

Vanessa hired Walter reluctantly as part-time gardener and odd-job man, thinking she was doing him a favour, when she would far rather get someone else – such as Mr White, 'the old man who brings the washing. He buys a new pony every week, Grace says, and he keeps hens and he's a jobbing gardener. If only I could employ him instead of the D[olt]! Isn't it tempting', she wrote to Angelica, who was staying with her 48-year-old lover Bunny Garnett. Walter did not relish being at the beck and call of Mrs Bell. By the following summer, as she wrote to her friend Jane Bussy, she had 'driven the Dolt with such an iron rod all these months that we really have plenty of cabbages . . . Poor man, I have no mercy on him.' Walter knuckled down and built goose pens, chicken runs and a pigsty for an old sow called Hannah who produced an annual litter of piglets. He dug and sowed new vegetable plots, pruned and fertilised the gnarled fruit trees, and Charleston became largely self-sufficient.

Clive Bell played his part too, dressing up like a country squire and coming back at the end of the day, rifle cocked over one arm, with rabbit, hare, pheasant or partridge dangling from his hand. These would be hung in the larder for a week before they could be cooked, and as Peter John remembered 'they were *high*. They'd be hanging with newspapers underneath to catch all the nasty drips. They really smelt terrible. The flies would be buzzing around the newspaper on the floor – and Grace dealt with it all.' Or else they'd be used for still lives, young cock pheasants hung up against a looking glass by artists Angelica and Quentin with a 'Do Not Disturb' sign propped up to warn off Grace.

The red and white cows continued to produce their thick, creamy milk, delivered to the kitchen straight from the dairy. While the nation sank its teeth into 'corned beef toad in the hole', or 'tripe au gratin'

(*Daily Express Wartime Cookery Book*), at Charleston there was – as Angelica remembered – 'a defiant abundance of food and drink'. The climax was her cordon bleu twenty-first-birthday dinner party in December 1939. 'Everyone was determined to make it a remarkable occasion, from Lottie, who slaved for a fortnight beforehand, to Vanessa, who thought of and organised it.' Oddly, she doesn't mention Grace.

Lottie Hope, Clive's cook, was 49 years to Grace's 36 at the start of the war and they knew each other of old. As young maids they had often shared a bed at Charleston, whispering about boyfriends in the dark. Lottie was all hot, dark intensity to Grace's cool, freckled calm. She was a foundling, left in a cradle on the doorstep of the hospital; that was why she was called Hope. Lottie drank, so the rumour went, and sometimes lost her temper with violence.

After five years of having the kitchen the way she liked it, Grace opened her door to Lottie and her strident laughter. Previously she had worked beneath Lottie as kitchen maid. Now she was cook-housekeeper: the king pin. This wasn't going to be easy.

Although the niece of a fellow servant remembered Lottie to be an awful cook (based on visits to Gordon Square in the 1930s), according to Quentin she was a gifted one, producing rich and elegant meals for Clive, who was something of a gourmet and had been known to order a butler from Fortnum's when entertaining at home. Grace's style was different. She is remembered for her good, unpretentious English cooking: succulent roast joints, wonderful soups, seed cakes, spotted dog. The two locked horns in a culinary battle that was to last a year and a half, each vying to out-trump the other with their wartime specialities.

As the Government sought to control every aspect of domestic life, so tensions mounted in communal households where ration books were pooled and commodities shared. How dare Lottie use up the precious sugar allowance on another wholly unnecessary iced cake? *Who* had been at young Peter John's ration of concentrated orange juice? Was it right that the best cuts went to the family, when rationing had introduced a scrupulous equality to the table? Not only food, but other goods too became hard to obtain: safety pins, knitting needles, saucepans, Vim. Sanitary towels, face powder, contraceptives, soap. Toothpaste, toilet paper, floor cloths, hairpins. Every intimate corner of domestic life was brought under official scrutiny. Charleston was not a particularly spacious country house: there were nine people sharing its rabbit warren of low-ceilinged rooms. The potential for petty grievances was high.

People were irritable, and they were fearful. Hundreds of East End children from Bermondsey had been evacuated to Lewes with satchels and gas masks (shoplifting, so they said, proliferated).[10] The wailing night sirens followed by the continuous flute-like all-clear began to be a fact of life in town. The Bells and their servants hunkered down behind the blackout smoking, knitting, keeping nerves at bay – the Bells by the dining-room fire, the servants next door in the kitchen. By the summer of 1940 a German invasion at Newhaven was expected imminently, the tension mounting inexorably after France's surrender in June. Virginia Woolf was close to hysterical: Leonard was a Jew – what was the point of going on living? Women everywhere felt near to breakdown. How would you save your child from German soldiers? A mother in Essex writing a diary for the Mass Observation Project decided she would put aside a bottle containing a hundred aspirins, which she would dissolve in milk and give to her four-year-old daughter if the Germans came.[11] Grace and Walter, sitting around the wireless for the six o'clock news, tried to keep such fears from their five-year-old son.

That summer, the blue skies of southern England were criss-crossed with smoke and fire from swarms of German Messerschmitts and British Spitfires: the Battle of Britain had begun. On the evening of 7 September, close to a thousand aircraft attacked London, lighting up the sky like a sunrise as the East End burned. The bombing continued for the next seventy-six nights. Vanessa Bell's studio at 8 Fitzroy Street was destroyed that September: most of her early work went up in flames.

Vanessa retreated physically and mentally within the four walls of Charleston, calming her nerves by painting. *Interior with Housemaid* is an early wartime work; more accurately, interior with housekeeper. Grace is slim, her hair bobbed, her posture young for a 36-year-old. She stands by Vanessa's mahogany writing cabinet, its pot of fountain pens contrasting with her own tool of work: a broom. It must have been hard to carve out the time to pose, what with the demands of the kitchen and her young son at her heels. Vanessa, who would nab anyone in the house for a life model, also painted the little boy; his was one of the first portraits done in her new attic studio. 'Peter John's not a very good sitter,' he remembered her tutting to Grace. 'He's so restless.' He was always desperate to get back downstairs to the kitchen and his mother.

News worsened daily. Bombs came close enough for the blacked-out windows to rattle. Outside, rolls of barbed wire cut off Grace's blackberry-picking walks along the cliffs. Life, necessarily, contracted. By the end of 1940 – a winter of power cuts, worsening queues and a dozen bombs dropped on Lewes – tensions at Charleston finally exploded. As Vanessa and the family sat at the round dining table one evening eating pot-roast pheasant, drinking French wine and making erudite conversation, there came the sound of raised voices from the kitchen across the hallway. Two women arguing – no, *shouting* at each other. There was a scuffle and a scream. Duncan put down his knife and fork and went to investigate.

'Terrific domestic upheavals' at Charleston, wrote Vanessa Bell to her old friend Jane Bussy after the event. Lottie had, she said, 'got at odds with the Higgens family (Grace and the Dolt) and our sympathies were divided. But when it came to the point of loud shrieks during dinner and terror lest a carving knife should be brought into play something had to be done.'

When forced to make a choice, Vanessa couldn't envisage life without her right-hand woman – and so it was Lottie Hope who was dismissed without a pension after twenty-five years in Bloomsbury. Grace won the battle over Lottie, but there were other discontents. She wanted more privacy: a separation between work and her own domestic life. Taking strength from her victory, she became more assertive. 'The Higgens family remain,' Vanessa continued,

but have a separate ménage of their own. Grace in fact has become a daily, and in consequence I cook the evening meal. The result is most of my stray thoughts are given to food, and in spite of all I must say we live very well . . . With unlimited quantities of milk, potatoes, bread, vegetables, apples, coffee etc, I don't want to make your mouth water, but one can do without Lottie's spate of iced cakes and not starve.

X

Small Pleasures

Peter John recalled nothing of the kitchen conflict when asked for his memories of the war. Grace's son was four years old when war broke out, ten years old when it ended. As an adult he could still picture himself lying in bed at night, looking up through the rusting attic skylight and seeing German doodlebugs zooming over Charleston en route to London.

As Grace walked her son across the fields to Selmeston school, they'd warily watch the dogfights overhead. 'All those planes, fighting in the air above our countryside. I wouldn't think of the danger,' he said. 'I was fascinated by what was going on in the air.' At the end of the school day Grace would leave the kitchen and walk to meet him. He had a little bicycle, and she'd push it all the way to meet him so he could ride the bike down Barleymow Hill home. 'We wouldn't see a car, in those days.' Once home, Peter John ran outside with a stick, 'shooting' at German planes flying low across the cornfields, chased by

British Spitfires, 'which petrified my mother because she thought they would shoot at me'. Grace had every reason to be anxious: a young Lewes mother had been fired at by a German plane as she pushed her six-week-old baby along in a pram.[12]

A searchlight was stationed near the farmhouse, run by a dynamo that thundered away at night. It was manned by the Home Guard, trigger-happy local men who would fire at low-flying enemy aircraft with a mounted gun. Grace would shout at them, furious: 'Of all the stupid things! You could hit one and blow us all up!'

That was Grace: outspoken, opinionated, instinctively pacifist. She had ambitions for her son, the spider-limbed Peter John. Working for the upper middle classes had changed her outlook on life. She decided to take him out of Selmeston Primary and send him to a private school in Lewes for a 'better education'; a 'mainly girls school' that took in boys. Broughton House School drilled him parrot-fashion in countries, capitals and rivers and coached him in sport, at which he excelled. He had no sense of being different to his classmates for being the son of a domestic servant. 'I was just another boy from the country.' This was a measure of Grace's standing with Vanessa, Clive and Duncan. She did not feel inferior, so neither did her son. Nor was he aware that the ménage at Charleston might be of interest to anyone. 'The Bloomsbury lot? They were just another family. "Bloomsbury" didn't mean anything to me at the time. There was no mention at school of them . . . I never talked about them, and no one appreciated or realised who they were.'

When Virginia Woolf committed suicide in March 1941 he was unaware of her great fame as a writer – he was, after all, just five years old. But he remembered vividly the change in atmosphere at Charleston at the time. Vanessa, 'fragile but not overwhelmed', broke the news to Duncan on his arrival from London. 'We all three clung together in the kitchen,' wrote Angelica, 'in a shared moment of despair, feeling that the world we knew, and the civilisation Virginia had loved, was rapidly disintegrating.' Was Grace – who rarely left the kitchen – a witness? Was she physically included in this family moment? Angelica, whose memory was selective regarding servants, doesn't say. Grace was so shocked by the news that she hid it from her small son. Some time later he found out that Virginia had drowned herself in the River Ouse.

Grace's voice is restored to us again in 1944, but her diaries have by this time shrunk in size – and scope. The little burgundy appointment books make no mention of the war. While the country tensely awaits 'D-Day' and the much-talked-of Second Front, Grace lists her outings – from *Alice in Wonderland* at Lewes Little Theatre, to a trip to the hairdresser's; from a dental appointment, to a jumble sale at Selmeston. She visits her friend Betty Hudson in Hurstpierpoint, takes part in a local ladies' darts match and sees her precious goslings hatch.

In April and May of that year, trippers were banned from the coastal zone from East Anglia down to Cornwall, and the roads were clogged with an endless stream of military traffic. Sherman tanks rolled down the steep streets of Lewes. 'Careless Talk Costs Lives' went the slogan, and Grace stuck to her own concerns. In any case, it was hard to keep a sustained interest in the larger picture of war and its various battles. The domestic front was too all-absorbing, with its ration books, registration cards, queues and petty domestic irritations. 'Try to run a home without saucepans, frying pans, dishcloths, floor cloths, toilet paper, brushes, Vim, fuel of any sort, and, of course, soap!' wrote Barbara Cartland in her memoir of the war years. 'We never had enough.'[13] Grace simply recorded day-to-day life, perhaps with a sharpened sense of gratitude for small pleasures.

In 1943 Vanessa painted her housekeeper working at the square kitchen table surrounded by soothing domestic items: mixing bowl, onions, scales, turnips. The atmosphere is serene; Grace rubs fat into flour unhurriedly. Nothing suggests we are at war. It is a nostalgic, idealised version of domestic life, painted with a yearning for peace and normality. It's also evidence of an unusually intimate relationship between mistress and cook-housekeeper: both silently at work, sharing this small space separately but harmoniously.

Many women had their lives changed immeasurably by the war. Those who experienced war work, including thousands of former domestic servants, were tested to their physical and mental limits in both nerve-racking and exhilarating situations. They travelled widely, mixed widely and had their horizons permanently expanded. If Grace had been ten years younger, her story might have been very different. Instead, her war was intensely parochial. At Charleston she looked after what were, in effect, four male drones. Duncan, 54 at the outbreak of war, carried on painting. Clive, 58, enrolled in the Home Guard – as did Quentin, 29, whose past history of tuberculosis disqualified him from active service. Walter was willing to join the Home Guard if he could belong not to the Firle, but the Selmeston corps, which met conveniently in his regular haunt, the Barley Mow pub. 'There is a great deal of feeling among the wives about the part the Barley Mow plays in the whole affair', Vanessa wrote to Duncan in 1940. As it had seemed unpatriotic to keep Walter on as a full-time gardener, he found a job in the brickworks at Berwick, a 'reserved occupation' that kept him from conscription. By 1942, when Walter was 48 years old, men up to the age of 51 were being called up to fight.

Grace would willingly have played her part by looking after an evacuee or two, since Lewes was bursting at the seams trying to accommodate them all. But the upper middle classes were notoriously chary about accepting East End children – it is hard to imagine Vanessa Bell sharing her studio attic space with a couple of bed-wetters from Bermondsey. No doubt Grace, soft-hearted and maternal, had her views, but these went unrecorded. Country houses all over Britain were doing their patriotic bit, after all, and soon the local big houses – Firle Place, Sheffield Park, Admiralty House, Southover Grange – were commandeered to billet British and Canadian troops.

But Grace's story of simply tending to a middling-sized house and its occupants was not untypical of many a woman's experience during the Second World War. *Good Housekeeping* reminded the housewife of her essential, even heroic contribution:

Yours is a full-time job, but not a spectacular one. You wear no uniform, much of your work is taken for granted and goes unheralded and unsung, yet on you depends so much . . . Thoughtlessness, waste, a minor extravagance on your part may mean lives lost at sea, or a cargo of vitally needed bombers sacrificed for one of food that should have been unnecessary . . . We leave it to you, the Good Housekeepers of Britain, with complete confidence.[14]

That jittery summer of 1944, Walter had a hernia operation, Vanessa Bell had a mastectomy for breast cancer and Quentin had his appendix out. Charleston became a place of recuperation – and Grace was back at the stove, caring for them all. 'Everyone here has come to the rescue', Vanessa wrote to Leonard Woolf in August, 'Grace doing all the cooking and others coming in to help, so that I need do nothing but live like a lady if I only knew how.' Whatever Grace's 'live-out' arrangement with Vanessa after the Lottie spat, she could not let her mistress continue cooking dinner for the family. From this point on, the balance of power between Grace and Vanessa slowly began to shift in the other direction. Vanessa needed her. Grace looked after her. From being a 'hopeless amateur', a girl who once travelled on the overnight train to Provence with her head in Mrs Bell's lap, Grace was now a mother figure looking after a fragile woman of 66.

XI

Vote Labour

Victory in Europe Day, 8 May 1945, was marked in this corner of East Sussex by a party held at Tilton House by Lord and Lady Keynes for their workers, local soldiers and friends. In torrential evening rain, beer, biscuits and cheese were handed out to the Wellers,

Wests and Higgenses and all farmhands, surveyed by a giant effigy of Hitler made by Quentin. Vanessa and her family hovered awkwardly on the outskirts, listening to 'a painful episode of songs by the Dolt which reduced nearly everyone to ill-suppressed giggles', as she wrote to Angelica. 'He assured us with deep passion and very flat notes that the would stand by us whatever befell.' Peter John Higgens, about to turn ten, remembered 'a bonfire on the hill, bananas and oranges, chocolate, a bran tub with treats', and in the midst of it all Lord Keynes, walking around like a squire, 'distinguished-looking with a little moustache and bushy eyebrows'. He also remembered seeing Mrs Bell smile 'for the first time' when Charlie, a cockney chef working at a nearby army camp, swooped in and gave her a smacking kiss.

By Vanessa's sixty-sixth birthday at the end of the month, Grace had been twenty-five years with Mrs Bell. A general election was called that July, the first for ten years. Election posters were stuck up in the porch: 'Vote Labour' for Vanessa, Duncan and Quentin, 'Vote Liberal' for Clive. Remarkably, Walter was also allowed space by this egalitarian household: he pinned up 'Vote Conservative'. Grace professed herself to be 'in between'. The house newspapers were similarly divided: *The Times* for Clive, *The Daily Worker* for Quentin and the *Express* for Walter. Vanessa's investigations into working-class 'specimens' had gathered pace during the war. She had taken a businesslike interest in pig breeding and joined the local Pig Keepers' Council – unlike sentimental Grace, who treated the pigs like pets and hated them being killed, though she jointed and salted them down herself on the scrubbed kitchen table. 'The curious thing,' Vanessa wrote to her daughter, 'is that though these rustics can really hardly read or write . . . they are in some ways very sharp indeed – too sharp, you may think.'

On 5 July 1945 Clement Attlee's Labour Party won a landslide victory, their first majority government. Post-war reforms were pushed through with determination. Labour Party membership had risen fourfold between the wars (the Rodmell branch was hosted monthly by Leonard Woolf at Monk's House). Labour promised full employment, a National Health Service and a 'cradle-to-grave' Welfare State. Its campaign message 'Let's Face the Future' had tapped into the nation's impatient mood for change.

In 1949 Grace suffered a series of headaches, but, like so many women used to putting up with complaints because medicine cost money, she did nothing about it. Vanessa Bell insisted she saw a doctor at the new NHS surgery in Lewes, all upholstered waiting-room chairs and free magazines. On her return Grace was found in tears in the hall: in a desperate voice, she announced she had just shut a toad in the door. Vanessa got the charlady, Mrs Stevens, to remove the corpse and asked what the doctor had said. Grace had asked for new glasses but had not mentioned the headaches, as she'd heard that Mrs Carter, the cook at Tilton, was going stone deaf, and she thought by comparison her headaches could not be mentioned. 'I very nearly made Grace go straight back to tell the doctor her own symptoms', wrote Vanessa to Angelica with fond exasperation. 'I suppose Grace will just go on being Grace.'

How did Vanessa, now an austere, silver-haired 70-year-old, view her housekeeper? Though Grace was 46, Vanessa still instinctively thought of her as the willing, flustered girl from decades back. She had never become 'Mrs Higgens' in her mistress's mind; never taken on that dignified mantle of the upper servant. Grace had kept the same hairstyle she'd worn to her job interview – bobbed, held with a side clip – and its girlishness made her look slightly batty, grey as she now was.

Forty-six: this was properly middle-aged in 1949. Grace was in the autumn of her life, and her character was not going to change. She was who she was: easily startled, prone to inappropriate shrieks of laughter, soft-hearted. She was the sort who would pull the babies' pram into the kitchen ('Poor little darlings'), when Angelica left her twins out in the cold for their nap: the sort who would give George the postman a daily cup of tea and a bun and listen to his news. Grace found it hard to sleep and would lie in bed reading – 'all kinds of books, as many books as she could' said her son – well into the small hours. She was garrulous, sociable and tactile, throwing out her hand and giving you a push when something made her laugh. She had a horror of grubbiness, loved neat and cheerful flowerbeds, spoke passable French – and was quietly ambitious for her only son.

Her pocket diary for June 1947 notes that 'Peter John sat for exams'. This was the all-important Eleven-Plus, the exam that would see him go either to grammar school or to Lewes County Modern. He passed, and Grace got bolder still. She settled on Christ's Hospital, a boys' public school in Horsham some twenty miles away, with a tradition of funding pupils from poorer backgrounds. It is an ancient school with an esoteric uniform (belted long blue coats, knee breeches, yellow stockings); the sort of school her employers might have chosen for their own children. Perhaps she was told about it by Duncan, Clive or Vanessa – or perhaps not, as they seem to have lumped Peter John together with Walter as another dolt. I imagine Grace catching the cross-country train from Lewes, her beanpole son in slightly too short grey flannel trousers with his hair smarmed down. Grace would have been in her customary hat (she never went on a journey without a hat), gloves and clip-on earrings. She always wore earrings. Outwardly, she would have been calm and confident, but her hands clasped tightly on her handbag would have hinted at her anxiety.

Peter John did not get into Christ's Hospital. He failed the interview. 'So, young man, are you looking forward to joining our historic school?' asked the patrician headmaster, leaning back in his chair and fixing Peter John with a kindly yet unwavering stare. 'No, sir,' Grace's son had replied. 'Actually, I'm not. I'm happy just where I am. I don't want to move at all.'[15] And Grace had her ambition for him crushed in one sentence. It had all been her own idea – but he was her husband's son.

John dropped the 'Peter' from his name, went to Lewes County Modern and became head boy, for though he wasn't the brightest, he was the best at sport. 'John 36 runs against Ringmer' reads Grace's diary one summer's day after that fated interview. 'John's lip split by cricket ball' a couple of years later. Sport was his salvation – in a way that it had never been for Quentin Bell, overweight, uncoordinated and miserable at public school. For all Grace's fierce ambition, perhaps John had known instinctively what was right for him.

XII

Modern Milestones

Grace wrote an exclamatory sentence in biro in her new Women's Institute diary on 11 January 1953: 'John out to tea with Diana Piper!' Her 17-year-old son was out on another date with the girl he would eventually marry. Diana Piper – rosy-cheeked, outgoing, vivacious – blew into the closed world of Charleston in that Coronation year and shook things up. She brought with her an outsider's perspective on the whole ménage, questioning Grace's unthinking loyalty to the family and prompting John to ask if his mother was being taken for granted. Diana Piper was the granddaughter of a servant: her grandfather had been a groom for Lord Gage at nearby Firle Place. She had left school at 15 to work with horses, felt beholden to nobody and was surprised to discover that somewhere like Charleston still functioned the way it did. 'I didn't like the way they spoke to Grace,' Diana remembered. 'It was very formal. All Victorian standards.'

That spring John walked her up the long cart track, 'puddles and all sorts', to the farmhouse. First she was greeted by Blotto, Grace's hairy mongrel, who slept in a half-barrel kennel outside the back door. John led Diana past the clutter of coats and boots into the kitchen. 'Grace was there, as she always was – it wasn't very often you went to Charleston and didn't find her there, either at the sink or at the table, cooking,' she said. The first thing that hit her was 'this awful concrete floor'. Grace had long waged a campaign to replace it with linoleum, but Vanessa Bell had a prejudice against lino. Diana remembered too the comforting smells of the kitchen – percolating coffee, home-made soup simmering on the Aga. She took note of the one-gallon geyser over the kitchen sink for washing up (with no washing-up liquid, though 'Fairy' had been around since 1950); and the fact that all the Higgens family laundry was done there by hand. The four squeezed into their tiny sitting room and played card games with much talk and laughter ('they both liked to talk a lot'), while Grace kept an ear cocked for the call from the dining room. Diana watched with wonder the ritual of serving another family.

'It was different to my own home,' she said. 'We were just a family, two brothers and a sister.' At Charleston there was this other parallel but subtly different world through an interconnecting door. 'You would feel you were shut in this little sitting room, in case the family came out while Grace was doing her cooking. After a while I would come into the kitchen and talk to her, and I could see how hard she worked.' Diana would watch Mr Bell enter to get his gin and tonic from the old Frigidaire, acknowledging her with a gentlemanly nod. Mrs Bell would also nod and say 'good evening', very formal. But if Duncan Grant came in, 'his face would light up if he saw people – he'd ask you questions, he was just *interested*'. Diana soon learnt, like her boyfriend John before her, to 'pop back into the sitting room quick' if it was anyone other than Mr Grant.

On 2 April 1953, Grace and Walter took delivery of a black-and-white television set at a cost of £60 – around £1,200 in today's money – paid for in instalments on the new 'hire purchase' scheme (£6 down payment). That year, over a million televisions would be bought in Britain, bringing the total to 2.7 million. It was a hefty object boxed in teak veneer, duly admired by visiting guests; an object that would come to dominate the little sitting room, enhancing their cut-off life at Charleston. From this point, Grace began to record world news in her diaries. On 2 June, a cold day of sheeting rain, the Coronation of Elizabeth II was watched by the Higgenses and their friends the Ramsays. 'Beautiful reception on Television from abbey', wrote Grace that night. Vanessa Bell and Mr Grant, neither of them royalists, marked the day in London with plover's eggs and champagne.

It was a rare occasion that got Vanessa to London these days. After the war Clive returned there, Duncan shuttled between the two and Vanessa stayed on at Charleston. She had become weary of socialising, dreaded London parties and succumbed apparently happily to her contracting horizons. Her style of painting had fallen out of fashion; now her young granddaughters gave her her greatest pleasure: Amaryllis, Henrietta, and twins Frances and Nerissa. Angelica's marriage – at 24, to a man twenty-six years her senior – was not a happy one. Her husband Bunny Garnett (an ex-lover of Duncan Grant's, by a classic Bloomsbury twist), played the field while she was stuck in Huntingdonshire in a big house with very little help. 'It's really terrible that all your possible servants have fallen through', Vanessa wrote to her in 1952. 'It seemed more hopeful when I was with you.'

While Vanessa's world shrank, her housekeeper's began to expand. The modern milestones of the post-war era are ticked off one by one in Grace's diaries. In 1948 she gets a Vactric, which runs about polishing floors 'as if by itself'; in 1953 she buys the television, has her hair permed ('not too bad'), acquires her own passport and flies off on her first package holiday to Paris with a crocodile-skin travelling case and her friend Ruby Weller ('Horrible room in Hotel'). In 1954 she pays her first instalment on the *Encyclopedia Britannica*; in 1958 she's travelling again, this time on a week's package holiday by coach to Venice with Ruby and Mrs Harland ('lovely place'); and in 1961, aged 58, is the proud owner of a 'wonderful Hoover-Matic' washing machine (costing £90, a present from Mr Bell).

Grace also took to visiting country houses now open to the public, thanks to the fledgling National Trust and the Historic Buildings and Monuments Act of 1953, which ruled that in return for repair grants, the public should get a measure of access. Grace would join her WI friends on motorbus expeditions to Wakehurst Place, Haremere Hall, Alfriston Clergy House and Polesden Lacey, running her practised servant's eye over the interiors ('very grubby' was her verdict on one). If Grace saw any irony in herself, a housekeeper, visiting such houses as a tourist, she didn't comment on it. She was a working lady on her weekly day off, enjoying the scenery, nail scissors at the ready for furtive plant cuttings.

There was a price to pay for breaking her bounds. Time and again Grace records getting back from a holiday to find the sink full of dirty dishes, or the fridge full of stinking meat. There was the occasion when she found her big cauldron of soup, left expressly on the Aga for the family, still bubbling foully on her return. 'Spent day scrubbing & cleaning,' Grace recorded on her return from Paris. 'Took six buckets of water to scrub kitchen, it was filthy.' Going to the Paris ballet, riding down the Grand Canal on a Venetian gondola – well, it cast something of a grey pall over daily life. John began to take note of the small disrespects paid to his mother, such as Quentin walking through from his pottery with his 'clodhopper boots covered in clay' just after Grace had scrubbed the tiled passageway from front to back door; or the last-minute announcements that there would be eight to dinner, requiring a bus journey into Lewes to buy more food. Few suppliers would deliver to Charleston now; the long, potholed track was too much for the delivery vans.

Grace wasn't a moaner. She might exclaim, 'What a waste of time!' but she seemed outwardly content. There were signs, though, that she wanted something more from life. When the war ended, the women of Britain desired only to put their energies into home – their own home. Home was what the men had been fighting for, symbol of so much hope and pride. For many women it was more than a simple wish for privacy. Home was who they *were*, their 'creative power base', a projection of their very identity. 'Four walls and a roof is the height of my ambition', wrote one Mass Observation diarist after the war.[16]

Charleston was home to the Higgenses, but it was not *their* home. When Diana Piper met the family in the early 1950s, Grace was already on a housing list to get a council bungalow. She had started thinking about a life beyond Charleston.

But there were few houses to be had. After the war, prices had quadrupled. While Grace had been salting away her tips, her earnings and the Bell Christmas presents of crisp five-pound notes, she and Walter did not yet have enough to buy a home in East Sussex. When Angelica's old nurse Nellie Brittain visited, boasting a husband in the police force, a son in the civil service and general prosperity, Grace was made uncomfortably aware of how comparatively poorly off she was. Walter was fed up too. 'He thought they put on her too much,' said John, 'especially in the evenings, when she'd like to watch a television programme or listen to the radio, and she'd be called on – "Grace?" – and she'd have to come out of the sitting room and go and see to their needs.'

Or they'd be discussing something at dinner and decide to get their housekeeper's point of view,

and she'd readily give it; talk it over in the kitchen. Duncan, or Quentin, would come back into the dining room and say, 'Grace thinks so-and-so' – and they'd laugh, and think maybe she did have a point . . . very often this would occur.

It was flattering, this dependency on her. They wanted her not just for her cooking but for her opinions. Yet this summoning of Grace might go on up to ten or eleven o'clock at night, and the couple began to crave more privacy.

Her solution was to buy the old family house in Banham, Norfolk; two farm cottages knocked together, bought cheaply from her parents in 1958 and in need of modernisation. Grace had kept in constant touch with her family, writing home weekly, visiting every summer and sending her son off for the school holidays. She harboured a dream of retiring there now that John, who had a steady job with a television repair company, looked set to marry Diana. She and

Walter could live among her extended family and contribute to the smallholding. But the dream was just that: a dream. For, as the years went by, Grace found it harder and harder to contemplate leaving her ageing charges at Charleston. Gradually, they had come to depend upon her for everything.

XII

A Circle Closing

John Higgens married Diana Piper on Cup Final day, 2 May 1959. As Nottingham Forest played Luton Town at Wembley, televised live on *Grandstand*, Grace and Walter hosted a crowded reception at the brick and flint Trevor Arms in Glynde following a traditional church wedding. Diana wore 'a white ballerina length lace & nylon dress', while bridesmaid Sally looked 'very sweet in a pink embossed nylon dress.' Grace was every inch the proud mother in grey suit and hat, still with faint social ambitions ('the Champagne was a great success'), and annoyed that Walter had forgotten his braces so he didn't look as smart as he could for the photos. The Bells were not there, though they sent a generous cheque. Four days later Vanessa took to her bed, dangerously ill. 'Mrs Bell's heart very bad', wrote Grace in her diary. 'Doctor said she must stay in bed & have no salt. Very worried.' Her mistress was three weeks short of her eightieth birthday.

Grace was now 56, a matronly figure in a flowered overall straining over her bosom and tied tightly round the waist, a rigid iron-grey permanent 'set' and rheumatic joints. Now that her son had left home, she began to use her diary to make sense of the life she had chosen for herself. It was too late now to change its course.

There was a mood of reckoning, of taking stock. 'Walter & I have been married 25 years & we have been very happy & very lucky', she wrote. 'We have a son, whom any mother or father would be proud of, & we have our health . . . we are indeed fortunate people.' Grace did not appeal to God to get her through; she'd go and eat a cream bun and get her hair permed ('looks very nice'). Events beyond her small world were beamed into the sitting room each evening on the six o'clock news, recorded in her diaries as they happened: student riots in Paris, first man on the moon, the Vietnam War, Cliff Richard singing 'Congratulations' in the 'Song for Europe' contest.

To the Bloomsbury set she was now known as 'The Angel of Charleston', a name coined by Duncan Grant. It was no longer Vanessa, famous hostess, but Grace who was the mainstay of the house. She had become indispensable. As 'the backbone of Bloomsbury' she held enormous power, but there is no sense of this in her diaries. Rather, she seems still helplessly beholden to the family and its needs. In the winter of 1960 Vanessa Bell took Grace back to the South of France for an open-ended sojourn, leaving the now retired Walter to fend for himself and Diana heavily pregnant with the Higgenses' first grandchild. 'They collared her,' Diana told me, 'and although Grace was quite outspoken she always felt she had to be there for them. She *had* to look after them.'

'I am very lonely', wrote Grace from La Souco, an ant-infested villa near Monte Carlo with leaking taps and broken light switches, '& would much rather be in Sussex with Walter, Blotto & Sam' (the dog and cat). 'Goodness I am bored.' While Vanessa and Duncan were setting up their easels and painting the view, Grace was fiddling about with the gardener's primus stove to heat soup and boil eggs because the house had run out of gas. Her attempts to get to know the gardener and his wife – Grace had a 'great capacity for friendship', according to her son, 'all types and all walks of life' – were noted with faint disdain by Vanessa. 'Grace, who gets in touch with *everyone*, has been talking in some peculiar language to the old people below and makes them give her oranges and grapefruit and anything she wants', she wrote to Jane Bussy, whose house they were staying in. 'I have impressed it upon her that they all belong to you and not to the old couple.' Grace noted in her diary that, 'Mrs Bell said I was not to talk to her [the gardener's wife], poor old dear, but I shall take no notice, I am glad of her to talk to. Still no letters from England. Rained hard all day.'

There were brighter moments, too – Prince Andrew's birth; everyone complimenting her chicken risotto; a wonderful spree in Ventimiglia with Angelica, now 42, bringing back 'a very smart twin set which would cost me about six pounds in England.' (How Grace loved to dress up after all that depressing wartime utility wear.) Like her 18-year-old self, she still had a nicely observant eye for detail: 'The coach driver raced round the corners, spitting out of the window,' and 'We have a leg of lamb for lunch, with as much meat on as Marlene Dietrich's leg.' But no longer did Mrs Bell have the power to reduce her to misery with a stern look. Grace was bored, but she was no longer intimidated.

Her mistress was infuriatingly vague on when they might return. After several enquiries from Grace, Vanessa took the unusual measure of entering her housekeeper's bedroom late in March to announce slightly sheepishly that they 'might stay on longer'. Was the boot now on the other foot? It appears that Vanessa was a little nervous of Grace's authority, and had entered her private space to reassert herself. 'Mrs Bell informs me she has changed her mind about returning to England,' wrote Grace. 'Extraordinary woman never says the same thing twice. I don't know what to do.'

Vanessa Bell died at home the following spring, in 1961. She was tended throughout the night by her housekeeper, who spooned warm broth into her mouth and kept vigil. 'So brave,' wrote Grace as the bronchitis worsened. 'When the doctor asked her how she was, she said much better, her breathing is terrible.' She made up the bed for the night and changed her mistress's nightshirt. Vanessa passed away at midnight – still 'Mrs Bell' to Grace and reserved to the last, though pathetically dependent. 'I shall miss her terribly,' she wrote. They had been partners for forty years – half a lifetime, longer than many marriages; and at such close but very separate quarters. They'd shared moments of raw grief and pure terror; of doting joy over grandchildren and proud satisfaction over vegetable plots. Both loved juicy steak, zinnias, sunshine, small babies. Neither could function without cleanliness and order in the home.

They were like two halves of the same coin – though not once had mistress and housekeeper been photographed together. Her relationship with Grace was in the end the most consistent thing in Vanessa Bell's life, providing more stability than her marriage to Clive Bell or her companionship with Duncan Grant, who could never love her in the way she wanted. Strange as it now seemed, these two women, on different sides of the class divide, had made a silent pact with each other – and on that last trip to France there had been the sense of a circle closing.

While others mourned the great artist, mother and muse in words and letters, the housekeeper had the job of clearing out her mistress's room. 'Had a bonfire & burnt Mrs Bells' mattress & lots of her clothes, & pillows. Cleaned out her room & got it ready for Mr Bell.' At Vanessa's interment on 12 April there was just Duncan, Angelica, Quentin and Grace at the graveyard in Firle. Grace was taken aback by the austerity of the ritual: 'There was no one there,' she wrote in her diary; 'no Clergyman, no flowers except what I and Angelica took, & no service, we did not go into the church, the undertakers just put the coffin into the grave, we looked into it & then left.' This, to her mind, was not a proper leave-taking.

XIV

Work, Work, Work

Charleston after Vanessa Bell was a different place, and Grace established a different relationship with her new master. Duncan Grant, 76, had not shared Vanessa's hermit-like tendencies, and their relationship had often been heavy going and guilt-laden. Now the house hummed to his gregarious nature. A breezy irreverence and sense of equality was enjoyed between Grace and her new master (though he always remained 'Mr Grant'). They took to watching the boxing together in the Higgenses' little sitting room. 'I cannot regard Grace as anything but a family appendage',[17] Duncan wrote to Bunny Garnett. She was emphatically not, to his mind, a servant. Although the regime relaxed somewhat, since Duncan didn't much care about cleanliness, the constant flow of house guests vastly increased her workload. Grace was by now desperate to retire.

The younger generation took the place over once again: Angelica's teenage daughters, their friends and boyfriends used it at will. Quentin, his wife Olivier and their three young children descended from Newcastle upon Tyne every summer holiday. For all of them, Grace and her rock buns spelt instant comfort. Clive Bell, 80, was too frail to do more than gaze wistfully at these miniskirted young girls, but he continued to arrive and depart with his garrulous companion, the artist Barbara Bagenal, until his death in 1964. Charleston still suffered from an erratic water supply, insufficient heating and freezing pipes in winter – at which time Duncan Grant would be ferried off to louche outposts in Morocco by one of his young male muses, leaving the Higgenses to their own devices. 'Terribly cold', wrote Grace in her diary, December 1961. 'No water in the house. Afraid everything is frozen. Impossible to get warm with our electric fire.' 'I think you would like this place', came a postcard from Duncan; 'Every sort of flower in the garden . . . the sun is really hot.' His status as an artist and his energy for painting continued undimmed – Grace was flattered by his 'marvellous' portrait of her, 'full of life, much too grand for me' – but his mind was growing erratic.

How much more of her life should Grace give to this household? Quentin's daughter Virginia Nicholson believed that Charleston's housekeeper must have loved her job, since by the 1950s it was 'a seller's market, servants were forever walking out. Grace chose to stay;

she made her life there.' She probably couldn't explain even to herself why she stayed for so long. Grace didn't expect her son's generation to understand the pull exerted over her by her employers for half a century. Such unwavering loyalty belonged to another era, and she had been schooled in her values by a generation more remote still. When her own father was gravely ill during her final trip to Provence in 1960, Grace had agonised in her diary over whether or not she should return home to Norfolk. In the end she decided not to, because 'he had always told me to stay with Mrs Bell'.

But Mrs Bell was now no longer there, and by 1968 she had had enough, judging by diary entries from her life as a 65-year-old:

21 February 1968: Mr Grant said Amaryllis wants to bring three friends down next weekend. I am so tired, & my back aches.

22 February: Aired downstairs room, and made up bed for Amaryllis. Told Mr Grant, why not get Henrietta [Angelica's second daughter, aged 23] to come as housekeeper, he said he did not want her. I am too old to keep working & would like to leave, so that I could sit down & rest.

23 February: Amaryllis & her friends did not arrive until ten thirty in the evening, the Dinner was spoiled.

24 February: Amaryllis brought another friend name Boots for the weekend with his sheep dog. Extraordinary young man.

25 February: Mr & Mrs Spender left afterwards for London. Mrs Spender is the daughter of Maxim Gorky. She is very charming & considerate & left me a large tip.

26 February: Amaryllis & friend left for London after lunch, they did not rise until lunchtime, very untidy couple.

1 March: Scrubbed through lower passage.

2 March: Scrubbed bathrooms lavatorys & hall, kitchen this morning.

6 March: Washed my hair. Quite white.

She was a relic from another era: an upper servant, a *housekeeper*, now having to 'do the rough' – the work of charladies – in a barely recognisable modern world. Grace's son John claimed she turned a blind eye to what went on upstairs at Charleston: 'It was something she became acclimatised to; that was the way of life.' But Diana remembered Grace's tight-lipped reaction when she'd make up two beds and find only one slept in: 'The permissiveness of some of the guests – that was not good.' In January 1961 Grace had bought a copy of *Lady Chatterley's Lover* to send to her aged mother Bessie (Penguin's second edition, produced after winning the Obscene Publications trial). '*Disgusting* book,' she wrote in her diary, heavily underscored.

The Sexual Offences Act of 1967 had made for greater tolerance, and perhaps Duncan had become a touch casual. On 25 March, a day that 'a black man from Brighton came to tea,' something inside her snapped. It wasn't the young men per se, but the endless traffic of unexpected visitors: the bed making, the catering. Grace braced herself and bravely told Mr Grant that she would be retiring at the end of the year. 'He is upset, said I should go for a holiday, but where can we go?' *When could they go*, with house guests from May through to September? 'I'm so tired, I wish I could go away & never come back', she wrote on 2 September, a day Amaryllis knocked a large bottle of black ink over sheets, pillow case and carpet. 'Work, work, work, & meals, so many people, Oh I wish my house was near a road so I could live in it.'

Grace's Norfolk house had proved to be a white elephant. They had spent every summer holiday overseeing renovations, but neither she nor Walter had ever learnt to drive, which made the plan of retiring to the empty Fens an unfeasible one. They returned from a restorative fortnight in Devon in late September to be shown round her old friend Ruby Weller's retirement cottage, 'full of nice furniture given her by her children & Lady Keynes'. Charleston had now fallen into disrepair, with rising damp and rainwater staining the vibrant frescoes of another, earlier era. Frescoes, by Grace's judgement, painted some fifty years ago. By the winter of 1970 she could take no more.

XV

The Angel Of Charleston

The Higgenses settled into their new 'chalet' in nearby Ringmer with surprising alacrity. It had cost them £6,950 (around £70,000 in today's money), and Grace had paid for it in cash – in part from the sale of her Norfolk house, in part from savings. Grace had played the stock market for many years, using Clive Bell's regular financial advice, and been rather successful at it. She clearly had a housekeeper's head for figures. There had been an 'insane' leaving party for her, remembered Virginia Nicholson, 'at a peculiar restaurant in Lewes run by one of Duncan's disreputable male friends'. A socially awkward group of around forty had got rather drunk, Grace included. She was free at last! Why, then, did she feel so anguished? 'Somehow I dread going to live in my new house', she confided to her diary. 'I hate the idea of leaving Charleston.' It had been her home for thirty-seven years. Duncan Grant, now an incontinent 86-year-old, had pleaded with her not to leave – 'poor old dear', wrote Grace; 'he is so helpless'. Quentin Bell had even suggested that she rent out her new house until a replacement couple could be found to look after Duncan – advice that had incensed John Higgens. Did they think they *owned* his mother? On 1 March 1971 – a fortnight after 'Decimal Day' – two lorries had loaded up a lifetime's possessions from the attic.

When Quentin's wife Olivier Bell visited Grace in her new home she was taken aback by how *modern* it all was. 'Spick and span all over,' her daughter Virginia recalled her saying. 'But full of these wonderful pictures she'd been given over the years. It seemed incongruous to my mother – but not to Grace. Olivier had assumed, because of Charleston being lovely and old, and everyone loving old and characterful houses, that Grace would have chosen a rustic cottage.' How little they really knew Grace, whom Olivier had always liked very much but viewed (so she told me) as 'part of the furniture'.

Of *course* Grace was going to choose the ease of a centrally heated home with yellow fitted carpets throughout, a Formica kitchen, gas hob and tea at the touch of a Morphy Richards button. These were her dues, her reward after Charleston. With her snappy little mongrel Dandy at her heels, Grace quickly slotted into community life in Ringmer, revelling in being able to walk to the shops, spend time with her granddaughters Jackie and Suzanne without racing back to prepare Mr Grant's dinner, and control her own destiny. (She never could get used to shopping for herself, writing 'every mortal thing' she bought down in her diary.) Walter pottered happily in his patch of garden, free from 'that lot' at last.[18]

For most career servants, this was the moment at which you might lose your identity. Stepping outside the protection of the big house, you were no longer defined by what you did or where you once lived. Unless you were kept on in an estate cottage and were nominally involved in the running of the house (as so many 'treasures' were), you were ejected into an indifferent universe. In 1971, being a former servant was not necessarily something you wanted to boast about. Yet wholly unexpectedly, Grace was to find herself courted in retirement as something of a curiosity. Her memories had acquired a market value. First came a documentary-maker a year before she left Charleston, a man who thanked her for 'all the scones and cups of tea' while he made his film about Virginia Woolf, which included a clip of the housekeeper reminiscing in the kitchen. 'I know you will look and sound superbly', he wrote.[19] The scene was dropped at the final edit and Grace was 'secretly a little pleased',[20] as the sudden attention was rather discomfiting.

Then came another film crew to make *Duncan Grant at Charleston*: it needed three takes for Grace to get her memories right as she stirred a pudding at the kitchen table, faltering over names and dates as the cameras rolled. Her voice is soft and careful, her accent mimicking that of her employers. 'Ay don't usually hev much time for modelling,' she told the film-maker.[21] Her everyday Norfolk vowels wouldn't do in front of company.

A few years later the writer and publisher Nigel Nicolson contacted her while editing the letters of Virginia Woolf. 'What a remarkable record!' he wrote in reply to what must have been a long letter from Grace. 'And what an important slice of English history you witnessed during all those years.'[22] *Important?* This is not how it might have seemed to Grace at the time, as she carried cans of hot water up creaking stairs to guests' bedrooms and scrubbed out the lavatory on their departure. But it gave a woman a sense of self-worth, actually to be sought out as a witness to 'history'. In 1979 she was interviewed again for a book on Vanessa and Duncan, then in 1980 for Vanessa Bell's biography. Grace was of increasing interest – if only as a conduit to the Bloomsbury Group.

There is no doubt that she'd enjoyed the frisson of glamour that came from being part of Bloomsbury, and this was probably one of the reasons she chose to stay for so long. The work was hard, but it could be interesting. Not many housekeepers were on such familiar terms with E. M. Forster that they wanted to call their dog 'Morgan' (gently discouraged by Mrs Bell); or had watched Sir Frederick Ashton 'leaping about Charleston Lawn with red Roses threaded in his hair'; or served George Bernard Shaw and Bertrand Russell her Queen of Puddings (sponge cake soaked in egg and milk, topped with jam and meringue). Yet there were other reasons for her steadfastness that outsiders couldn't begin to guess at.

By the time of Grace's retirement, Walter, John and Diana Higgens were united against the Charleston regime and had made their views known to her. John struggled to understand her loyalty when 'they expected so much of her, for so little. I thought she should give it up'. His father Walter 'didn't like to show unwilling against the family, but he did think that they used to take my mother for granted, and she shouldn't have done all what she did do, and not for so long. She at times was treated like a skivvy.'

The truth was that after fifty years of service, Grace was unable to separate her narrative from the Bells'. Her connection with this family predated her marriage to Walter by fifteen years; her photograph albums were filled with pictures of Bloomsbury children and grandchildren, who continued to visit and write to her in retirement like a favourite aunt. This had been not so much a job as a vocation. There was a sense – unpalatable to John, Walter and Diana – that her employers were more 'family' to Grace than her own people. Every letter sent to her by the Bells and Mr Grant she kept as having an emotional value. Most contain instructions; others reveal a touching mutual affection. 'I thought of you as I eat a *wonderful* steak(!)', Vanessa wrote from Iseo in Italy, 1952; 'just right. Thick & *juicy*.' Later, from Venice, she sent impressionistic word sketches to her housekeeper from her bedroom window: 'three boys, practically naked, rowing a boat about the Canal at 7pm'. After Vanessa's death Grace had received a letter from Angelica, together with a cheque

for more than what I originally told you because I feel sure that is what Nessa would have wished, if she had realised how little money can buy these days . . . The actual amount has nothing to do with her fondness for you & her reliance on you, which as you know was unmeasurable – but she would have been happy to think it might be spent on something that would make life easier for you.

Grace's blue biro has heavily scored out the three-figure amount: she didn't want anyone to find out how much she'd been left. When Duncan Grant died in 1978, aged 93, he left her £500 – the equivalent of £5,000 today. 'I did not expect it', wrote Grace, 'as I did not think the poor darling had much money.'

Grace would occasionally grumble, but she did not consider herself exploited. To think this would be to deny a lifetime's work its validity. She continued to fill her scrapbooks with press cuttings on the circle and, when tracked down by journalists seeking to denigrate 'Bloomsbury' (as had become fashionable), she was staunchly loyal. 'I was just happy to spend my time with them,' she told a *Sunday Times* reporter in 1981, three years after Duncan Grant's death. 'They were my kind of people.' In retrospect, viewed from the dignified comfort of her three-piece suite, hers had been a 'marvelous' career. If she had a blind spot in her memories, then it suited her.

It also suited the Bell–Grant household to idealise their housekeeper. She would be addressed with fond irony as 'Amazing Grace'; 'The presiding genius of Charleston', or 'The Angel of Charleston' – as if her work was a divine calling and it were simply a matter of sprinkling fairy dust around to change the sheets, peel the onions, scrub the passageways and wash the dishes. With nicknames like these, how could Grace complain? For all that her son saw her 'treated as a slave', doing 'ongoing, unrewarding work', *she* was the Angel of Charleston, and so it was work worth doing. Advantage had undoubtedly been taken of Grace's cheerful nature – but she was complicit in the deal.

Grace developed breast cancer in 1983, aged 79 – and, unlike Vanessa Bell, she did not survive it. Walter had died a year earlier at 88. Their deaths coincided with the restoration of Charleston, steered by Quentin Bell and his wife Olivier. John and Diana Higgens were among the first tourists in 1986, and it was a bizarre experience. All looked so familiar. John wanted to reach out a hand and touch things to bring back memories, but 'You mustn't touch!' said the guide. 'You mustn't sit on any chairs!' He was surprised by the 'over-the-top' descriptions of objects he hadn't given a second glance – the red Omega Workshop dining chairs, the pictures on the walls, the painted mantelpieces. But when the group moved into the kitchen, he knew he was on solid ground. Ticked off for pulling out the old kitchen drawer where he used to keep his toys, John felt he had to speak up. 'Excuse me,' he said, 'I don't think certain things are correct.' The floor, he told them, had once been concrete, not these square terracotta tiles. The walls had been covered in ugly lead pipes, the original sink was much lower and smaller and there was no modern, gas-fired Aga but an old brute, 'a so-and-so to get alight', that required stoking with coke. The Charleston curators' obsession with authenticity hadn't made it into the kitchen. This dark little room, once the hub of the house, had been given a tasteful makeover.

The other tourists looked at John Higgens with new interest – this tall, diffident man who might be able to get them one step closer to Bloomsbury. 'It did strike me as rather strange, their interest in me,' he reflected. 'I didn't assume that I was important at all. Obviously my mother was an important person here, but people seemed to think that I might know certain things.' The room he'd grown up in was essentially gone, but his mother was commemorated with a plaque behind the Aga. Quentin the potter had glazed some tiles in tribute to the cook-housekeeper who had given his family half a century of her life: 'Grace Higgens, née Germany, 1904–1983, worked here for fifty years & more. She was a good friend to all Charlestonians.' It was the Bloomsbury equivalent of a gravestone in the family churchyard.

Actually Grace was born in 1903, but it was the spirit of the thing that mattered: she hovered over the farmhouse still, a benevolent angel in flowered nylon housecoat, duster in one hand, soup ladle in the other. For John, this was one step towards redressing the balance. 'I think in their own way they really did like her and love her,' he later concluded – 'in some sort of fashion, to the best of their ways.'

Epilogue

Nicky Garner of Holkham Hall, Norfolk 2013

Applicants will be required to be conscientious, reliable and discreet at all times.

ADVERTISEMENT FOR HOUSEKEEPER, HOLKHAM HALL, 2007

Something Almost Military

Nicky Garner drives through the Triumphal Arch in her black Nissan Note. It's 8.30 a.m. and she's running late. Two miles to go – into the deer park, over the cattle grid, a curve to the right and there it is: a severe Palladian slab in yellowish brick, crisp against its green parkland, straight off the eighteenth-century architect's page. She swings into the immense gravel forecourt and climbs out: a diminutive, youthful figure in biker boots, tight black trousers and quilted gilet.

She enters Holkham Hall through the porter's door and makes straight for her small office in the service wing. Neatly pinned certificates, from firefighting to tower-scaffolding safety, line its walls. Her desk faces the butler's, but Daniel Green isn't in yet. Last night's corporate banquet must have gone on late. She logs on: several emails from 'Lady C', one from the new flower-arranging lady, one from the enterprises manager. A discreet Aztec tattoo is visible on Nicky's right hand as she clicks away with her computer mouse.

This is the head housekeeper. Many things about Nicky's role today would be unimaginable to the women in the pages of this book. Most obviously, just now, that she shares an office *with a man*; that she is expected to *make her own tea* from an electric kettle; and that Her Ladyship is so constantly in touch, with such a stream of *informal* correspondence. The photograph of Nicky's two young sons pinned to the wall might catch the eye of Dorothy Doar, dismissed for requesting six weeks' maternity leave back in 1832. Nicky lives locally with her family, and it is unthinkable that she might desert them as Mrs Doar and Mrs Wells were forced to do in the nineteenth century.

Her priorities lie outside the Triumphal Arch, and it might seem obvious, looking at the calm, unflustered face of Holkham's housekeeper, that there is little drama or tragedy in her world. She is not crushed or bowed down by her job. She has to suffer none of the random injustices and upheavals of her predecessors; her life is not lived on the edge, or riven by crisis. Nicky Garner is the last in the line of this great tradition – and, thankfully, outwardly her life could not be more different.

She has put the morning aside to take me on a tour of the house, now closed to the public for winter. As we walk through the vast rooms (faded red flock wallpaper; Gainsboroughs and Guido Renis at every turn), she talks of her goals for the 'closed season.' This year she's putting her four girls on to the Saloon, the South Drawing Room, the South Dining Room, the Classical Library, the Manuscript Library and the Long Library. All six staterooms are to be 'deep-cleaned' by April next year when the house reopens to the public, and Nicky will lead the work from the top plank of the scaffolding, her 'Museum Vac' slung over one shoulder like a handbag, inching her way down the seventeenth-century Flemish tapestries with her suction nozzle.

I ask if she's always this hands-on. 'Absolutely. I will help clean the chandeliers, the canopies on the beds, the pictures, the picture frames. Everything you can see, everything you can touch, we take care of.' Is there a pride in doing this kind of work? 'Absolutely!' This is Nicky's favourite word, and it suits her: definite, deliberate. 'I'm not just cleaning. I'm conserving. I'm making a difference.' A walkie-talkie sticks out of her back pocket and as we walk, it crackles with news of distant estate business. Everyone at Holkham is *connected*. Nicky has a purposeful walk – forward leaning, proprietorial. Her dark brown eyes sweep each room, checking the closed shutters, the carpet pile, the fenders, the door handles ('Lord and Lady Coke like to see very shiny, very brassy door handles and fireguards').

The house as a whole is one very great work of art, crammed with the extraordinary spoils of the 1st Earl of Leicester's eighteenth-century Grand Tour. Daily Nicky's girls stride with their cleaning boxes past Poussins and Titians, Van Dycks and Canalettos to tackle the sagging Georgian furniture, the priceless silver plate and porcelain, the sixty Roman sculptures dotted around the place (one in a guest bathroom, peering voyeuristically down at the bath). It is an awe-inspiring place to work – and to visit, for Holkham is open to the public three days a week, seven months a year. Thirty thousand visitors tramp through these rooms annually. Add to this a heritage-industry programme of corporate jamborees, banquets, weddings, festivals and fairs, all requiring 'some serious overtime' from domestic staff, and you get a picture of the reinvented English country house that none of our previous housekeepers would recognise.

Nicky Garner is part of this reinvention. Her role is extraordinarily multifaceted: she's waging war on the moth infestation, she's digitally cataloguing the contents of the Fabric Room, she's showing corporate guests to their bedrooms. But Holkham Hall is also a family home, and for Nicky the Cokes (pronounced 'Cooks') come before all else.

Having resurrected the stories of servants long dead, I was fascinated to see this relationship with a family in action. It surprised me to find a twenty-first-century housekeeper with so much invested emotionally in her job. Central to this reverence – and reverence is not too strong a word for what Nicky feels – is the housekeeper's relationship with her mistress. Nicky is Lady Coke's right-hand woman – she is her eyes, her ears and her constant prop.

Today the old master-servant relationship is closer than ever – the service wing is just a door away from Lady Coke's Aga, and communication just an email or phone call away. 'I tell Nicky to call me whenever she wants to talk,' says her mistress – and she does, frequently. Back in the mid-nineteenth century, Holkham employed sixty indoor servants. Today it has just six full-time and nine part-time staff, and there is a greater dependency on them than ever. Hanging in the corner of the laundry room is a flimsy Bellville Sassoon vintage dress in cream chiffon that Nicky will repair by hand. The modern housekeeper is as much lady's maid as head housemaid; nothing should be beneath her. But if the prestige of the role is consequently lower, such intimacy brings its own rewards. 'I'm up close and personal with Lady Coke's clothes, her shoes, her children,' says Nicky. She'll even feed her mistress's Black-headed Caique parrot, Basil. 'I'm part of an extended family. I feel appreciated and very much looked after.'

Crackle crackle goes the walkie-talkie.

'Nicky, it's Lady Coke, are you receiving?' The voice is light, friendly, not obviously posh.

'Yes, go ahead Lady Coke.' Nicky's accent is faintly Norfolk, faintly primary-school teacher. She emanates dependability.

'Nicky, do you know where I could find some fabric to decorate the Santa's grotto?' Holkham is preparing for its Christmas opening.

'Yes of course, Lady Coke, there are some nice bits in the store cupboard in the laundry.'

'That's brilliant, Nicky; would you be able to gather them all up and leave them outside my kitchen, please?'

'Yes of course, Lady Coke, I'll do that straight away.'

'Nicky, that's *brill*, thank you.'

The housekeeper is above all a *giver of comfort*, physical and emotional, and her fundamental reward is being appreciated. It is a specifically female transaction, and it is a timeless one. The same relationship did not – and does not – exist between the master of the house and the butler. Lady Coke is conscientious about praising Nicky Garner. She is a great believer in the handwritten thank-you note, the box of Thornton's chocolates after a big event. It makes a difference. It helps transform a potentially complicated relationship into something mutually satisfying and pleasurable. But it is a delicate relationship all the same, and it is at the heart of the stories I have told here.

Think of Dorothy Doar, welcoming her long-absent Regency mistress to Trentham Hall with roast partridge and apple tart back in 1831; and of Sarah Wells at Uppark, pulling off a High Victorian house party at the age of 69, her efforts ignored by her mistress: 'Miss F very quiet . . . Miss F never asks if I am tired.' Remember Ellen Penketh before her sudden fall from grace, collaborating with her mistress on each triumphant bout of Edwardian entertaining at Erddig, her Charlotte russe invariably chosen for dessert because she did it *so well*. Then there is the greatest charmer of them all, housekeeper Hannah Mackenzie, flying 'like a bird' to those Wrest Park First World War surgeons, in the absence of any praise from her mistress, attending to their needs until they were 'tied to her little finger'. And think of Grace Higgens, the 'treasure', whose diaries noted every tip, every kiss bestowed on her cheek, every compliment for her cooking – in part because they were so rare.

In 2007 Lady Coke had placed an advertisement on the Holkham Hall website for a housekeeper. She, her husband and their four children had recently moved into this austerely beautiful palace set in 25,000 acres on the windswept North Norfolk coast. Along with the house they inherited the old staff that had worked for Viscount Coke's father, the 7th Earl of Leicester – some since the age of 16. 'I was given no book of tips from my mother-in-law,' says Lady Coke. 'I would have asked for advice, but I didn't know what to ask.' It was an 'incredibly daunting' period, she remembers, adjusting to the scale of Holkham and working out how to run it as a business. 'There was a certain resistance to change among the staff. We weeded out those who didn't have the right attitude.' To Lady Coke, this elusive *attitude* is all.

'Suitable applicants will be required to be conscientious, reliable and discreet at all times', read the advertisement. 'Excellent references and a good previous employment history are essential.' Lady Coke also used an employment agency, but she soon discovered that if you mentioned Holkham Hall it either put people off, or it made them apply for the wrong reasons. 'If you recruit someone to live in, they often have ideas about being in a position of power. They're hands-off, managerial. I want someone to be hands-*on*, not afraid of getting down on their knees if necessary.'

The story of Lady Coke – Polly – echoes the story at Erddig Hall a century earlier, when new chatelaine Louisa Yorke moved into the big house. Neither Polly, a milliner by profession, nor Louisa, a parson's daughter, were to the manor born. Both women came unexpectedly to these big houses set in remote rural parts of England. Those who served 'the Hall' – Erddig in North Wales, Holkham in North Norfolk – came from families who had done so for generations. Each mistress (decisive, creative, on the cusp of 40) blew in as the agent of change. It was never going to be easy.

'Oh! The trouble of the servants at Erddig', Louisa Yorke wrote in her diary in 1902. 'The new Housekeeper Mrs Osmond is to leave at once. She will do no work except arrange flowers!' And so it turned out at Holkham. They came and they went: older women with a certain self-importance, 'lady housekeepers' who would not roll up their sleeves and who alienated their staff. They had the wrong *attitude*. Polly Coke might not have been born to the role (her mother, the fashion designer Belinda Bellville, still thinks it a good joke that her chaotic daughter should have ended up mistress of Holkham). But she knew that the housekeeper was essential to the happiness of her home. Like Louisa Yorke before her, Lady Coke decided to ignore the recruitment agencies and go with her instincts.

There are qualities you can list on a CV, or pick up on at interview, but there is something indefinable about a good housekeeper. In Nicky's case you could argue that it is genetic. Nicky comes from the Butters clan – and Butters, historically, were born to serve. Her great-grandfather Henry Butters was a lifelong Hall handyman. His son, Fredrick Butters, was a footman and under-butler. Great-aunt Althea worked in the estate office after the Second World War, then as a room steward welcoming the first public visitors to Holkham in 1950; she married Albert Butters, another Hall handyman who doubled up as a footman. Auntie Sheila Gibson, 'very particular, a bit of a clean freak', was housekeeper to the 7th Earl of Leicester in the 1990s.

Nicky was born in 1979, eight years after Grace Higgens retired from Charleston. It was thought, back then, that treasures like Grace were the last of their kind – and that, with their passing, the fortunes of the English country house had waned. In 1955 these houses were being demolished at the rate of one every five days. By 2000, one in five (some 1,500) had gone. Those that survived had to adapt to a new world – and a different sort of servant. The Duke of Westminster was incensed to be taken to an industrial tribunal in 2002 by his former housekeeper Mrs Hewson, who claimed unfair dismissal from Eaton Hall, Cheshire because her face 'no longer fitted'. It was countered that she had 'harassed' her underlings and spread 'malicious gossip'.¹ Mrs Hewson lost the case, and the Duke won a High Court injunction banning her from revealing details of his private life.

This is the sort of tale to make blue blood run cold, for the house-keeper's position is, above all, one of trust. 'They see me in my dressing gown. They see me shouting at my husband,' says Lady Coke, who finds the lack of privacy one of the hardest things about her new life. But she had a gut feeling about Nicky Garner, a part-time cleaner at Holkham Hall with a forthright, personable manner and strong work ethic. 'Not at all the stereotype; the sort you might go and have a beer with.'

Nicky is not the stereotype – she's young, she's of her time, she has her Aztec tattoo (and four more, she wouldn't say where). But for all the immediate differences, I think my five earlier housekeepers would still recognise her as *one of them*. She has the same obsessive, literal-minded attention to detail; the same character that can't step back from the job. They would nod approvingly at Nicky's mantra, 'Methodical, adaptable and logical'. There is something almost military about her. 'I've always been ridiculously methodical,' she says, flipping open a folder and showing me her annual graph on moth reduction (down fifty per cent in the staterooms and Statue Gallery).

When summoned to Lady Coke's office in 2011 and offered the top job, Nicky wasn't sure she could do it. She has always viewed herself as a grafter – 'someone who works really hard but never gets anywhere'. She was intimidated by the title Head Housekeeper, wondering if she shouldn't be called Cleaning Supervisor instead. But, as she soon discovered, cleaning was the most straightforward part of her role.

'Grateful, tearful and slightly petrified', she signed up for a trial period. 'It was such an *honour*. I felt I had a lot to prove.' But unlike our previous housekeepers, it was never assumed that she would do it all by herself. The daunting responsibility of running Holkham Hall was not placed squarely on her shoulders, but shared by a network of senior staff – estates director, enterprises manager, collections and security manager, cook – with the Cokes just as closely involved. Nicky's previous job was in catering, but her mistress didn't seize the opportunity and make her cook-housekeeper, as Louisa Yorke did with Ellen Penketh. Today that would be seen as exploitation. Portuguese cook Maria is in charge of the family and big events, while mistress *and* master like to cook in their own kitchen. If indifferent fare is served up to important visitors, it is the enterprises manager, not Holkham's housekeeper, who takes the rap.

As a child, Nicky used to picnic in the grounds of Holkham Hall like any other tourist, and she found it hard to believe that somebody actually *lived* there. Like a castle in a fairy tale, it fascinated her. 'It was so *huge*. And I was so tiny.' Today, as she swings her car down the avenue and sees the great house before her, 'I think, Wow! I *work* in there.' None of her forebears had the same daily experience of a fresh perspective on their place of work. They lived in the house; they spent their days in its service quarters. They could never step back from it.

Nicky feels awe, and she also feels pride. Perhaps not for a hundred years has this great house been so well looked after, and she is part of its renaissance. There is a level of luxury and an attention to detail throughout – from the little silver vases of flowers in each bedroom, to the crisply laundered linen napkins at the breakfast table – that can only be attained by a highly motivated professional team.

The Hall has a long tradition of hospitality. In 1822 it was said to be 'always full and very like an Inn, for people arrive without any previous notice and seem to stay as long as they like'.[2] Even in the dark days of the Second World War and its aftermath it kept up appearances. When James Lees-Milne visited in June 1947 on behalf of the National Trust, he found it to be 'superbly kept up, all the steel grates, for instance, shining brightly, the work of one devoted daily', despite the fact that Lady Leicester had a nervous breakdown 'brought on by the anxiety and worry of keeping up Holkham with practically no servants. What these wretched landowners have to go through!'[3]

Male Cokes have always been house-proud, even housekeeperly. In the 1950s and 1960s the 5th Earl of Leicester would go and check the lavatory paper and the writing paper in all the bedrooms, to his wife's exasperation. Polly's husband Tom, Viscount Coke (son of the 7th Earl), is equally fastidious. He checks the fridge; he goes through the recycling bins. In Holkham's public spaces 'he'll pick out a cobweb at one hundred miles. He's got more quirks than Lady Coke,' says Nicky. 'He hates chemicals. He's definitely one for the brass. He's fanatical about linseed oil.'

Nicky must train her four girls in the Holkham Hall ways, such as Lady Coke's obsession with the level of water in the flower vases. 'My new girl Claire is *petrified*. Petrified that she'll bump into Lord or Lady Coke; that she'll get something wrong.' Victorian maids caught at work would once feign invisibility. Today, the down-to-earth Cokes would be mortified if their staff thought them unapproachable – but these old upstairs-downstairs reflexes are, not surprisingly, hard to lose when you work in a house as historically grand as this.

If Nicky Garner and Polly Coke had met as strangers, say, while walking their dogs on the white sands of Holkham beach, there would be none of this standing on ceremony. They would be two local mothers – one small and sturdy, the other tall and willowy – equally entitled to ownership of this ravishing stretch of British coastline. Class distinctions are less immediately obvious today. But once the big house is brought into the equation, the setting seems to demand a different sort of protocol. Polly winces when journalists use the title Viscountess Coke, but there is no getting away from it. The heft of Holkham Hall enforces this slightly absurd world of lords and ladies, housekeepers and butlers. Nicky and Polly are both playing a role, and each has had to work hard at her part.

Nicky has been sent on many a human resources training course, from people management to etiquette. Lady Coke is blunt about her housekeeper's foibles: 'She can be too chatty, overfamiliar. She's had to learn when to hold back, to learn the manners of a different generation. For example, I don't want her saying goodbye to guests at the same time that Tom and I are seeing off our friends. But she doesn't mind being told.'

'It's all part and parcel,' Nicky shrugs. 'I've learnt through trial and error.' She still has excruciating moments – such as the time she gave Lady Coke a grateful hug in return for a present. 'I thought, Oh God, I'm going to get a warning now.' But she didn't. Lady Coke hugged her back and told her not to worry. 'Still, I walked away and thought, I shouldn't have done that.' Does she sometimes feel as if she's bowing and scraping? 'Yes, especially when I'm apologising. And it has to be "Lord and Lady Coke"; I've learnt not to overstep the mark. It's a humble position; there is a lot of yes sir, no sir.' But Nicky thrives on all this; she *likes* working for what she calls 'high-ranking people'.

When I asked Lady Coke if I might spend a day with her housekeeper, she first sought Nicky's permission. It wasn't what she might say that bothered Lady Coke; she just wanted to make sure her housekeeper would be comfortable appearing in a book. Nicky, for her part, was honoured. 'I'm quite excited, to say the least. Thank you so much for giving me this opportunity,' she'd emailed back to her mistress – who was, in turn, rather touched. Such transparency did not exist a century previously. In 1907, the Yorkes of Erddig Hall were *mortified* to have the workings of their household exposed in court. Servants 'getting above themselves' were once firmly to be discouraged, and an instinctive reticence was the result. Hannah Mackenzie lost her job for forgetting her place at Wrest Park in 1915. Grace Higgens was hesitant talking to journalists about Charleston even in her retirement.

But Nicky is very much a talker, and shows every sign of becoming a Holkham Hall 'character', a fixture like her aunts Althea Butters and Sheila Gibson before her. Does she see herself here in twenty, even thirty years' time? 'Absolutely! If I ever leave I'll be dragged out kicking and screaming.' But while Polly's tenure at the Hall will pass into history, in time becoming the story of the 8th Earl and Countess of Leicester, Nicky's most probably won't. She might be remembered anecdotally for her obsession with moths, or for the green and gold she revealed in the tapestries by introducing the Museum Vac. She might even get her portrait painted, a new Coke tradition introduced by the 7th Earl in 1993. But who will be able to discover the story of Nicky Garner in a hundred years' time?

This book has shone a light on a handful of women who, for the most part, did not make it into history. It has resurrected them as human beings rather than as footnotes in the archives: real women with opinions, hopes, anxieties and crises. Many were erased from the story of the big house, and I like to think that in tuning into their faint voices, in sifting through the evidence, I've helped to set the record straight. There were many hundreds of such women working in the basements of our great houses throughout the nineteenth and early twentieth century; these are just five representative stories. Read together, they form a salute to the dedication, tenacity and sheer hard toil of the housekeeper, and an attempt to give her back the dignity she was largely denied in life.

Prologue

1 'At Holkham Hall': Adeline Hartcup, *Below Stairs in the Great Country Houses*, p. 93.

2 'A goody sort': *Below Stairs*, p. 89.

3 'The under-maids': Eric Horne, *What the Butler Winked At*, p. 65.

4 'Out of Dickens': ed. Merlin Waterson, *The Country House Remembered*, p. 42.

5 'Faithful and excellent': Wilton Household Regulations, quoted in Jeremy Musson, *Up and Down Stairs: The History of the Country House Servant*, p. 148.

Part 1: Dorothy Doar

The Sutherland Collection at the Staffordshire Record Office (SRO D593) is my source for all family and servant correspondence, estate ledgers, floor plans, wage books and miscellaneous records, unless otherwise stated.

1 The Leveson-Gowers' wealth and houses, guest comments: Eric Richards, *The Leviathan of Wealth: Sutherland Fortune in the Industrial Revolution*.

2 'Pigmy and dingy': Gervas Huxley, *Lady Elizabeth and the Grosvenors, Life in a Whig Family 1822–1839*.

3 'Jewellery worth £3,622. 8s. 6d.': *The Leviathan of Wealth*.

4 'I rushed to the potager': 19 November 1828. *Letters of Harriet, Countess Granville, 1810–1845*.

5 French appendix: Samuel and Sarah Adams, *The Complete Servant*.

6 'Strictly abstain from all conjugal intercourse': *The Diaries of Sylvester Douglas*.

7 'Encourage Sellar in trouncing these people': *The Leviathan of Wealth*.

8 'As good as a play': Thomas Creevey, *The Creevey Papers*. Entry from 1833.

9 'A delightful voyage': Letters of Elizabeth, Countess of Sutherland and Marchioness of Stafford, to her husband George, Marquis of Stafford (later 1st Duke of Sutherland) during her visit to Sutherland. SRO D6579/11/1–41.

NOTES

10 Samuel and Sarah Adams, *The Complete Servant*. (1825)

11 'She must be able to undertake': correspondence to James Loch, SRO D593/K/3/1/5.

12 'Every shilling we have': James Loch to William Lewis, SRO D593/K/1/3/20.

13 The Potteries: *Employment of Children and Young Persons in the District of the North Staffordshire Potteries and on the Actual State, Conditions and Treatment of Such Children and Young Persons*; report by Dr Samuel Scriven, submitted 1841, published 1843.

14 1840 wages book for all four houses: SRO D593/R/4/3.

15 Dunham Massey: Pamela Sambrook, *A Country House at Work*.

16 Mrs Ingram's vouchers, 1874: SRO D593/R/10/7.

17 'Little things': Julia McNair Wright, *The Complete Home*, quoted in Asa Briggs, *Victorian Things*.

18 List taken from the 1826 inventory of household furniture at Trentham Hall, SRO D593/R/7/10b.

19 'Best yellow soap': Mrs Ingram's vouchers.

20 A list for the value of meals: Mr Vantini's accounts books 1833–38, Household Disbursements. SRO D593/R/1/8.

21 1803 linen inventory, Trentham Hall. SRO D593/R/7/2.

22 The Countess of Carlisle: Dorothy Henley, *Rosalind Howard, Countess of Carlisle*.

23 An 1864 entry from Jane Welsh Carlyle, *Letters and Memorials*. Jane Welsh Carlyle was a letter writer, diarist and wife of essayist Thomas Carlyle.

24 Foundling Hospital. John R. Gillis, 'Servants, Sexual Relations and the Risks of Illegitimacy in London, 1801–1900'. *Feminist Studies* vol. 5, no 1, Spring 1979.

25 *Bucks Herald*, *Lloyd's Weekly Newspaper* and *Sheffield Independent* between 15 and 29 December 1849.

26 'A liberal use of their sticks': *Staffordshire Advertiser*, 4 February 1832.

27 ''This is our time!': *Bath Chronicle and Weekly Gazette*, 5 April, reporting on the court case for the October 1831 Bristol and Bath riots.

28 Charles Dickens, *Sketches by Boz*, 'Gin-Shops', Chapter XXII. Published 1833–6 in newspapers and periodicals.

29 'Her Ladyship desires me to say': letters from Loch to Lewis and Lewis to Loch, from SRO D593/K/3/1/18 and D593/K/3/2/12.

30 'You will excuse my troubling you': miscellaneous correspondence with James Loch, SRO D593/K/1/3/20.

31 Ball at Ashburnham House: *Morning Post*, 13 April 1832. All further court and social reports mentioning the Marchioness of Stafford are taken from London's *Morning Post*, May 1832.

32 'Disastrous news from London': Mr Lee to James Loch, SRO D593/K/1/3/20.

33 Thomas Creevey, *The Creevey Papers*.

34 'An astounding hissing and yelling': *Staffordshire Advertiser*, 19 May 1832.

35 *Domestic Servants As They Are & As They Ought To Be: A few friendly hints to employers by a practical mistress of a household. With some revelations of Kitchen Life and Tricks of Trade.*

36 Samuel and Sarah Adams, *The Complete Servant*.

Part 2: Sarah Wells

Copies of the five diaries of Sarah Wells are kept at the West Sussex Record Office (WSRO), MSS 41,235–9. I have dated extracts only where relevant or meaningful.

Other material comes from personal observation at Uppark today, and from these books: Margaret Meade-Fetherstonhaugh and Oliver Warner, *Uppark and Its People*, for Harry Fetherstonhaugh's marriage to Mary Ann Bullock, and the subsequent reign of Frances Fetherstonhaugh and Ann Sutherland at Uppark. Margaret Meade-Fetherstonhaugh inherited the house in 1930 and spoke to those who remembered the High Victorian era. Most archives used for the book were destroyed in the fire of 1989. H. G. Wells, Volume I of *Experiment in Autobiography: Discoveries and Conclusions of a Very Ordinary Brain (Since 1866)*, for Sarah Wells's life and employment and her son's visits to Uppark. H. G. Wells, *Tono-Bungay*, an autobiographical novel in which Uppark is recreated as 'Bladesover' and Bertie Wells is 'George'.

1 Quoted in Pamela Horn, *The Rise & Fall of the Victorian Servant*, p. 58.

2 H. G. Wells, *Experiment in Autobiography*, p. 110.

3 *The Journal of Mrs Arbuthnot*, pp. 423–4.

4 'Servants included . . .' from 1851 census.

5 Accounts from Frances Bullock Fetherstonhaugh's bank books, WSRO Uppark MSS 234–9. Staff lists and payments from Box of Accounts (twenty-six bundles for year 1880), Uppark MSS 861.

6 Taken from the 1881 and 1891 census.

7 *Mrs Beeton's Book of Household Management*, p. 19.

8 Box of Accounts (twenty-six bundles for year 1880), WSRO Uppark, MSS 861.

9 'There came and went on these floors . . . a peer of the United Kingdom': *Tono-Bungay*, p. 13.

10 'O God how dull I am!' Letter to A. T. Simmons quoted in Geoffrey West, H. G. Wells, p. 71.

11 'Take it to Petworth': Christopher Rowell, *Uppark* (The National Trust, 1995), p. 33.

12 'Winds, wet ways and old women': Letter to Miss Healey, quoted in H. G. Wells, p. 71.

13 Frances Bullock Fetherstonhaugh's bank books, WSRO Uppark MSS 234–9.

14 Box of Accounts (twenty-six bundles for year 1880), Uppark MSS 861.

15 *The Sphere* – quoted in Frank Dawes, *Not in Front of the Servants: Domestic service in England 1850–1939*, p. 21.

16 'Report of the Metropolitan Commissioners in Lunacy to the Lord Chancellor, Presented to both Houses of Parliament by Command of Her Majesty'. *The Westminster Review*, vol. 43, March–June 1845, pp. 162–92.

17 *The Lancet*, 19 August 1905, p. 546.

18 Janet Oppenheim, *Shattered Nerves*, p. 5.

19 Crichton-Browne, *Education and the Nervous System* (1883). quoted in *Shattered Nerves*, p. 200.

20 Eric Horne, *More Winks, Being further notes from the life and adventures of E. Horne*, p. 46.

Part 3: Ellen Penketh

Much of my material comes from the diaries of Louisa Matilda Scott (later Mrs L. M. Yorke), 1885–1909, kept at Flintshire Record Office, Erddig MSS, D/E/2816.

Other documents consulted in this archive (Erddig MSS, GB 0208 D/E) include:

Housekeeper's Petty Cash Accounts 1902–27 (D/E/463)
Mrs Yorke's Household Accounts 1902–18 (D/E/464)
Estate Cash Book 1904–24 (D/E/2365)

For the history of Erddig and descriptions of Meller and the Yorke family, I have consulted Merlin Waterson's *The Servants' Hall: a domestic history of Erddig* as well as talking to Mr Waterson. As the National Trust's Historic Buildings Representative at the time of Erddig's handover, he spent much time with Philip Yorke III before Philip's death in 1978.

For details of guests and entertaining I have consulted the Yorkes' visitors' book (1902–14) kept by the National Trust at Erddig.

For Ellen Penketh's hearing at Wrexham Magistrate's Court and her trial at the Ruthin Assizes, I have used the detailed reports in the *Wrexham Advertiser* (27 September and 5 December 1907) and the *North Wales Guardian* (6 December – an edition kept by the Yorke family, now in the Erddig archive, D/E/2754).

I have filled in the gaps in Ellen Penketh's life using the National Census; the Female Nominal Roll at Shrewsbury Prison (1905–21) held at Shropshire Archives, SA 6405 and the Home Office Identity and Passport Service for her death certificate.

Details on Ruthin Gaol and its regime come from material and archives on display (now open as a museum, www.ruthingaol.co.uk).

1 D/E/2820 Letter from Philip Yorke II to Mr Campbell, 15/11/1877.

2 Butler's letter to Mr Hughes, 9 December 1897, Erddig MSS, D/E/595.

3 'Between 1901 and 1911, the number of maids aged 14-plus willing to go into service dropped by over 62 per cent': Pamela Horn, *Life Below Stairs in the Twentieth Century*, p. 12.

4 '. . . inevitably a source of friction': E. S. Turner, *What the Butler Saw*, p. 238.

5 '. . . by lowering a key in a basket': according to maids interviewed by Merlin Waterson for *The Servants' Hall*, this was what Ellen Penketh's successor Miss Brown used to do.

6 *Mrs Beeton's Book of Household Management*, 1901.

7 'Footman left for impudence': 11 September 1903. 'The groom is a worry but I will make him leave the house at 10pm'; 10 January 1904. D/E/2816.

8 'At moments when a glass of barley-water might have been acceptable': J. B. Priestley, *The Edwardians*, p. 61.

9 Sara Paston-Williams, *The Art of Dining*, p. 334.

10 'The doll in the blue knitted wool dress [in the dolls' house] was dressed by a Miss Penketh who was stone blind. She was sister to the thief Cook who was at Erthig for many years'. From *Facts and Fancies: A description of Erthig, Denbighshire* by Louisa Matilda Yorke 1863–1951. This typed manuscript is kept at Erddig.

11 '. . . one never knows when they will turn nasty': Vita Sackville-West, *The Edwardians*, p. 30.

12 As reported by the *Wrexham Advertiser*, Thursday, 5 December 1907. Mr Davies was called as first witness on the second day at the Ruthin Assizes.

13 Annie Kennedy, *Memories of a Militant*, on her first imprisonment in Holloway. Quoted in ed. Joyce Marlow, *Votes for Women: The Virago Book of Suffragettes*, p. 41.

14 *The Criminal Prisons of London, and Scenes of Prison Life*, p. 194.

15 Mr Artemus Jones was made King's Counsel in 1919 and a judge of the County Court in 1930. The practice of the judge offering a defendant a dock brief would have allowed Ellen Penketh to pick any barrister then in court to defend her for a very small sum, if any. My thanks to Victor Tunkel of the Selden Society for information on court practice during this era.

16 'Like many other country-house cooks, Mrs Penketh made free with the whisky and cooking sherry. "She's at it again", John Jones the footman was overheard to remark to Frank Lovett, as she approached unsteadily along the basement passage': Merlin Waterson, *The Servants' Hall*, p. 191. The anecdote comes from interviews between Waterson and the teetotal Philip Yorke III (who was two years old at the time of Ellen's trial), and former maid Bessie Gittins, who joined Erddig in 1909 as a nursery maid, two years after Ellen's departure.

Part 4: Hannah Mackenzie

The privately held diaries and photographs of Nan Herbert, 'Scrapbooks 1909–1916', are the basis for my story. Andrew Hann and Shelley Garland's guidebook *Wrest Park* (English Heritage, 2011) is useful on the house's history and contents. For details on nursing during the First World War, I consulted the Royal London Hospital Museum, together with Sue Light's excellent website www.scarletfinders.co.uk.

BLARS – Bedfordshire and Luton Archives and Records Service.

1 Extracts from King George V's diary quoted in J. B. Priestley, *The Edwardians*, p. 284.

2 H. G. Wells, *Mr Britling Sees it Through*. 'outside English experience' . . . 'thoroughly at war', p. 208; 'something like competition', p. 250.

3 Caroline Dakers, *The Countryside at War 1914–18*, p. 39.

4 *Mr Britling Sees it Through*, p. 207.

5 *The Bedfordshire Times*, 11 September 1914.

6 Quoted in material at the Royal London Hospital Museum.

7 *The Bedfordshire Times*, 21 August, 4 September.

8 Obituary for Sir Sydney Beauchamp in the *British Medical Journal*, 3 December 1921. He was knocked down and killed by a 'motor omnibus' in Pall Mall, aged 60.

9 'A Scotsman on the make', in J. M. Barrie's play *What Every Woman Knows*, Act II (1908). 'Almost painful in its intensity': Lisa Chaney, *Hide-and-Seek With Angels: A Life of J.M. Barrie*, p. 104.

10 Writing to Millicent, Duchess of Sutherland 12 January 1917, quoted in Janet Dunbar, *J.M. Barrie: The Man Behind the Image*, p. 285. The play was *The Old Lady Shows Her Medals*, adapted into the film *Seven Days' Leave* (1930) starring Gary Cooper.

11 Letter to Lord Lucas, 30 March 1916. Ed. Viola Meynell, *Letters of J. M. Barrie*.

12 Nurse's autograph book. First World War. Imperial War Museum, Documents 351 (private papers).

13 *Independent*, 28 December 1914.

14 John Buchan, *These for Remembrance: Memoirs of Six Friends Killed in the Great War*, p. 22.

15 Barrie to Charles Turley Smith, *Hide-and-Seek With Angels*, p. 309.

16 Cynthia Asquith, *Portrait of Barrie*, p. 2.

17 Letter to Nan Herbert, September 1916, on the death of Raymond Asquith.

18 *From Eyes of Youth* (1943), quoted in Richard Davenport-Hines, *Ettie: The Intimate Life and Dauntless Spirit of Lady Desborough*, p. 22.

19 Balfour to Mary Elcho (later Lady Wemyss), August 1891. *Ettie*, p. 44.

20 *Woman's Life*, October 1920. Quoted in Virginia Nicholson, *Singled Out: How Two Million Women Survived Without Men after the First World War*, p. 97.

21 To Mrs Hugh Lewis, 1 September 1915. *Letters of J. M. Barrie*.

22 *The Times*, 4 December 1916.

23 Lady Herbert to Mr Surtees, 17 August 1917. BLARS L 26/1516

24 'They just went on the same': Grant, Howard. Transcription of oral history interview with Tara Kraenzlin, 23 February 2001. The Preservation Society of Newport County Archives (PSNCA).

25 'A stalwart, heavy British'... 'individual shepherd's pies': Massé Smith, Geneviève (Charles Massé's daughter). Transcription of oral history interview with Barbara Shotel, 16 August 2000. PSNCA.

26 Cornelius Vanderbilt Jr, *Queen of the Golden Age: The Fabulous Story of Grace Wilson Vanderbilt*, p. 310.

27 'Everybody pitched in': Coleman, Patricia (daughter of Norah Kavanagh Sarsfield). Transcript of oral history interview with Tara Kraenzlin, 5 August 2001. PSNCA.

Part 5: Grace Higgens

These notes are very much intended for the general reader rather than scholars of Bloomsbury. For background material on Charleston and its inhabitants during Grace's era, I consulted the following: Quentin Bell and Virginia Nicholson, *Charleston, A Bloomsbury House and Garden*; Frances Spalding, *Vanessa Bell*; Angelica Garnett, *Deceived with Kindness*; Quentin Bell et al., *Charleston Past and Present*; interviews with John and Diana Higgens by Joyce Duncan, 2004, NLSC Artists' Lives series, British Library. Quotes from Henrietta Garnett come from Stewart MacKay, *The Angel of Charleston* (British Library, 2013). All letters from Vanessa Bell quoted in the text are found in Regina Marler, ed., *Selected Letters of Vanessa Bell* (Bloomsbury, 1993), unless otherwise specified.

I give dates rather than reference numbers to Grace's diary entries, and only when this seems important. The Higgens Papers are kept at the British Library (Add MS 83198–83258). Letters written to Grace are part of the Higgens Papers.

I interviewed Diana Higgens, Anne Olivier Bell and her daughter Virginia Nicholson in June 2013. Grace's son John Higgens sadly died of cancer in April 2013, aged 77.

1 'Awesomely noble': Frances Partridge, quoted in *Charleston Past and Present*, p. 142.

2 'Splendid, devouring, unscrupulous': Virginia Woolf to Vanessa Bell, 16 February 1919.

3 'Oh, skivvies!': Margaret Powell, *Below Stairs*, p. 173.

4 'Lady Astor's personal maid': Rosina Harrison, *Rose: My Life in Service*.

5 'Laundry maid Nesta MacDonald': Pamela Sambrook, *The Country House Servant*, p. 207.

NOTES

6 Harold Nicolson, *Diaries and Letters 1930–1964*. 28 June 1936.

7 'Dear Mr Bell': Grace Higgens to Clive Bell, May 1934. Modern Archive at King's College, Cambridge: 'Maid at Charleston 1920–1970'.

8 'Please forgive me writing to you': Grace Higgens to Vanessa Bell, 1937. Modern Archive.

9 'Servants all over the country': see Virginia Nicholson, *Millions Like Us*, p. 17.

10 'Shoplifting proliferated': *Lewes Remembers the Second World War*.

11 'A mother in Essex': *Millions Like Us*, p. 62.

12 'A young Lewes mother': *Lewes Remembers the Second World War*.

13 'Try to run a home': Barbara Cartland, *The Years of Opportunity*, p. 134.

14 'Yours is a full-time job': *Good Housekeeping*, August 1941.

15 'I'm happy just where I am': author interview with Diana Higgens.

16 'Creative power base . . . height of my ambition': *Millions Like Us*, p. 351.

17 'A family appendage': Duncan Grant to Bunny Garnett, 13 October 1971. Frances Spalding, *Duncan Grant*, p. 479.

18 'Every mortal thing . . . that lot': author interview with Diana Higgens.

19 'Scones and cups of tea . . . superbly': Christopher Mason to Grace Higgens, June 1969, Higgens Papers.

20 'Secretly a little pleased': Richard Shone to Grace Higgens, January 1970, Higgens Papers.

21 'I don't usually have much time': Grace Higgens interviewed for *Duncan Grant at Charleston*, dir. Iain Bruce, 1969. Charleston Trust Recordings, British Library (C1180).

22 'What a remarkable record!': Nigel Nicolson to Grace Higgens, 11 May 1978, Higgens Papers.

Epilogue

1 *Daily Telegraph*, 23 February 2002.

2 'Very like an Inn': Adeline Hartcup, *Below Stairs in the Great Country Houses*, p. 79.

3 'A nervous breakdown': James Lees-Milne, *Diaries, 1942–1954*, p. 288.

Acknowledgements

Many people have helped in the process of writing this book. At the early research stage, Andrew Hann of English Heritage, Helen Lloyd of the National Trust, Jeremy Musson, Virginia Nicholson, Pamela Sambrook and Merlin Waterson kindly let me pick their brains. For the individual stories, my thanks to the following:

For the Prologue set at Hatfield House, I'm grateful to the Marquess of Salisbury and archivists Vicki Perry and Sarah Whale. For the story of Dorothy Doar at Trentham Hall, Pamela Sambrook generously alerted me to Mrs Doar's letter in the Sutherland archive; thanks also to the sleuth-like Beryl Holt, and to staff at Staffordshire Record Office.

At Uppark for Sarah Wells, thanks to Helen Roadnight for her patience with my queries about the house; also to Sophie Chessum and James Rothwell of the National Trust, staff at the West Sussex Record Office, and the University of Illinois Rare Book and Manuscript Library. At Erddig for Ellen Penketh's tale, Jill Burton was exceptionally generous with her research and in egging me onwards. Thanks also to Graeme Clarke and Sara Lewis of the National Trust; Beryl Jones, distant relative of housekeeper Harriet Rogers; staff at Flintshire Record Office, Denbighshire Archives and Shropshire Archives; Victor Tunkel of the Selden Society, George Turnbull of Manchester Transport Museum, Wrexham County Borough Museum, and Ruthin Gaol.

For Wrest Park and Hannah Mackenzie, I am indebted to Nan Herbert's family, also to her great-granddaughter Hannah Palmer for encouragement. The help and enthusiasm of Andrew Hann at English

ACKNOWLEDGEMENTS

Heritage was fundamental; thanks also to Wrest Park's committed volunteers Mike Brown, Jane Heywood and Debbie Radcliffe. Ross Mackenzie, Hannah's great-nephew, was warmly hospitable; researchers Jo Foster and Catherine Tremain left no stone unturned; Barbara McMahon checked J. M. Barrie's diaries at Yale; Caitlin Emery and Holly Collins of Newport Mansions Preservation Society hunted for Hannah among the Vanderbilts. For fleshing out Cecil Argles, the land agent who fell for Hannah, my thanks to Judith Argles, Charles Marsham Argles and Mike Turner. Sue Light of www.scarletfinders.co.uk was helpful on British military nurses, as were staff at Bedfordshire & Luton Archives & Records Service, and the Imperial War Museum Collections.

For Charleston and Grace Higgens, I'm exceptionally grateful to Anne Olivier Bell, Diana Higgens and Virginia Nicholson for their hospitality and memories. Alistair Burtenshaw, Darren Clarke and Wendy Hitchmough at Charleston were helpful; gardener Mark Divall let me poke around his attic flat and Grace's kitchen. For the Epilogue set at Holkham Hall, thanks are due to Viscountess Coke for her trust in letting me into her home, to housekeeper Nicky Garner for her time and patience, and to Celia Deeley and Christine Hiskey.

I regret that many wonderful (and splendidly named) housekeepers within living memory did not, in the end, make it into this book. Mrs Tricker (and her sparring partner, the nanny Florence Screech) at Merevale Hall in Warwickshire were brought to life for me by Sir William Dugdale, an interview kindly set up by his children Laura, Matthew and Matilda. Mrs Lickiss, the last remaining servant at Haigh Hall, Lancashire during the Second World War, was crisply evoked by the Earl of Crawford and Balcarres and his brother the Hon. Tom Lindsay. For memories of Dorothy Dean, first housekeeper at Chatsworth asked to look after the public, I am grateful to the Dowager Duchess of Devonshire, Helen Marchant and Christine Robinson. Clare Macpherson-Grant Russell, Lord Lieutenant of Banffshire, shared memories of family treasure Mrs McCardie, housekeeper at Ballindalloch Castle, who dropped dead of a heart attack days after retiring, aged 73, after fifty years' service.

Judy Macdougall had fascinating stories of housekeeping in the laid-back seventies at a large National Trust house in Buckinghamshire, her tenure coming to an abrupt end when her master remarried. I dearly wish it were possible to tell this housekeeper's tale, but most of the participants are still alive.

More general thanks are due to Karen Wiseman at Blenheim, Rachel Boak, Juliet Carey and Colette Warbrick at Waddesdon, the Marquess of Cholmondeley and Sam Lloyd at Port Lympne, Matthew Beckett of www.lostheritage.org.uk and Tracey Jewitt of Greycoats Agency. I am grateful to the staff of the National Archives, the British Library, the Foundling Museum, the Museum of Brands, the Museum of London and the Royal London Hospital Museum. Thanks also for advice, leads and general encouragement from Jacqueline Aldridge, Catherine Bailey, Dirk Bennett, Hattie Ellis, Oren Gruenbaum, Christina Hardyment, Fiona Hill, Sue Hills, Pam Ingleby, Elisabeth Jay, Natasha Kerr, Bronwen Riley, Katie Roden, Michael and Judy Watson, Jane Whetnall and Hannah Williams. Several friends read chapters and gave feedback: Lucy Brewster, Fiona Napier, Penel Lee and Rachel Doyle. Especial thanks to Sophie Carter, Casilda Grigg and Catherine Tremain – and to my husband Nick Glass for his invaluable criticism and steadfast encouragement.

Graham Coster commissioned this book and steered it to fruition: I am grateful for his wise insights and spot-on instincts. At Aurum, I'd like to thank my unflappable and meticulous editor Melissa Smith, together with Charlotte Coulthard and Iain Macgregor; also my copy editor Jenny Page. The book could not have happened without the enthusiasm and drive of my agent Georgina Capel.

When I started researching *The Housekeeper's Tale* in 2010 my children were aged four and one; they soon learned to parrot back at me my exasperated refrain, 'I'm not a servant!' It has sometimes seemed more than a little ironic to be writing about housekeepers *without* a housekeeper, so I'd like to thank the women whose help has enabled me to work: my child-minder Jasminka Livaja from Croatia, and my Brazilian cleaner Marcia Santos.

Bibliography

All archives consulted are listed in the notes section.

Georgian (Trentham Hall)

Creevey, Thomas. *The Creevey Papers* (John Murray, London, 1903)

Dickens, Charles. *Sketches by Boz* (first published 1833–6 in newspapers and periodicals, pbk edn: Penguin, London, 1995)

The Diaries of Sylvester Douglas, Lord Glenbervie (2 vols, Constable, London, 1928)

Letters of Harriet, Countess Granville, 1810–1845 (Longmans, Green & Co., London, 1894)

Henley, Dorothy. Rosalind Howard, Countess of Carlisle (Hogarth Press, London, 1958)

Horn, Pamela. *Flunkeys & Scullions: Life Below Stairs in Georgian England* (Sutton Publishing, Stroud, 2004)

Huxley, Gervas. *Lady Elizabeth and the Grosvenors, Life in a Whig Family 1822–1839* (Oxford University Press, 1965)

Richards, Eric. *The Leviathan of Wealth: Sutherland Fortune in the Industrial Revolution* (Routledge & Kegan Paul, London, 1973)

Vickery, Amanda. *Behind Closed Doors: At Home in Georgian England* (Yale University Press, New Haven and London, 2009)

Victorian (Uppark)

Briggs, Asa. *Victorian Things* (Batsford, London, 1988, pbk edn: Penguin, London, 1990)

Flanders, Judith. *Consuming Passions: Leisure and Pleasure in Victorian Britain* (Harper Press, London, 2006)

——— *The Victorian House: Domestic Life from Childbirth to Deathbed* (HarperCollins, London, 2003)

Hall, Michael. *The Victorian Country House* (Aurum Press, London, 2009)

Horn, Pamela. *The Rise & Fall of the Victorian Servant* (Sutton Publishing, Stroud, 1990, pbk edn: 2004)

May, Trevor. *The Victorian Domestic Servant* (Shire Publications, Oxford, 2011)

Meade-Fetherstonhaugh, Margaret and Oliver Warner, *Uppark and Its People* (George Allen & Unwin, London, 1964, pbk edn: Century, London, 1988)

Oppenheim, Janet. *Shattered Nerves* (Oxford University Press, 1991)

Rowell, Christopher. *Uppark* (National Trust, 1995)

Summerscale, Kate. *Mrs Robinson's Disgrace: The Private Diary of a Victorian Lady* (Bloomsbury, London, 2012)

Wells, H. G. *Experiment in Autobiography Vol. I: Discoveries and Conclusions of a Very Ordinary Brain (Since 1866)* (Gollancz, London, 1934)

Wells, H. G. *Tono-Bungay* (Macmillan, London, 1909)

Edwardian (Erddig)

Arthur, Max. *Lost Voices of the Edwardians* (Harper Perennial, London, 2007)

Crow, Duncan. *The Edwardian Woman* (George Allen & Unwin, London, 1978)

Garnett, Oliver. *Erddig* (National Trust, 1995)

Marlow, Joyce, ed. *Votes for Women: The Virago Book of Suffragettes* (Virago, London, 2001)

Priestley, J. B. *The Edwardians* (William Heinemann, London, 1970, pbk edn: Penguin, 2000)

Sackville-West, Vita. *The Edwardians* (The Hogarth Press, London, 1930, pbk edn: Virago Press, London, 2009)

Streatfeild, Noel, ed. *The Day Before Yesterday: Firsthand Stories of Fifty Years Ago* (Collins, London, 1956)

Waterson, Merlin. *The Servants' Hall: a domestic history of Erddig* (Routledge & Kegan Paul, 1980, pbk edn: National Trust, 1993)

First World War (Wrest Park)

Asquith, Cynthia. *Portrait of Barrie* (James Barrie, London, 1954)

Buchan, John. *These for Remembrance: Memoirs of Six Friends Killed in the Great War* (privately printed, London, 1919, reprinted: Buchan & Enright, London, 1987)

Chaney, Lisa. *Hide-and-Seek With Angels: A Life of J.M. Barrie* (Hutchinson, London, 2005, pbk edn: Arrow Books, London, 2006)

Dakers, Caroline. *The Countryside at War 1914–18* (Constable, London, 1987)

Davenport-Hines, Richard. *Ettie: The Intimate Life and Dauntless Spirit of Lady Desborough* (Weidenfeld & Nicolson, London, 2008)

Dunbar, Janet. *J.M. Barrie: The Man Behind the Image* (Collins, London, 1970)

Marwick, Arthur. *The Deluge: British Society and the First World War* (The Bodley Head, London, 1965)

Meynell, Viola, ed. *Letters of J. M. Barrie* (Peter Davies, London, 1942)

Vanderbilt Jr, Cornelius. *Queen of the Golden Age: The Fabulous Story of Grace Wilson Vanderbilt* (McGraw-Hill, New York, 1956)

Wells, H. G. *Mr Britling Sees it Through* (Cassell & Co., London, 1916)

Interwar, Second World War and post-war (Charleston)

Bell, Quentin, et al. *Charleston Past and Present* (The Hogarth Press, London, 1987)

—— and Virginia Nicholson. *Charleston, A Bloomsbury House and Garden* (Frances Lincoln, London, 1997)

Calder, Angus. *The People's War: Britain 1939–45* (Random House, London, 1992)

Cartland, Barbara. *The Years of Opportunity* (Hutchinson, London, 1947)

Garnett, Angelica. *Deceived with Kindness* (Chatto & Windus, London, 1984)

Kynaston, David. *Modernity Britain: Opening the Box, 1957–59* (Bloomsbury, London, 2013)

Lees-Milne, James. *Diaries, 1942–1954* (John Murray, London, 2006)

Lewes Remembers the Second World War (Lewes U3A Publications, 1995)

Light, Alison. *Mrs Woolf and the Servants* (Penguin, London, 2007)

MacKay, Stewart. *The Angel of Charleston* (British Library, London, 2013)

Marler, Regina, ed. *Selected Letters of Vanessa Bell* (Bloomsbury, London, 1993)

Nicholson, Virginia. *Among the Bohemians: Experiments in Living 1900–1939* (Viking, London, 2002)

——. *Millions Like Us* (Viking, London, 2011, pbk edn: Penguin, London, 2012)

——. *Singled Out: How Two Million Women Survived Without Men after the First World War* (Viking, London, 2007, pbk edn: Penguin, London, 2008)

Nicolson, Harold. *Diaries and Letters 1930–1964* (Atheneum, New York, 1980)

Seebohm, Caroline. *The Country House: A Wartime History, 1939–45* (Weidenfeld & Nicolson, London, 1989)

Spalding, Frances. *Vanessa Bell* (Weidenfeld & Nicolson, London, 1983)

——. *Duncan Grant* (Chatto & Windus, London, 1997)

General

Aslet, Clive. *The Last Country Houses* (Yale University Press, New Haven and London, 1982)

Bailey, Catherine. *Black Diamonds* (Penguin, London, 2008)

Briggs, Asa. *A Social History of England* (Pelican Books, London, 1987)

Burnett, John, ed. *Useful Toil: Autobiographies of Working People from the 1820s to the 1920s* (Allen Lane, Penguin Books, London, 1974, pbk edn: Routledge, London, 1994)

Cannadine, David. *Class in Britain* (Penguin, London, 1998)

——. *The Decline and Fall of the British Aristocracy* (Yale University Press, New Haven and London, 1990)

Davidoff, Leonore. *Worlds Between: Historical Perspectives on Gender and Class* (Polity Press, Cambridge, 1995)

Dawes, Frank. *Not in Front of the Servants: Domestic service in England 1850–1939* (Wayland Publishers, London, 1973)

Gerard, Jessica. *Country House Life: Family and Servants 1815–1914* (Blackwell, Oxford, 1994)

Giles, Judy. *Women, Identity and Private Life in Britain 1900–50* (Macmillan, London, 1995)

Girouard, Mark. *A Country House Companion* (Century Hutchinson, London, 1987)

——. *Life in the English Country House* (Yale University Press, New Haven and London, 1979)

Hardyment, Christina. *From Mangle to Microwave: Mechanisation of the Household* (Polity Press, Cambridge, 1988)

Hartcup, Adeline. *Below Stairs in the Great Country Houses* (Sidgwick & Jackson, London, 1980)

Horn, Pamela. *Life Below Stairs in the Twentieth Century* (Sutton Publishing, Stroud, 2001)

Kerr, Robert. *The Gentleman's House, 1864* (reprinted in facsimile, Johnson Reprint Corporation, New York, 1972)

Lethbridge, Lucy. *Servants: A Downstairs View of Twentieth-century Britain* (Bloomsbury, London, 2013)

Malos, Ellen, ed. *The Politics of Housework* (Allison & Busby, London, 1982)

Masters, Brian. *Great Hostesses* (Constable, London, 1982)

Musson, Jeremy. *Up and Down Stairs: The History of the Country House Servant* (John Murray, London, 2009)

The National Trust Manual of Housekeeping (National Trust, 2011)

Paston-Williams, Sara. *The Art of Dining* (National Trust, 1993)

Sambrook, Pamela. *The Country House Servant* (National Trust, 1999)

——. *Dunham Massey: A Country House at Work* (National Trust, 2003)

——. *Keeping Their Place: Domestic Service in the Country House* (Sutton Publishing, Stroud, 2005)

Sykes, Christopher Simon. *Country House Camera* (Pavilion Books, London, 1987)

Steedman, Carolyn. *Labours Lost: Domestic Service and the Making of a Modern England* (Cambridge University Press, 2009)

Tinniswood, Adrian. *A History of Country House Visiting: Five Centuries of Tourism and Taste* (Basil Blackwell, Oxford, 1989)

Turner, E. S. *What the Butler Saw: Two Hundred and Fifty Years of the Servant Problem* (Penguin, London, 1962)

Waterfield, Giles, et al., eds. *Below Stairs: 400 Years of Servants' Portraits* (National Portrait Gallery, London, 2004)

Waterson, Merlin, ed. *The Country House Remembered: Recollections of Life Between the Wars* (Routledge & Kegan Paul, London, 1985)

Worsley, Giles. *England's Lost Houses* (Aurum Press, London, 2002)

Reports and academic papers

Gillis, John R. 'Servants, Sexual Relations and the Risks of Illegitimacy in London, 1801–1900' (*Feminist Studies* vol. 5, no 1, Spring 1979)

Hann, Andrew. *The Service Wing at Audley End House* (English Heritage: Properties Historians' Report, 2007)

Jay, Elisabeth. 'The Enemy Within: The Housekeeper in Victorian Fiction', in A. M. Kilday and N. Nanfasse (eds), *Social Deviance in England and France 1830–1900* (Cahiers Victoriens et Edwardiens de la SFEVE, pp. 247–60, 2004)

Published memoirs and diaries

The Journal of Mrs Arbuthnot (Macmillan, London, 1950)

Balderson, Eileen. *Backstairs Life in a Country House* (David & Charles, Newton Abbot, 1982)

Balsan, Consuelo. *The Glitter and the Gold* (Heinemann, London, 1953)

Bankes, Viola. *A Kingston Lacy Childhood* (The Dovecote Press, Wimbourne, 1986)

Bath, Marchioness of. *Before the Sunset Fades* (The Longleat Estate Company, Warminster, 1951)

Bedford, Duke of, John. *A Silver-Plated Spoon* (The Reprint Society, London, 1959)

Cooper, Lady Diana. *The Rainbow Comes and Goes* (1958, republished Century, London, 1984)

Cullwick, Hannah and Elizabeth Stanley, ed. *The Diaries of Hannah Cullwick: Victorian Maidservant* (Virago Press, London, 1984)

Dugdale, Bill. *Settling the Bill* (Endeavour, London, 2011)

Gorst, Frederick. *Of Carriages and Kings* (W. H. Allen, London, 1956)

Harrison, Rosina. *Rose: My Life in Service* (Cassell, London, 1975)

Horne, Eric. *What the Butler Winked At, Being the Life and Adventures of Eric Horne (Butler), for Fifty-seven Years in Service with the Nobility and Gentry* (T. Werner Laurie, London, 1923)

—. *More Winks, Being further notes from the life and adventures of E. Horne* (T. W. Laurie, 1932)

King, Ernest. *The Green Baize Door* (Kimber, London, 1963)

Lanceley, William. *From Hallboy to House Steward* (Edward Arnold & Co., London, 1925)

Lewis, Lesley. *The Private Life of an English Country House: 1912–1939* (Sutton Publishing, Stroud, 1998)

Powell, Margaret. *Below Stairs* (Peter Davies, London, 1968, pbk edn: Pan Macmillan, London, 2011)

Rennie, Jean. *Every Other Sunday: The Autobiography of a Kitchenmaid* (Arthur Baker, London, 1955)

Sykes, Christopher Simon. *The Big House: The Story of a Country House and Its Family* (HarperCollins, London, 2004)

Welsh Carlyle, Jane. *Letters and Memorials*, ed. J. A. Froude (Longmans, Green & Co., London, 1883)

Wyndham, Ursula. *Astride the Wall: A Memoir 1913–1945* (Lennard Publishing, London,1988)

Contemporary conduct books, manuals and reports

Adams, Samuel and Sarah. *The Complete Servant* (Knight & Lacey, London, 1825)

Anon. *The Housekeeper and Butler's Guide* (London, 1853)

Beeton, Isabella. *Book of Household Management* (Ward, Lock & Co., London, 1861)

Campbell, Lady Gertrude Elizabeth and Colin Campbell, *Etiquette of Good Society* (Cassell & Co., London, 1893)

Cassell's Book of the Household, vol. 2 (Cassell & Co., London, 1890).

Firth, Violet. *The Psychology of the Servant Problem: A Study in Social Relationships* (Daniel, London, 1925)

The Housekeeping Book of Susanna Whatman (Geoffrey Bles, London, 1956, pbk edn: National Trust, 1988)

Index